T0244683

Victor D. Cha is Professor of Government at Georgetown University and holds the Korea Chair at the Center for Strategic and International Studies in Washington, DC. **Ramon Pacheco Pardo** is Professor of International Relations at King's College London and the KF-VUB Korea Chair at Free University of Brussels.

Further praise for *Korea*:

"Enjoyable, engaging, timely and often surprising ... The perfect starting point for anyone interested in a fascinating people, culture and part of the world." Steven Port, *Get History*

"Anyone looking for a modern history of North and South Korea will find this the best available." Brandon Palmer, *Pacific Affairs*

"Readers are quickly brought up to speed on over 4,000 years of history, from current day issues all the way back to ancient conflicts ... A helpful introduction." Oliver Jia, *NK News*

"An enjoyable read that will appeal to those who have fallen under the sway of South Korea's not-inconsiderable soft power and have a curiosity about its estranged sibling to the north." Joshua Huminski, *Diplomatic Courier*

"A highly engaging book ... The authors share their decades of research, observations, and engagement with Koreans, North and South." Jay Song, *Australian Outlook*

"A highly readable history of the Korean peninsula ... A must-read to understand how one ill-informed moment in history led to an ongoing human tragedy and geopolitical challenge." Anna Fifield, Asia-Pacific editor, *Washington Post*

"Victor Cha and Ramon Pacheco Pardo have done the nearly impossible: they have managed to write a succinct and readable history of Korea over the past hundred years that does full justice to this complicated and fascinating story." Sue Mi Terry, Director of the Asia Program and the Hyundai Motor-Korea Foundation Center for Korean History and Public Policy, Wilson Center

"The authors begin their book by posing this question: 'What circumstances led the same people to live in such starkly different conditions?' This in fact is a question which often dogs casual Korea watchers. If you are one of them, this is one of the best books I can recommend to you. Among other things, it was written by two of the most qualified Western observers of the two Koreas." Ahn Ho-young, Chair Professor of North Korean Studies, Kyungnam University, and ROK Ambassador to the United States (2013–17)

KOREA

A NEW HISTORY OF
SOUTH AND NORTH

VICTOR D. CHA
RAMON PACHECO PARDO

YALE UNIVERSITY PRESS
NEW HAVEN AND LONDON

For information about this and other Yale University Press publications, please contact:
U.S. Office: sales.press@yale.edu   yalebooks.com
Europe Office: sales@yaleup.co.uk   yalebooks.co.uk

Set in Adobe Caslon Pro by IDSUK (DataConnection) Ltd
Printed in the United States of America.

Library of Congress Control Number: 2024934836

ISBN 978-0-300-25981-0 (hbk)
ISBN 978-0-300-27870-5 (pbk)

A catalogue record for this book is available from the British Library.

10 9 8 7 6 5 4 3

In memory of Victor's dear friends and mentors, Fred Hiatt, Bob Jervis, Jim Morley, and James Reardon-Anderson

To Ramon's wife Mina and daughter Hannah

CONTENTS

ILLUSTRATIONS

Plates

8. Surrender ceremonies in Seoul, September 9, 1945. Official U.S. Navy Photograph, National Archives (80-G-391464).

9. Establishment of South Korea as an independent country, 1948.

10. Crossing the 38th parallel, 1950. National Archives (NAID: 541822).

11. South Korean refugees crossing paths with US troops, 1950. akg-images.

12. Syngman Rhee, *c.* 1939. Harris & Ewing photograph collection, Library of Congress Prints and Photographs Division, Washington, DC (LC-DIG-hec-26756).

13. Park Chung-hee, *c.* 1961. Alamy.

14. Kim Il-sung, 1946.

15. Women working at a factory, South Korea. Colaimages / Alamy.

16. Kim Il-sung and Kim Jong-il, mid-1960s. CPA Media / Alamy.

17. South Koreans arrested during the Gwangju Uprising, 1980. Sadayuki Mikami / AP / Shutterstock.

18. Seoul Olympic Games inauguration ceremony, 1988. Bob Daemmrich / Alamy.

19. Protests during the Asian financial crisis, 1997. Choo Youn-Kong / Getty Images.

20. The first inter-Korean summit, 2000. Kyodo News / Getty Images.

21. Park Geun-hye, 2013. National Archives of Korea, Korea Open Government License.

22. One of the protests of the "Candlelight Revolution," 2016. Lee Jin-Man / AP / Shutterstock.

23. Propaganda posters along Podunamu Street, Pyongyang, 2008. Hemis / Alamy.

24. Agricultural workers in North Korea, 2018. Torsten Pursche / Alamy.

25. Grand People's Study Hall, 1989. akg-images / Pansegrau.

26. Arirang Mass Games parade, 2019. Dita Alangkara / AP / Shutterstock.
27. Still from *Parasite*, 2019. BFA / Alamy.
28. Samsung Electronics headquarters in Seoul. Newscom / Alamy.
29. Blackpink on stage at a fan meeting, 2022. PA Images / Alamy.
30. North Korean missile test, 2022. UPI / Alamy.
31. US President Donald Trump meets with Kim Jong-un, 2018. White House / Alamy.
32. View towards the Ryugyong Hotel in Pyongyang, 2018. iStock / chintung.
33. Seoul at twilight, 2020. iStock / tawatchaiprakobkit.

Figures

Readers will find the following online at https://www.yalebooks.co.uk/page/detail/korea/?k=9780300259810

NOTE ON THE KOREAN TEXT

Romanization of the Korean language has long suffered from a lack of a single, agreed-upon standard for spelling, which is why you will variously see "Kim Jong Il," "Kim Jong-Il," and "Kim Chŏng-il" in the press and academic publications. The book at hand uses something of a mishmash of different standardized Romanization techniques. For names and places that will be familiar to many readers, such as "Kim Il-sung," "Kim Dae-jung," and "Pyongyang," Revised Romanization is used. For names of people and places less familiar to the casual observer, Revised Romanization is mostly employed, with some use of McCune-Reischauer Romanization. And for those who aren't acquainted with Korean, Chinese, or Japanese names, it bears pointing out that in nearly all cases (with the exception of a few, whose names are widely known and/or used in the reverse order, such as Syngman Rhee), Korean, Chinese, and Japanese names are written in their traditional order, with the surname first and the given name last.

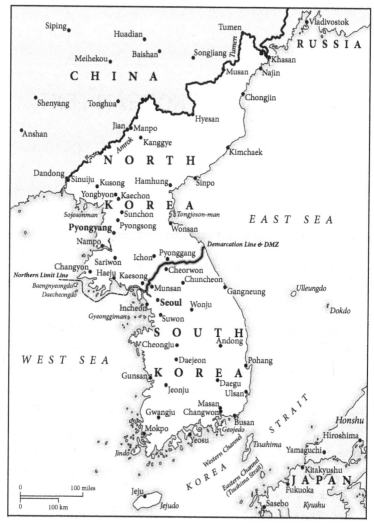

Map of North and South Korea.

INTRODUCTION

In 2007, Victor Cha found himself in a Blackhawk helicopter flying from the demilitarized zone (DMZ) that separates North and South Korea to the capital city of Seoul for a meeting with then-president Roh Moo-hyun. He was returning from a few days of negotiations with counterparts in North Korea as a member of the National Security Council staff at the White House, and was to brief the South Korean president about the meetings. It was his first trip to North Korea. He had not gone to the country as an academic. Being hosted in a VIP guest house and chauffeured to and from meetings, Victor was struck by the orderliness and cleanliness of the capital city of Pyongyang. Though the buildings and infrastructure of the city seemed dated by a few decades due to North Korea's stagnant economy, life certainly looked livable. It was only when his handlers drove Victor from Pyongyang to the DMZ for his return trip to the South that he saw the true squalor of the country. Bar a couple of military vehicles, there were no cars on the road during the hours-long drive.

Barren fields on both sides of the highway boasted no evidence of mechanized farming, only an occasional ox and plow (and some machine-gun nests). Just visible from the car were distant apartment buildings in the city of Kaesong, North Korea's second-largest metropolis. They lacked windows, adorned only with tarp to protect from the elements of early spring.

Boarding the military chopper on the southern side of the DMZ, his control officer handed Victor a schedule of meetings for the day, but as he stared at the piece of paper, he could not get these parting images of North Korea out of his head. Within a few minutes of take-off, the traveling party flew over a sprawling factory complex. Victor asked what it was, and the control officer told him it was one of Samsung Electronics' factories, prolific producer of high-end phones, HDTVs, and consumer appliances owned by households around the world. They then came within sight of the densely packed, gleaming skyscrapers of downtown Seoul. A colleague once described Seoul as a twenty-four-hour global city not unlike New York. Victor had seen the skyline of the city many times before, of course, but not after having just spent time in North Korea. His immediate thought was that the windowless buildings in Kaesong and the state-of-the-art structures in the south were both built and occupied by Koreans, the same Koreans, compatriots who were divided not by any choices of their own.

How did this happen? What circumstances led the same people to live in such starkly different conditions? There are no genetic differences between the Koreans in the north and the Koreans in the south to account for this disparity of development. Is this what politics can do to people and to a country?

The story of Korea is unique and original. For Korea has a long and rich history. The mythical foundation of the country dates back to 2333 BCE, when Dangun established Gojoseon (Old Joseon). Today, both North and South Korea celebrate *Gaecheonjeol* (National

Foundation Day) on October 3 to commemorate Dangun's establishment of the country. This, of course, is a legend. But the proto-
states that eventually resulted in the creation of Korea do date back
millennia. Along with its neighbors China and Japan, Korea can
credibly claim to be one of the oldest countries in the world.

From 57 BCE until 668, the kingdoms of Goguryeo, Silla, and
Baekje occupied the whole of the Korean Peninsula and parts of
Manchuria. This was the Three Kingdoms period. Silla then unified
these kingdoms as well as most of the Korean Peninsula under its
rule. This was the start of the Northern and Southern States era, with
Balhae in the north and Silla in the south. This period would end in
935. It would be followed by the first kingdom that unified the whole
of the Korean Peninsula, Goryeo, which would last until 1392.

In 1392, Taejo of Joseon took power and established the Joseon
dynasty. The dynasty would go on to rule Korea until 1910. A period
of over five hundred years that, inevitably, left an imprint in modern
Korea. Confucianism became the official religion and determined the
way in which life was organized, with clear divisions between rulers
and ruled, men and women, parents and children, and elder and
junior. Today, the legacy of Confucianism still affects the politics and
society of North and South Korea. Also during the Joseon era, Korea
had to fend off periodic invasion—or at least intervention—attempts
by China and Japan. Today, the two Koreas still strive to forge their
own path independent of the influence of external powers. And under
the Joseon dynasty, Korean culture flourished to levels unseen previously. This culture continues to influence the (South) Korean movies,
dramas, and pop songs that the world has learned to love.

In this book, we focus on Korea's modern history. A period roughly
covering the late nineteenth century up to the third decade of the
twenty-first century. The two of us have decades of accumulated
experience researching, teaching, and talking about Korea, and the

two Koreas into which the country is divided today. We have also worked for or supported the work of government. Thanks to these experiences, we have had access to policymakers, politicians, civil society leaders, academics, and researchers from South and North Korea. Our innate curiosity and family circumstances have also given us access to "regular" folks, especially in South Korea but also, within limits, in the North. This book stems from all these experiences.

Take the case of Ramon Pacheco Pardo, the co-author of this book, who hails from a country that historically has had limited interest in Korea, or the rest of the Asian continent for that matter. When Ramon first announced that he was to move to South Korea, his friends organized a farewell party. These friends went around bookstores and searched on the internet for days and days, so that they could gift him a book to better understand the country he was going to be moving to. It has to be said, it was a labor of love and friendship for which Ramon will always be grateful. His friends ended up finding two relevant books: a South Korea tourist guide book, and a book nominally about North Korea that was as much about China. That was the state of interest about (South) Korea in his country back then.

Twenty years later, K-pop bands Ateez, Blackpink, and Monsta X have filled out stadiums in Ramon's home country of Spain. Family, friends, and acquaintances often ask about the films *Parasite* or *Train to Busan*, TV shows *Squid Game* or *Extraordinary Attorney Woo*, boy band BTS or global hit "Gangnam Style." They also ask about North Korea in general or the Kim family in particular, Pyongyang's latest nuclear test or tirade against Seoul and Washington, the country's latest economic problems or the regime's latest execution. The point is that there is growing interest in the two Koreas, which seems to have no end. Even in countries that in the past focused their attention elsewhere.

Readers may still wonder what led us to write this book. Sure, our work focuses on Korea and we have personal links with the country. But so do many others. We do have an answer to that question. Simply put, we believe that there is a need for a book grounded in academic research that is accessible to the general public. The modern history of Korea, pre- and post-division, has gone through many twists and turns. This can make it difficult to follow. With this book, we hope to provide the readers with a detailed and analytical introduction to Korean history, so that they can gain deeper knowledge about where North and South Korea currently are and why they are there today. Both Koreas have become well known globally, albeit for very different reasons. Our hope is that with this book the reader will be able to understand why this is the case.

We do not wish to claim that Korea and the Koreans are misunderstood. But we do think that they are less understood than comparable countries, whether in Asia or in the West. Take the case of North Korea. A common question that we are asked is why it is the most isolated country in the world as of 2023. Facile explanations such as the character of the Kim family ruling the country since its establishment or Korea's past history as a "hermit kingdom" do not hold. We have to look beyond them. Or take the case of questions we are often asked about South Korea, such as why its culture seemingly came out of nowhere to become globally recognized or how it was able to go from poor to rich in the span of only three decades.

As we discuss in this book, the roots of these developments lie in the modern history of Korea. In other words, Korea and the Koreas may not be misunderstood, yet we need a book that allows us to understand them better. This is our aim here. We argue that Korea's modern history has been an odyssey driven by inexorable forces of geography, power, and resilience. To put it simply, Korea, both North and South, has been victim of its own geography, sandwiched in the middle of the great states of East Asia and beyond. It has navigated balance-of-power politics, however, and has demonstrated an uncanny resilience. Whether this is North Korea surviving a famine that killed up to 10 percent of its population in the 1990s, or South Korea recovering from the financial crisis in 1997, Korea and Koreans have found a way to survive, and in some cases, thrive.

And how have Korea and the Koreans resisted and thrived against all odds? In this book, we argue that there is no single explanation. Over time, unified Korea, South and North Korea, and the Koreans living on both sides of the 38th parallel have evolved. However, we do believe that Korea has grown stronger when its people and its leaders have had a sense of common purpose and have remained united, as was the case in North Korea throughout the 1960s–1970s or in South Korea's post-Asian financial crisis. Conversely, we argue that Korea has been at its weakest when internal divisions have allowed outside powers to exercise their influence, as was the case in the early twentieth century leading to colonization by Japan. And sometimes, certainly, divisions between the people and the leaders have resulted in a stronger Korea, such as the democratization process in the 1980s in the South.

In this book, we recount this story in unique and novel ways, drawing from personal experiences in and around US, Asian, and European governments, oral interviews, journalistic accounts, and traditional research materials. We believe that this new history of Korea we have penned is different from any other because we view it from American, Korean, and European perspectives. In this sense, this transatlantic collaboration is a first for a history book on Korea.

It only remains for us to thank those who have made this book possible. The authors would like to thank the Center for Strategic and International Studies (CSIS) and the Academy of Korean

Studies. This work was supported by the Laboratory Program for Korean Studies of the Ministry of Education of the Republic of Korea and the Korean Studies Promotion Service at the Academy of Korean Studies (AKS-2021-LAB-223002). We are appreciative of the research support we received for this book from many able individuals. Seiyeon Ji managed our many drafts between Washington, DC, London, and Seoul, and helped review the different chapters with her excellent research skills. Victor also thanks Andy Lim, Minchi Hyun, Hwijin Jung, and ByeongKyu (Colin) Jun, and Ramon thanks Jonathan Chen, ByeongKyu (Colin) Jun, Hyewon Kang, and Ju-Hyun Kim for their research assistance. At Yale University Press, we are indebted to Jo Godfrey, Rachael Lonsdale, Frazer Martin, Kristy Leonard, and Katie Urquhart for their support and enthusiasm for the project from commission to publication.

1
BALANCE-OF-POWER POLITICS
AND THE OCCUPATION
THE NINETEENTH CENTURY TO 1945

It is customary for guests at the White House who are there for a meeting with the President of the United States to wait in the Roosevelt Room. Sitting diagonally across the hallway from the Oval Office, it is a windowless meeting space that was originally the office of Theodore Roosevelt when the West Wing was built in 1902, and thereafter expanded by Franklin Delano Roosevelt (FDR). Portraits of both presidents hang on the north and south walls.

On this particular occasion, Victor Cha was escorting a high-level South Korean official for a meet-and-greet with the president. As is so often the case with the US president, it was a busy day, and he was about ten minutes behind schedule. As the visiting party was held in the Roosevelt Room, the White House protocol officer cheerfully offered the guest and his three-person entourage a quick tour of the historic room. Our guest politely accepted, and the protocol officer proceeded to talk about the history of the room, and about how President Nixon named it after Teddy Roosevelt in 1969. She then explained the tradition of how Republican administrations would hang Tadé Styka's *Rough Rider* portrait of their party's Roosevelt over the mantel, and Alfred Jonniaux's portrait of Franklin Delano Roosevelt (FDR) on the south wall. When the Democrats held the White House, the portrait positions would be switched (this stopped with Clinton). As she walked us around the meeting table in the center of the room to the closed door opposite the Oval Office, we stood in front of a small glass-encased gold medal suspended on the wall. The protocol officer explained proudly that this medal was the Nobel Peace Prize awarded to Teddy Roosevelt for brokering the Treaty of Portsmouth that ended the Russo-Japanese War. While the protocol officer was smiling, Victor looked for a reaction from the guest. For Koreans, Roosevelt's Nobel Prize is synonymous with the US selling out Korea to Japan—after a secret agreement made between Washington and Tokyo granting Japan a sphere of influence over Korea in return for a US sphere of influence over the Philippines. The guest nodded attentively, affixed his gaze on the medal, then moved on, glancing at his watch.

The meeting with the president went as planned, but days later, a left-wing South Korean news website's (incorrect) report stole the headlines. The article cited an unnamed source who stated that the White House insensitively displays in the Roosevelt Room a copy of the secret Taft–Katsura agreement that led to Japan's colonization of Korea. As untrue as this was, it spoke to the raw emotions that still surround this period in history.

* * *

Korea's history is its geography. It is a 680-mile-long, 220-mile-wide mountainous peninsula attached to two great powers in Asia, China and Russia, and which juts out across the sea to another, the Japanese archipelago. This location, combined with Korea's relatively smaller size in the region, perennially encourages geopolitical designs by the great powers to dominate Korea. For centuries, China sought influence over Korea to protect its rear flank against aggression. For centuries, Japan valued Korea as a land bridge to continental Asia. And for centuries, Russia defended a smaller border of Korea than China, but coveted the peninsula's ice-free ports to the Pacific Ocean. Even today, these geopolitical impulses, however muted by modernity and development, will always be a part of Korea's story.

China was the first to gain influence over Korea from the seventh century, making it a satellite of China's civilization. Korean culture, philosophy, and customs were heavily beholden to China for centuries. The Mongols rolled into Korea in the thirteenth century and ravaged the country for a hundred years, using it as a base of operations to attack Japan. China returned to dominate the peninsula from the fourteenth century and Korea became once again a tributary of the Middle Kingdom, and one that wholly adopted Chinese ways of art, culture, and philosophy, which some have described as a Korea that was "more Confucian than Confucius." This was a period of great civilization for Korea that lasted 150 years until it was disrupted by Japan. The samurai armies of Toyotomi Hideyoshi invaded in 1592 for several years, during which the Japanese robbed Korea of many treasures, artworks, and cultural artifacts. With the help of China Koreans fought to expel the invasion, but then the country closed in on itself, even as it stayed tied to China. Seeking to avoid the turmoil of its region, Korea became known as the "hermit kingdom."

Korea had a king in 1864 but he was only 12 years old. The country, governed by a dying dynasty in its last throes, was run by the father of King Kojong, Yi Ha-ung or the Taewon'gun, as the de facto regent. He ruled for a tumultuous decade between 1864 and 1873 when Korea was racked by internal dissent and external predation. Korea had a population just shy of 10 million and boasted a

Neo-Confucian society that was rich in culture, but socially strati-fied. *Yangban* were the privileged landowners and officials of the country. The *jungin* were the noble class of technicians, artisans, engineers, doctors, and musicians. The *sangmin* were the commoners who lived as farmers, laborers, and the military. The lowest class were the *cheonmin* whose place in life ranged from slaves to criminals.

The people and leadership of the country debated fiercely over how best to strengthen the country. While China and Japan had opened to the West in the mid-1800s, the Taewon'gun and tradi-tional Confucianists, including *yangban* and the *jungin*, wanted to maintain the "hermit kingdom," isolating Koreans from the modern-ization waves of the Western "barbarians." This "reject heterodoxy, support orthodoxy" school rebuffed Western demands for trade rela-tions and saw Catholicism's appeal to commoners as a threat to rule. The "hermit kingdom" rejected overtures by ships arriving from England in 1832, France in 1846, Russia in 1854, and the US in 1866. In the last case, an American trading ship, the *General Sherman*, was destroyed by fire and its crew massacred.

Countering this orthodox school were forces for enlightenment, who advocated for an open door policy to the outside world. These progressives, including the commoner classes and some sections of the *yangban* and royal family, yearned for a strong and independent Korea and believed the only way to achieve this was through refor-mation of the existing socio-economic system. As early as 1862, these forces launched a revolt against the existing hierarchical social structures and unequal economic system. The revolt would be quelled, but more would follow over the following decades. Elites sympa-thetic to the situation of the lower classes promoted the opening of schools to educate the population, advocated for the use of easier-to-learn *hangeul* instead of Chinese characters, called for the abolition of slavery, or advocated for lower taxes on the peasantry. They were impressed by Japan's modernization, and wanted Korea to adopt Western technologies, convert to Christianity, and open relations with Japan and the United States. The end of the Taewon'gun's rule in 1873 led to more debates about progressive reform divided between those who pushed for complete opening and those traditionalists who wanted to adopt Western technology but maintain traditional Korean values—so-called "Eastern ways, Western machines." In the end, the royal family supported changes to existing structures, abolishing slavery and building new infrastructure, but the reforms were too little, too late. The internal strife had weakened Korea and by then Japan has become the ascendant power in Asia.

Korea faced a choice in the late nineteenth century. On the one hand, the country could follow China in opposing foreign intervention, keeping its traditional organization of the economy, politics, and society, and, more generally, closing itself to the outside world. On the other hand, Korea could follow Japan in accepting the arrival of Western powers to East Asia, pursuing a policy of industrialization and changes to society and politics, and, essentially, opening to the changing world around the Korean Peninsula. The decision that Korea made would determine the fate of the country.

The Balance of Power in Nineteenth-Century East Asia

Japan had always seen the territory of Korea as important to gaining a foothold on mainland Asia. In 1876, Japan exhorted Korea to sign the Kanghwa Treaty. The ostensible purpose of the treaty was to gain access to Korean ports for trade, but the most important strategic aspect was its role as the first step in Japan's designs to open up Korea. By executing the first Western-style treaty with Korea, Japan was able to deal with Korea as an independent sovereign state and thereby challenge China's traditional dominance on the peninsula.

The Kanghwa Treaty created concerns on the part of the Chinese, who, in 1882, dispatched about 4,500 troops to the peninsula.[1] This, in turn, created resistance among reform-minded nationalists who wanted to assert Korean independence from China and inspire change akin to Japan's Meiji Restoration for their country.[2] The resulting Kapsin Coup of 1884 pitted Japan-backed modernizers like Kim Okkyun, who learned from their time abroad of Korea's desperate need to modernize, against China-backed Confucian traditionalists. The internal chaos led to a direct clash of forces between China and Japan on the peninsula. The Convention of Tientsin in 1885 managed to stave off escalation into a wider conflict temporarily as both sides agreed to withdraw troops and provide prior notification of any future intervention.

In spite of the agreement, both China and Japan still vied for power on the Korean Peninsula. In 1894, the Donghak Rebellion, a peasant uprising against poor economic conditions, corruption of the Joseon (Yi) dynasty royalty, and foreign interference, prompted both powers to set foot on the peninsula again, this time with troops. The ensuing Sino-Japanese war reflected a classic power transition war between the rising challenger and the declining hegemon, which Japan won. The Treaty of Shimonoseki in 1895, drafted by a former American secretary of state, John W. Foster, required China to acknowledge the formal independence of Korea.[3]

After disposing of Chinese influence in Korea, widespread modernization policies inspired by Japan came to the country known as the Kabo reforms. The unpopularity of these measures in some segments of society, including the "top-knot" edict (requiring Koreans to cut off the traditional top-knot and don Western attire), provided the opportunity for Russia to gain influence to pursue their traditional interests on the peninsula. Most important for Czar Nicholas II was access to warm-water ports for commerce and for build-up of a navy commensurate with the Russian empire's status as one of the largest territorial powers in the world. After the Japanese conspired with a Korean faction in the assassination of Queen Min in October 1895, King Kojong looked to Russia for safety, moving under the cover of night to the Russian legation along a path that now constitutes the back wall of the US ambassador's residence in downtown Seoul. The Russians provided protection to the Korean king for nearly a year, thereby cementing a position on the peninsula close to the leadership. Japan—which already felt threatened by Russia's support of China in the Sino-Japanese war and its participation in the Triple Intervention (requiring Japan to return the Liaodong Peninsula to China)—entered into negotiations, and, in an omen of things to come, the two parties even considered a division of Korea into spheres of influence at the 38th parallel. However, in the end, Japan could not countenance a challenge to its influence in Korea and staged a surprise attack on the Russian navy at Port Arthur in February 1904, eventually sinking every Russian ship in the navy's Pacific Fleet and then pushing the Russians out of Manchuria. The Russo-Japanese war was the first victory of an Asian power over an occidental power (it was also one of the first wars where the number of battle deaths outnumbered that of deaths by disease) and constituted a tremendous source of pride for Japan.

Russia conceded defeat to Japan at the Treaty of Portsmouth in 1905. The peace agreement, mediated by US President Theodore Roosevelt, gave Japan control of Korea, southern Manchuria, and the southern half of Sakhalin Island. Roosevelt persuaded Japan not to demand an indemnity from Russia in pressing for a final peace agreement. For Koreans, what mattered most about this settlement was the prior secret agreement between Secretary of State William H. Taft and Japanese Foreign Minister Katsura Taro, in which the US agreed to concede any interest in Korea in exchange for Japan recognizing a US sphere of influence in the Philippines. The ultimate importation of European balance-of-power politics to Asia, where great powers traded the fates of smaller ones, the Taft–Katsura agreement is still remembered in Korea as profound betrayal by the United States, even as the peace treaty won Theodore Roosevelt the Nobel Peace Prize, as described in this chapter's opening vignette.

America's rationale for abandonment of Korea at the turn of the twentieth century probably made little sense to most Koreans. The decision stemmed from a combination of paternalism and lack of interest. Roosevelt, beset with the imperialist mindset, firmly believed that Korea was incapable of governing itself as the Joseon dynasty crumbled from within. Roosevelt assessed then, "we cannot possibly interfere for the Koreans against Japan. . . . They could not strike one blow in their defense."[4] Roosevelt also firmly believed that the burden of Korea should not belong to the United States. Korea mattered to the US only as a pawn in great power politics. Therefore, selling Korea down the river in exchange for Japanese acknowledgment of US dominance of the Philippines met with little opposition in Washington. Indeed, seventeen years later, the United States would do the same thing when Secretary of State Charles Hughes refused to raise with Japan the issue of Korea's cries for independence after the March 1st Movement because the stakes of reaching a deal with Tokyo at the 1921 Washington Naval Conference to delimit Japan's military build-up far outweighed those of Korean independence.[5] American Christian missionaries in Korea, such as Homer Hulbert and Horace Allen, tried to convey the inadvisability of the policy. Allen, who later became head of the US legation in Korea, was recalled in 1905 over his opposition to the Taft–Katsura agreement. Hulbert was eventually expelled by the Japanese in 1907 prior to the formal Japanese annexation of Korea in 1910. Roosevelt refused to hear either man's entreaties as his decision was firm. His own words convey the strength of his convictions:

Korea is absolutely Japan's. . . . Japan could not afford to see Korea in the hands of a great foreign power. She regarded her duty to her children and her children's children as overriding her treaty obligations. Therefore, when Japan thought the right time had come, it calmly tore up the treaty and took Korea, with the polite and businesslike efficiency it had already shown in dealing with Russia, and was afterward to show in dealing with Germany.[6]

Within a period of ten years, Japan succeeded in expelling the Chinese from Korea by defeating them in the Sino-Japanese war, and weakening Russian influence through victory in the Russo-Japanese war. It obtained tacit agreement from the United States not to interfere with its designs for the peninsula. Despite repeated pledges to respect Korean territorial integrity in the Treaty of Shimonoseki, the 1902 Anglo-Japanese Alliance, and a prior 1898 agreement with Russia, Japan saw the path cleared to take over. In 1905, Japan made Korea a protectorate, which established the legal foundation for its domination. It dissolved the Korean army and gave Japan full authority over Korea's internal administration. And on August 22, 1910, it formally annexed Korea as a colony. As was the case with almost every other imperial grab in world history, Japan's rationale took the same imperial tone of bringing "civilization" to the masses:

In order to sweep away evils rooted during the course of many years as well as to secure the well-being of the Korean Imperial family, to promote the prosperity of the country, and at the same time to ensure the safety and repose of Japanese and foreign residents, it has been made abundantly clear that, the protectorate system being unable to achieve these aims, Korea must be annexed to the Empire and brought under the direct administration of the Imperial Government.[7]

9

Our brief rendering of these events highlights one of the most enduring themes with regard to Korea. The country's fate, as was the case in the late nineteenth century, is inextricably tied to the vagaries of its external environment. This environment is characterized by three immutable traits.

The first relates to Korea's *geostrategic location*. The Korean Peninsula sits at the intersection of the major powers of Asia. An appendage of continental Asia bordering China and Russia, and across the sea from Japan. This position makes Korea potentially an invaluable asset, or, if unduly influenced by another, a threat to all. It is a land bridge for Island Japan's access to the Asian mainland, or it is a "dagger" pointed at the heart of Japan. A friendly Korea gives both China and Russia comfort that their rear flank is secure, but an unfriendly one creates vulnerabilities. Korea's position is unenviable in this sense; it lives in a tough neighborhood of large powers—not unlike that of Poland in Europe—and this geostrategic fact will never change.

The second trait relates to *relative power*. In addition to occupying a critical location, Korea does so as a relatively weak state compared with its neighbors. This is, of course, a function of geographic size and population, but it also relates to domestic politics. For most of the nineteenth century, as balance-of-power politics swirled around the peninsula, the country was internally disjointed and factionalized as a result of a host of factors, including corruption of the Joseon dynasty court and acrimonious battles between those who wanted to ride the wave of Western modernizers and the Confucian traditionalists. This internal weakness made Korea vulnerable to forces from the outside. As noted earlier, Roosevelt saw a linear relationship between Korea's weakness and the need for one of the great powers to control it. To quote an old adage, Korea was treated as a "shrimp among whales."

The final trait relates to the *intentions* of the larger powers. The external players in East Asia all want to exert influence over Korea's fate. This could be by choice, in the sense of offensively minded power grabs over a weak neighbor. Or it could be by necessity, in the sense that the powers see Korea's alignment as important to their defensive security needs, rather than any predatory goals.

What all of this amounts to is a Korean Peninsula in East Asia that is valued *strategically, but not intrinsically.* That is, the designs of great powers to control Korea in the late nineteenth century were not about craving something intrinsically special about Korea, its land, its economy, its culture, or its people. The motivations were cruder than that and stemmed from an underlying desire not to allow any other competing power to control it. That is, in the balance-of-power politics of the period, Korea's strategic value was in not allowing it to fall into the other's camp. A weak Korea was a power vacuum in search of Russia, China, or Japan to fill it. Of course, Korea's value today has appreciated significantly from those early days, but the same core calculation still drives the thinking of the neighboring players—the best Korea is one that is friendly to it.

The Occupation Period, 1910–45

The Japanese occupation of Korea from 1910 to 1945 is a difficult and painful period for many Koreans. Conversations about it can quickly become emotional, even among the most professional of colleagues. Victor recalls participating in his first trilateral meeting as a White House official with Korean and Japanese counterparts in a South Korean foreign ministry meeting room. The discussion became heated over a perceived slight by one of the Japanese colleagues, causing a Korean counterpart to lunge out of his chair, shouting and jabbing his finger in the direction of the Japanese official. Victor grabbed the Korean official's belt from behind his suit jacket just as he propelled his torso across Victor's seated position at the table. He recalls jotting in the margins of his notes, "History is alive."

And yet it is impossible to talk about Korea in a modern context without reference to this period. After all, the occupation made up nearly half of Korea's twentieth-century existence, so much so that many aspects of Korea today are directly or indirectly rooted in this period. An entire generation of Koreans, mostly grandparents today, were educated and became literate in Japanese while never formally learning their mother tongue. The loss of sovereignty for thirty-five years is bound to affect a nation's conception of self and what it means to be Korean. The two most important national holidays today, *Samiljeol* and *Gwangbokjeol*, celebrate Korean patriotism by remembering the struggle against Japan.

There were three phases to Japanese occupation of Korea. The initial period, from 1910 to 1919, characterized by some scholars as the "Dark Period," saw the brutal repression of Korean politics and society, as well as the squashing of any dissident efforts to assert independence.[8] The ensuing middle years, from 1919 to 1931, what we term the "Suasion Period," saw a kinder and gentler Japanese administration of its colony that relaxed some of the unpopular controls and even birthed a mini-renaissance of Korean identity in commerce and culture. The final period until the end of World War II was the "Assimilation Period." These years witnessed the harshest policies of the occupation as Japan mobilized for war in China and the Pacific. In particular, the efforts to wipe out Korean identity by a wartime Japanese government left the deepest indelible imprint on Koreans today.

The government structure of the occupation was one of absolute, centralized, and total control. Scholar Gregory Henderson termed it "colonial totalitarianism."[9] Power was located in a massive bureaucracy run by the governor-general, Terauchi Masatake, who was technically part of the home ministry back in Tokyo, but held absolute executive, legislative, and judicial authority over all issues pertaining to Korea. As an imperial appointee, the governor-general reported directly to the emperor and held the power of appointment over all officials down to the local village level. Basically, everything was decided by the governor-general.

Through this apparatus, Japan sought to stamp out all forms of Korean resistance in the initial years of the occupation. The bloodiest repression took place in the years between the protectorate treaty in 1907 and the annexation in 1910. In Korea and China, Japan launched "pacification campaigns" in cities and the countryside to root out the independence fighters. Also known as "righteous armies" in Korea, these fighters were the primary form of armed resistance, organized loosely as bands of peasants, many of them holdovers from the Donghak Rebellion. These groups grew in number after the dissolution of the Korean army in 1905. They used guerrilla tactics to disrupt the colonial administration, targeting communications and transport infrastructure. The assassination of former prime minister Ito Hirobumi in October 1909 by An Jung-gun at a railway station in China reflected the work of these freedom fighters and, at the time, the last gasp of Korean efforts to resist the imminent annexation. The pacification campaigns killed over 17,000 independence fighters during these interregnum years between protectorate and annexation.

Another target of colonial repression during the Dark Period was political leaders. Japan sought to purge all prominent Korean nationalists and to deter others from taking up the mantle of independence. In 1912 alone, more than 50,000 people were arrested for illegal political activity and assembly.[10] The public trial of the Case of One Hundred Five in 1911 was typical of the methods used. Nationalists were rounded up on the pretext of a conspiracy to assassinate

13

Governor-General Terauchi Masatake. Claiming that the assassination plot was part of a bigger conspiracy, the colonial police arrested more than 600 people and ultimately indicted 100, including important members of the Korean nationalist leadership. Among those indicted were prominent leaders of *Sinminhoe* (New People's Association), formed in 1907 to promote cultural activities, education, and native economic development. While the association was not involved in the assassination attempt, the incident nevertheless provided a convenient basis to target organized resistance movements and to discourage others from considering resistance.

A major instrument of repression was the curbing of basic civil rights and freedom of expression. In order to control an occupied population, Japanese authorities banned the right to organize and heavily censored publications. The 1907 Newspaper Law, the 1907 Peace Preservation Law, and the 1909 Publication Law were just some of the measures designed to ban the right of assembly, any form of political organization, and the circulation of Korean-language publications. These laws were designed to suppress both the catalysts for and the organization of any political resistance.

The primary means by which Japan enforced these policies was through the colonial police. This was a large force relative to the population (for example, compared with the force employed by the French in Indochina), which was endowed with significant power, including the power to arrest, adjudicate, and render punishment on the spot. Their methods were often brutal, and they became a hated symbol of the occupation. In 1910, there were 6,222 military and civilian police under the governor-general. By 1922, this number had more than tripled, to 20,771, and had more than tripled again by 1941 to reach over 60,000 police.[11] What made the legacy of the police even more bitter was that a good part of the force was made up of Koreans hired by Japanese colonial authorities to overcome the language barrier, and for their familiarity with the local terrain. Roughly half of the police force was Korean, and the colonial thought police frequently employed an extensive network of native informers. Many of these were from lower classes in pre-colonial Korea, which tore even further at the social fabric of the occupied population, as these colonial police were now imbued with power in a society that formerly shunned them as outcasts. Complicating this dynamic further, some of the police had little choice but to join the force lest they or their family members be detained.

For Koreans, life under Japan's occupation was one of discrimination. Those who held positions in the colonial bureaucracy had some privileges, but no Korean was immune from social bias. Though the Japanese made up only 3 percent of the population, they enjoyed all of the benefits. Koreans, on the other hand, regularly paid a separate and higher interest rate on borrowed money, made about one-half of the wages of their Japanese counterparts, and still paid higher taxes.

The March 1st Movement

The harsh curtailment on freedom of expression in colonial Korea could not prevent a well of resentment against Japanese rule that found expression in the *Samil* (March 1st) Movement in 1919, a nationwide peaceful demonstration against the Japanese occupation. On the morning of March 1, 1919, thirty-three nationalists at the core of the movement signed a declaration of independence that was read in Pagoda Park, in central Seoul, and dispatched to the governor-general. All signatories were promptly arrested. Unarmed demonstrators made their way to the Japanese colonial headquarters and clashed violently with the police. The demonstrations started in Seoul but fanned out to the countryside along the main railway lines from Seoul to Uiju, Wonsan, and Busan. They continued sporadically for over a month involving between 1 and 2 million citizens.[12]

The Japanese authorities were taken by surprise at the united show of resistance, which they proceeded to brutally put down. The police fired on unarmed demonstrators and tortured Koreans in public. The Japanese sent for reinforcements, which arrived in April, and undertook a campaign attacking villages and destroying Christian and *Cheondogyo* churches. In one case, known as the *Jeam-ri* massacre, they targeted Christians in villages by locking them in a local church and setting it on fire.[13] Numbers of deaths are unclear. Japanese reports cite some 500 fatalities and about 12,000 arrests in the ensuing month, but Korean sources record 7,500 deaths and over 45,000 arrested.[14]

Several factors in tandem led to the March 1st Movement. First, events on the international scene—in particular, the emergence of a new post-imperial world order in the wake of World War I, and Woodrow Wilson's Fourteen Points calling for national self-determination of all people—inspired Koreans to give voice to their aspirations for liberation from Japanese rule. They believed that their protests would resonate with the international community. Excerpts from the March 1st independence declaration illustrate the inspiration to Koreans of a new post-World War I order that would favor their liberation from Japan:

We hereby declare that Korea is an independent state and that Koreans are a self-governing people. We proclaim it to the nations of the world in affirmation of the principle of the equality of all nations, and we proclaim it to our posterity, preserving in perpetuity the right of national survival. We make this declaration on the strength of five thousand years of history as an expression of devotion and loyalty of twenty million people. We claim independence in the interest of the eternal and free development of our people and in accordance with the great movement for world reform based upon the awakening conscience of mankind.... For the first time in several thousand years, we have suffered the agony of alien suppression for a decade, becoming a victim of the policies of aggression and coercion, which are relics from a bygone era. How long have we been deprived of our right to exist? How long has our spiritual development been hampered? How long have the opportunities to contribute our creative vitality to the development of world culture been denied us? ... Behold! A new world is before our eyes. The days of force are gone, and the days of morality are here.[15]

Second, a union of internal activist groups, including students and religious groups (like the *Cheondogyo*), worked to organize covertly. Third, Koreans in exile, who had left the country during Japan's occupation and who had advocated for Korean independence abroad, pleaded the Korean case before the international audience. Syngman Rhee, head of a Korean nationalist association in Hawai'i, brought a petition to Washington and wrote to Woodrow Wilson to plead Korea's case, but received no reply. He took out an ad in the *New York Times* demanding President Wilson recognize Korea as independent.[16] Korean nationalist Kim Kyu-sik, living in China, attended the Paris Peace Conference to lobby the victors for Korean independence. Korean nationalists in Japan also assembled in secret and presented a petition to the Diet and the Korean governor-general.[17]

Finally, the pent-up emotion and nationalist sentiment found a catalyzing event in the mass funeral for the death of Emperor Kojong, the last king of an unoccupied Korea, who was forcibly deposed by Japan's colonial authorities.

The March 1st Movement, in retrospect, failed to achieve its goals. The demonstrations were completely suppressed, and Korea did not win independence. Moreover, despite Wilson's call for self-determination, the movement did not win the sympathies of the international community. As the then German consul remarked, "It's a shame but no one I think will send a gunboat [to help Korea]."[18]

So why is the March 1st Movement remembered as such an important part of Korea's history? It was the first mobilization and expression of Korean resistance on a mass level. Prior to this event, there proliferated unorganized and scattered resentment by radicals and elites, but as Eckert et al. state, *Samil* awakened "the entire nation to the accumulated political, cultural, and economic inequities inherent in Japanese imperial rule."[19]

The method of protest was also quite significant. The *Samil* movement was led by religious figures, students, and activists in a national peaceful demonstration. This was juxtaposed to the violent suppression by Japanese authorities, thereby wholly delegitimizing Japanese rule and giving the Korean resistance the moral high ground. As will be discussed, this impacted not just Koreans but also the Japanese, who became more conscious of the optics of their policies going forward after 1919.

The *Samil* movement also spurred a temporary union of disparate indigenous and external nationalist groups. In Japan, Korean students organized to demand independence. In Korea, *Cheondogyo*, Buddhists, and Christians united for the purpose of calling for liberation. In April 1919, disparate nationalist groups in exile formed the Korean Provisional Government in Shanghai with Syngman Rhee as president. The movement also helped to enforce a stronger sense of a unique Korean identity. It was significant not just for the opposition to Japanese rule but because the movement was led by Koreans as individuals rather than as Japanese imperial subjects. In sum, the March 1st Movement represented a focal point of unity of indigenous groups, external groups, progressives, conservatives, students, religious leaders, radicals, and elites in the history of Korea's struggle for independence. Prior to this movement, the groups were fractured and unorganized; moreover, afterwards they would suffer the same fate, even beyond liberation and ultimately up to the Korean War. *Samil* manifested the crystallization of unified Korean full-throated expression of nationalism, liberation, and anti-Japan resentment like no other.

The period after the March 1st Movement saw liberalization during the middle "Suasion Period" (1919–31), as colonial authorities tried to put a kinder and gentler face on the occupation. Japanese Governor-General Hasegawa Yoshimichi took responsibility for allowing the loss of control of the Korean colony and was replaced by Saitō Makoto. The temporary relaxation of restrictions during this middle period of the occupation led to a renaissance of sorts in colonial Korea, with a proliferation of social and cultural groups. Daily newspapers like *Donga Ilbo* and *Chosun Ilbo* flourished,[20] as did various literary fora in which public discussions about national identity could take place. In 1921, educators created the Korean Language Society to keep the teaching of *hangeul* alive and preserve literacy in Korean. The movement standardized grammar and spelling, and sought to create a Korean-language dictionary. Despite these efforts, many Koreans born during the later Assimilation Period would only have the benefit of formal education in Japanese and not their native language. Though many of this generation are now in their late 80s or early 90s, they are readily identifiable as they still recite multiplication tables in Japanese.

Groups during this renaissance period of colonial Korea also sought to preserve Korean industry. The *Joseon Mulsan Jangnyeo Undong* (Korean Production Movement, 1923–4) encouraged citizens to "buy Korean" to help homegrown businesses that were getting crowded out of the market by the flood of Japanese imports. The motto of "our livelihood with our products" manifested the desire to maintain an indigenous Korean industrial base that could form the basis of an independent national economy in the future. As well-intended and well-organized as this movement was, it met with challenges—Japanese companies bought out many large Korean producers; consumers grew tired of paying higher prices for lower-quality Korean-made goods; and leftist independence activists criticized the capitalist nature of the endeavor.

In the immediate aftermath of the March 1st Movement (between 1920 and 1922), the number of Korean groups ballooned from 985 to 5,728.[21] They all had to be careful to walk the fine line between celebrating and preserving the Korean identity, while avoiding advocating resistance, or independence.

Assimilation Period

Japan's acceptance of the promotion of Korean identity was not out of goodwill; rather it was part of an effort to persuade Koreans to internalize a belief that Koreans were cousins of Japanese, and therefore part of a "master race" and subjects of the emperor. However, as Imperial Japan went to war in China and the Pacific from 1937 to 1945, this suasion strategy transformed into a draconian effort to erase Korean culture and identity. It was during these years that Japan enacted a number of policies that are remembered by Koreans as the most unforgiveable practices of its colonizer, which carried legacies that continue to mar contemporary relations.

From 1925, with the Peace Preservation Law enactment, Japan started to restrict Korean cultural activities. The target was "cultural" activities because all political activities had already been banned. In 1934, the new Rescript on Education ordered the de-emphasis of Korean culture and banned the use of the Korean language in schools and in public offices. Incentives for Japanese to learn Korean were eliminated. The colonial authorities redoubled efforts to inculcate Koreans from a young age to internalize the imperial narrative. Every morning, Korean students were to sing the Japanese national anthem, raise the Japanese flag, and bow deeply to the flag while pledging allegiance to the emperor. The 1935 Shinto Shrine Order mandated all Koreans to practice the state religion in schools and workplaces.

After the Marco Polo Bridge Incident of 1937, marking the start of Japan's aggressive designs on Manchuria, a 1938 governor-general report called for "*Naisen Ittai*" (Japan–Korea One Body), which mandated policies to culturally assimilate Koreans. From 1940, the governor-general shut down all Korean-language newspapers except the *Maeil Sinbo*, which was used as a tool to convey imperial messages. After the military altercation at the Marco Polo Bridge, for example, the *Maeil Sinbo* published articles endorsing Japan's actions by famous Korean poet Yun Ch'i-ho and historian Ch'oe Namson.[22] One of the most hated elements of Japanese assimilation policies was the 1940 Name Order Edict ("*Sōshi-kaimei*"), which required Koreans to give up their names and take on Japanese names. By 1944, around 84 percent of Koreans had lost their names (a 1946 Name Restoration Order during the US military occupation reversed this).[23]

Between 1932 and 1945, tens of thousands of Korean, Chinese, Southeast Asian, and European women were forced to serve Japanese soldiers in "comfort stations," mainly in Japanese-occupied China. Some of these girls were barely teenagers and were either forcibly abducted or told lies that they were being recruited to train as nurses. They were then sent to brothels and forced to have sex with soldiers in filthy, violent, and disease-ridden conditions. The Japanese government destroyed documents at the end of the war, so there is no official record (though scholars have unearthed some), and controversy continues to this day over denials by some Japanese that the practice ever existed, and over two agreements between Japan and Korea to compensate these victims, which are deemed insufficient by Koreans.

And between 1938 and 1945, millions of Koreans were conscripted as part of a National Mobilization Law. Around 1.5 million were uprooted from their homes and sent to China and Japan, and another 2 million were moved within Korea to serve the Japanese war effort. Many slaved through seventeen-hour workdays in mines and died in accidents in unsafe conditions working for Mitsui, Mitsubishi, Sumitomo, and other Japanese big businesses (*zaibatsu*). About 80,000 were in Hiroshima and Nagasaki when the US dropped the atomic bombs. These issues continue to haunt contemporary relations. Some argue that neither the Korean nor the Japanese governments have done enough to compensate these victims. Moreover, South Korean court rulings in 2018 decided that claims of compensation could still be made by victims against Japanese companies, despite the reparations settlement in the 1965 normalization treaty between Japan and Korea.

Double-edged Sword

During the opening ceremony of the 2018 PyeongChang Winter Olympics in South Korea, as the Japanese athletes entered the stadium, an NBC television analyst remarked, as the cameras panned to the country's prime minister Shinzo Abe in attendance, "[Athletes] representing Japan, a country which occupied Korea from 1910 to 1945, but every Korean will tell you that Japan is a cultural, technological, and economic example that has been so important to their own transformation." These words by the commentator, Joshua Cooper Ramo, sparked an uproar on social media and demands for Ramo's firing for "culturally insensitive" remarks, for which NBC later apologized.[24] The response to Ramo's remark underscores how sensitive and raw emotions remain when any semblance of credit is given to Japan for playing a role in Korea's modern development.

Many, if not all Koreans are wholly unwilling to accept that the occupation period did anything good for the nation. Indeed, even if they were to admit to this, those gains would be far outweighed by Koreans' suffering, their inhumane treatment by colonial authorities, and the usurpation of their national sovereignty for nearly half a century. However, a history of this period would be deficient if it did not enumerate some of the development that took place in colonial Korea. We call this "double-edged" development because, although all that Japan did to Korea was exploitative in nature and designed for Japan's benefit, it nonetheless did provide the country with certain benefits.

Education is a good example of a double-edged development. Japanese colonizers saw education as one of the primary means by which to control and assimilate the Korean population. It sought to revamp the Korean education system entirely in its own image. It instituted curricula in public schools teaching Japanese values and the importance of respect for and service to the emperor. Japanese was taught as the primary language, with Korean as the secondary language. History textbooks were rewritten to positively reflect on Japan and the legitimacy of its rule over Korea. The purpose was to educate a generation of Korean youth to be obedient citizens and a literate labor force, to eradicate Korean identity, and to internalize Japanese goals. This was a blatant effort at thought control for political purposes.

In the process of implementing this plan, Japan built hundreds of schools in the Korean colony and enrollment increased dramatically from the pre-colonial times, when education was the privilege of the elite *yangban* class. Literacy among the Korean population during the colonial years increased from 20 percent in 1912 to over 60 percent by 1940. Elementary school enrollment during the occupation went from 35,630 in 1911 to 1.1 million in 1938; middle and high school enrollment went from about 1,000 in 1911 to almost 26,000 in 1938; and total school enrollment (including college) went from a paltry 110,000 in 1911 to 1.38 million in 1938. Vocational school enrollment went from less than 1,000 students in 1911 to over 22,000 in 1938. Even girls were given the opportunity for schooling—fewer than 1,000 were enrolled in 1911, and more than 20,000 were in school by 1938. The total number of schools grew fivefold from 2,000 in 1911 to over 5,000 in 1938. The number of universities in Korea grew from 5 to 17.[25]

The double-edged impact of the occupation was also evident in the economy. Not only did Japan bring many trappings of a modern capitalist system to Korea for its own benefit, but this also indirectly benefited the Korean economy. In the later years of the occupation, as Imperial Japan mobilized for war, it built a modern network of transport (roads, railways, dams, ports) and communications infrastructure in its Korean colony. It built hydroelectric plants, steel mills, and chemical plants—which were state-of-the-art in the world at that time. The purpose was to link Korea and Manchuria into a single integrated economy to fuel the war effort. But at liberation, Korea was endowed with paved roads, railways, and telegraph infrastructure more advanced than most other countries in Asia. Investment in the public railroad system accounted for more than one-half of total public investment, with public railroads increasing from 1,006 miles in 1910 to 2,819 miles in 1942. By 1945, there were 1,130 train engines, 2,016 passenger cars, and 15,247 cargo trains. Between 1941 and 1945 alone, more than 200 engines, 652 passenger cars, and 3,990 boxcars were imported from Japan; in comparison, Korea produced more than 20 engines, 99 passenger cars, and 7,000 boxcars during the years from 1930 to 1944.[26]

Similarly in agriculture, while Japan ravaged the Korean countryside, and exploited and extracted mineral deposits and timber, colonial Korea was also exposed to modern irrigation and mining techniques. In northern Korea, particularly during Japan's war mobilization, the country was exposed to the development of heavy industry and tool, and machinery production. Indeed, this concentration of industrial development was the source of North Korea's economic advantage over South Korea at liberation. In southern Korea, Japan forced the expansion of the cotton industry, which was not traditional in Korea, through land expropriation and the use of dislocated labor.[27] This industry was then used to serve the metropolis, in this case Osaka, which was Japan's cotton center.

Basically, Japan's self-serving development of its Korean colony helped to start to transform a traditional, inefficient, agrarian economy into what one day would become a modern, urban, and industrial one. In 1910, the Korean economy was 95 percent agrarian (agriculture, fishing) and 3.5 percent manufacturing. By 1940, 60 percent of the economy was agrarian and 22 percent was manufacturing. In 1905, industry in Korea (manufacturing, gas, and electric power) was underdeveloped, with enterprises focused mostly on traditional handicraft and cottage-industry type. After 1910, however, the number of industrial companies increased significantly, from 25 in 1910 to 1,541 in 1940.[28] The number of industrial factories also increased from 151 in 1910 to 14,856 in 1943. Investments in the industrial sector were particularly pronounced in manufacturing, with the number of manufacturing companies increasing from less than 5 in 1905 to 1,964 in 1941. Within manufacturing, heavy and chemical industries (metal, machinery, and fertilizer manufacturing) saw the greatest expansion in investment under Japanese rule, increasing from an insignificant level in the early years to 36 percent of investment in 1941. The number of chemical manufacturers increased from 393 in 1929 to 1,588 in 1938, and the number of chemical factories increased from a negligible number in 1905 to 144 in 1941. Similarly, the number of metal and machinery companies, which were virtually non-existent in 1923, increased to 234 in 1941. Investment in the electric power and gas industries also expanded rapidly, and both industries played an important role in Korea's industrialization. In 1906, there were two electric power companies in Korea. This number increased to sixty-two in 1932 before being consolidated into twenty-one in 1937. This came at a tremendous expense to Koreans in terms of social dislocation, especially labor conscription; but in the process, Korea was introduced to economic efficiency, technical training, and business management when compared with the agrarian and backward economy of the Joseon dynasty.

All Koreans feel that the occupation was unjust and hold Japan accountable for wrongdoings over half a century later. The recent court cases in South Korea, calling for Japanese companies to pay compensation for labor conscription policies in the 1930s, is only the latest example of the continuing story of injustice. Imperial Japan justified its actions at the time, and showed no sense of remorse. In addition to the view that it was part of Japan's larger manifest destiny to rule Korea, and all of Asia, the colonial narrative propagated was that Korea's annexation represented the consummation of a natural union between the two peoples because of geographic propinquity, historical and cultural ties, and *"Nissen Yuwa"* (Japan–Korea harmony). The Korean colony was part of Japan's larger Greater East Asia Co-prosperity Sphere, in which Koreans would occupy a special place in the bosom of the Japanese empire.

To achieve *"Nissen Yuwa,"* Korea and Koreans had to be assimilated into a Japanese identity. And while these policies were introduced in the Suasion Period, their most notorious manifestations were during the war period. As noted above, the 1934 Rescript on Education, the 1935 Shinto Shrine Order, and the 1940 Name Order Edict reflected the ultimate attempt at identity absorption as it required all Korean subjects of the empire to adopt Japanese names. The reality was that Korean colonial citizens were the subject of social and institutional discrimination. Imperial Japan viewed Koreans as racially inferior, subject to discriminatory treatment under the law, in society, and in the colonial bureaucracy. In the latter case, Japan needed Koreans to help administer the colony, but their positions were often at the lowest levels. Similarly, the Name Order Edict was couched by imperial authorities in the language of harmony and removing any distinctions between Korean and Japanese, but the government recorded clearly which "Japanese" citizens were of Korean descent. Thus, beneath the rhetoric of inclusion lay practices of exclusion and hypocrisy.

There were many painful legacies of the occupation for Koreans, foremost among them the sex slaves ("comfort women") and labor conscription policies. One of the more conflicted legacies related to the way in which colonial co-optation strategies succeeded in winning the complicity of many Koreans from all parts of society. As noted earlier, Japan co-opted the lower class in Korea by using them to fill the ranks of the colonial police. They became one of the most controversial symbols of the occupation.

Another co-opted group were conservative elites. Many of the *yangban* aristocracy and former government officials were bought off by being given noble titles, fat pensions, and in some cases, a position on the Central Advisory Council, which was a rubber-stamp advisory board to the governor-general. Of the 84 noble titles offered to elites in 1910, only 8 were refused, and over 3,000 pensions were disbursed.[29] While many of these elites opposed Japan's usurpation of Korean sovereignty, the promise of a title and social status at a time when life as they knew it was under assault and uncertain was hard to turn down.

A third target of co-optation was landowners. While Japan seized all land held by Korean royalty, it instituted a Western legal system that required proof of title to the land. This forced squatters off property, but it enabled the majority of medium and large landowners to retain titles to the land. This was a form of co-optation as these families, fearful of losing everything, were not just relieved but empowered by a formal legal title system of ownership. By co-opting the aristocracy, elites, officials, and police, Japan's policies effectively took away the basis of leadership of any Korean resistance movement.

These policies of co-optation managed to pit Koreans against Koreans, and this is perhaps one of the most painful legacies of the occupation period besides colonization itself. It is inconceivable for Koreans to believe that their elites and political leaders collaborated with the Japanese. Indeed, it was heart-wrenching for many Koreans to contemplate a new identity, a new life, and new ambitions under a Japanese system. They had no idea that the occupation would end thirty-five years later. To them this was the permanent new reality. Yet others clung to their old identity, and were left without opportunity in their resistance. This naturally raised questions about what it meant to be Korean and to be a patriot—some believed this meant resistance to the bitter end, while others believed it meant to effect change through the system rather than in opposition to it. These social divisions became obvious in the aftermath of the *Samil* movement. Radical groups led by labor and students saw Korea's future salvation only through revolution, while moderates sought to build the foundation for Korea's eventual independence within the bounds of the Japanese system. These divisions were accentuated between nationalists who chose to stay in the country and those who left after Japan's takeover to establish governments-in-exile. The legacies of colonization and these divisions would tear at the fabric of the nation for decades thereafter.

2
LIBERATION, DIVISION, AND WAR
1945 TO 1953

The US delegation arrived on the northern side of the Joint Security Area one hour earlier than the appointed time after the two-and-a-half-hour drive from Pyongyang. It was early spring, and the morning air was cool. The delegation had just finished three days of negotiations with the North Korean military over the return of prisoner of war (POW)/missing in action (MIA) remains from the Korean War. They were to cross over the cement military demarcation line (MDL) in the Joint Security Area to awaiting US and South Korean military forces—the same place where Donald Trump would embrace Kim Jong-un thirteen years later.

Because the Joint Security Area sits at the most heavily militarized border in the world, regulations stipulate the precise time for the permission to cross, and it cannot be crossed before or after that time. Having checked to see that the pelican cases carrying the POW/MIA remains had arrived in the trail van, Victor Cha wondered what they would do with the hour remaining before they could cross. Their North

Korean interlocutor then asked, "Dr. Cha, would you like to see where the armistice was signed?" The scholar in Victor could not be suppressed, and he nodded approvingly. Victor got back in the car and after a short three-quarter-mile ride, arrived at a small, one-story white structure with brown wood trim. The unadorned room was unoccupied except for three green felt-covered tables and two white chairs in the center. On each table sat the flags of the Democratic People's Republic of Korea (DPRK) and the United Nations (UN), with a glass case memorializing the documents and writing instruments used to sign the Korean War armistice on July 27, 1953. Victor stared at the tables, cognizant that few Westerners would have a chance to view this piece of history cloistered in North Korea. While the conflict came to a close in 1953, the war has never ended officially. Only a ceasefire, signed and sealed at this table, keeps the peace. Victor thought about the millions of casualties over the course of this three-year conflict, which ended at the 38th parallel, the same place that it had started. As Victor walked to the car, he turned back for a final glance at the building that sat peacefully in the most heavily mined piece of real estate on the face of the planet. He wondered whether a peace treaty officially ending the Korean War would ever happen in his lifetime.

* * *

Liberation and Division

To our good and loyal subjects: After pondering deeply the general trends of the world and the actual conditions obtaining in our empire today, we have decided to effect a settlement of the present situation by resorting to an extraordinary measure. We have ordered our Government to communicate to the Governments of the United States, Great Britain, China and the Soviet Union that our empire accepts the provisions of their joint declaration. To strive for the common prosperity and happiness of all nations as well as the security and well-being of our subjects is the solemn obligation which has been handed down by our imperial ancestors and which we lay close to the heart ... the war situation has developed not necessarily to Japan's advantage, while the general trends of the world have all turned against her interest. Moreover, the enemy has begun to employ a new and most cruel bomb, the power of which to do damage is, indeed, incalculable, taking the toll of many innocent lives. Should we continue to fight, it would not only result in an ultimate collapse and obliteration of the Japanese nation, but also it would lead to the total extinction of human civilization.[1]

With these words broadcast by Japanese Emperor Hirohito over the radio to his imperial subjects and to the world, the thirty-five-year occupation of Korea ended abruptly. Japan's unconditional surrender to Allied forces—formally signed on September 2, 1945, and ending World War II—came without any forewarning to Koreans. What had seemed like eternal subjugation to foreign colonizers was finished. Koreans harbored great aspirations with its newfound liberation, but independence brought more challenge than opportunity, and once again subjugated the country to external balance-of-power forces that determined Korea's fate. Few could have imagined at the time that national liberation from the hated Japanese would be followed by national division, and then a fratricidal war.

Japan's defeat in World War II suddenly released the Korean Peninsula from a system that had been in place for almost four decades. This would have immediate consequences for liberated Korea. The first was acute social dislocation as a result of dramatic population transfers. At the end of World War II, there were over 2 million Koreans in Japan, 1.4 million Koreans in Manchuria,

600,000 in Siberia, and 130,000 in China. The end of Japanese colonial labor conscription policies permitted about 1.5 million Koreans to return home from Japan, and over 500,000 from China, Manchuria, and Siberia.[2] These movements led to the sudden overpopulation of urban centers, as well as over 1.8 million internally displaced persons across the peninsula seeking to reconstitute their lives as they knew them prior to the occupation.[3]

The second consequence of Japan's surrender for liberated Korea was acute economic dislocation. Colonial authorities ran an efficient and productive war economy for the Japanese empire which all suddenly ground to a halt. Between 600,000 and 850,000 Japanese in Korea returned to their home country, creating a massive brain drain of managers, technicians, and other experts.[4] Over 90 percent of industrial property in colonial Korea was now suddenly unattended and unowned. Farmlands were rendered infertile by overcropping and the heavy use of chemical fertilizers by the Japanese. Koreans sought to rebuild the economy with the colonizer's departure, but the country essentially went from a fully functioning, full-employment war economy run by Japan to an economy without direction, management, or technical expertise. Unemployment rose to nearly 50 percent within two years,[5] with unfortunate social consequences. Rising rates of criminal behavior, homelessness, and alcoholism were the unfortunate social ramifications for the masses who thought that liberation would bring them much more.

"In Due Course"

Koreans naturally thought that the liberation of the country would mean independence as a nation-state. After all, that was Korea's right before the external powers conspired to usurp its sovereignty at the turn of the century. But as World War II drew to a close, the Allied powers, wary of a weak Korea in the face of balance-of-power politics, sought a different fate for Korea. Koreans on the peninsula and from abroad in China and the United States tried to change this fate, but to no avail.

FDR faced a dilemma as he mapped out US strategy at the end of the Pacific War. He believed that Imperial Japan should relinquish all its colonies, but he did not necessarily want them all to become independent. Nor did FDR want the United States to expend limited resources and political capital, or to be responsible for them, because his main theater of concern was Western Europe. At the same time, however, the US did not want these former colonies to return to European subjugation, nor to succumb to growing communist influence from the Soviet Union. The concept that emerged under these circumstances was an international trusteeship or guardianship for Korea, with independence to be granted "in due course" at some point in the future.

At the Third Washington Conference in May 1943, FDR discussed with British Foreign Secretary Anthony Eden the disposition of Japan's colonies after the war. They agreed that Manchuria and Formosa (Taiwan) would be returned to China. FDR also first broached the trusteeship formula for Korea and Indonesia as an interim stage after liberation and before self-governance was granted. The following November, at the Cairo conference, involving the United States, Britain, and China, FDR stated his view that the period of tutelage for Korea should last for forty years, which elicited ambivalent responses from British Prime Minister Winston Churchill and then Chairman of the Nationalist Government of China Chiang Kai-shek. Wanting to reinstate China's traditional influence over an independent Korea, the latter advocated recognition of a newly independent Korea run by the Korean Provisional Government-in-exile in China (Chiang, however, eventually deferred to Washington because of his need for US assistance). In the end, the three leaders agreed to trusteeship language that would postpone Korea's independence: "The three Great Powers, mindful of the treacherous enslavement of the people of Korea, are determined that, *in due course*, Korea shall become a free and independent country."[6]

Stalin was brought into the conversation at the Tehran Conference in November–December 1943 and then again at the Yalta Conference in February 1945; but he, like Chiang, was ambivalent about FDR's insistence on a long period of trusteeship for Korea because he too wanted to wield influence over a Korea independent from Japan. The leaders all agreed to an informal consensus of about five to ten years with the US, Soviet Union, China, and Britain as the guarantors. Cooperation among the Allied powers envisioned in the trusteeship formula reflected an agreement to disagree about Korea's fate—over which Koreans had little say—and would eventually give way to Cold War tensions and American and Soviet military occupation of Korea.

FDR's insistence on trusteeship until his death in April 1945 stemmed from a combination of balance-of-power politics, lack of interest, and paternalism. The last thing that the US wanted in Asia after the Pacific War was more conflict created by regional powers like China and Russia jockeying for influence over a newly independent and weak Korea. After all, each had gone to war over Korea at the end of the nineteenth century. Trusteeship could hold these forces in check for a period of time. Trusteeship also seemed like the best answer for a problem that could not be afforded constant US attention. Because the main theater for postwar reconstruction was Europe, the US had neither the time nor the resources to nation-build anywhere else in Asia except Japan. Indeed, discussions about Korea among the leaders at Cairo and Yalta were almost an afterthought. Trusteeship provided a convenient way to place the issue on the backburner. Finally, an overriding paternalism, laced with racism, informed American attitudes.

Even though Korea had been an independent sovereign country for thousands of years before the Japanese occupation, US policymakers completely unfamiliar with Korea's history assumed that the country could not govern itself after Japan's departure. Secretary of State Edward R. Stettinius Jr., in the middle of conversations about Korea in 1945, was reportedly unable to locate the country on a map.[7] A January 1945 British Foreign Office report on Korea concluded, "The Korean people have had no experience in the organization and working of national representative institutions or in the execution of higher administrative tasks."[8] Washington policymakers did not reach similar paternalistic conclusions regarding similarly positioned countries in Europe. As one author observed when comparing US attitudes toward Austria and Korea after Germany and Japan's defeat:

> little doubt existed about the intrinsic capacity of Austrians to govern themselves. . . . The appearance and behavior of Austrians was far closer than Koreans to those of the Americans who tried to shape the postwar world. As one top U.S. official confided to his diary during a January 1946 visit to the peninsula, "Korea was a strange land, with strange-looking people."[9]

The enthusiasm for trusteeship in Korea, in Africa, and in Indochina was informed by Americans' self-perceived success in the Philippines, which progressed under fifty years of tutelage before Ivy-league Westerners felt comfortable that brown-skinned subjects could be trusted to govern themselves.

Division and Occupation (Again)

Plans for trusteeship soon gave way to Cold War balance-of-power politics as the US and the Soviet Union jockeyed for position on the

Korean Peninsula. Soviet leader Joseph Stalin declared war against Japan and entered the Pacific War on August 8, 1945, three months after the defeat of Nazi Germany and two days after the US dropped an atomic bomb on Hiroshima. Soviet forces advanced against Japan's Kwantung Army in Manchuria and assaulted enemy forces near Wonsan, Korea on August 12. These forces succeeded in taking Pyongyang on August 24. Concerned that Moscow would take the entire peninsula, the US proposed a division of Korea into two occupation zones to which the Soviets agreed. The decision about where to bisect the country was left to a junior colonel named Charles Bonesteel, who worked on the Strategy Policy Committee at the Pentagon. Bonesteel was given 30 minutes to come up with a dividing line for the occupation zones on the Korean Peninsula. While the Soviets were already in Pyongyang, the closest US forces available to receive the Japanese surrender were 600 miles away in Okinawa, Japan. Bonesteel had to find a line as far north as possible that the Soviets would accept. If Moscow did not accept the dividing line and instead took Seoul, there was little that the United States could do. Using a *National Geographic* magazine map of Korea, Bonesteel looked for a dividing line that kept Seoul in the US occupation zone, but could not find a readily identifiable geographic marker. Instead, he saw the 38th parallel and recommended that.

The 38th parallel was imposed by the United States without any regard for Korea's physical attributes. The border arbitrarily divided many natural features—over 75 streams, 12 rivers, over 300 local roads, 8 highways, and 6 rail lines. The division would also wreak economic havoc on the country. It put farmland in the South but fertilizer production in the North. It put some manufacturing in the South but raw materials and electricity generation in the North.[10] Korea, which had just been liberated from decades of foreign occupation, had no say in an agreement between the two powers that arbitrarily divided millions of Korean families between the Soviet and American sectors. They could only find solace in the stated plans for the two Koreas to be unified eventually under UN-supervised elections, as promised by the United Nations.

Why Stalin agreed to the US proposal when he could have taken the entire peninsula remains unclear (the US had a contingency plan to land at Busan if the Soviets took Seoul, but for what purpose was not entirely clear). One possible explanation is that Stalin never intended to take all of Korea. With only two divisions dispatched to Korea, Stalin may have been deterred from advancing further against the nine Japanese divisions still deployed there (having taken heavy losses in the amphibious assault on Wonsan). Another is that the US proposal to divide Korea at the 38th parallel was interpreted as similar to the proposal for spheres of influence that Japan offered in the early twentieth century. Stalin may have wanted to avoid repeating the same mistake of his predecessors, of rejecting the proposal, and then losing the war. A third plausible explanation is that with the US nuclear monopoly at this time, Stalin may have been deterred from resisting. Finally, he may have believed that cooperation with the United States on Korea might afford the Soviet Union a larger role in the occupation of Japan.

American and Soviet Occupations

The US and Soviet occupations of Korea were not particularly well-executed operations. They were carried out with minimal preparation and with limited knowledge of the complex political dynamics playing out in the aftermath of liberation. Each great power sought a stake in Korea not because it valued Korea's economy, people, resources, or culture intrinsically, but because it did not want the country to fall into the other's hands.

The US occupation of Korea was run by General John R. Hodge, who had much combat, but little political and administrative experience running a military occupation. Hodge had no familiarity with Korea, and none of the West Point polish of his counterpart in Japan (General Douglas MacArthur). As head of XXIV Corps in Okinawa, Hodge received orders on the day of Korean liberation to occupy the US sector south of the 38th parallel to receive the Japanese surrender. There were other generals with more experience in Asia, like Joseph Stilwell and Albert C. Wedemeyer, but Hodge was chosen because he was physically closest to Korea, hence making him the only US general chosen to run a military occupation based on shipping time. He was assigned a political adviser from the State Department, H. Merrell Benninghoff, who also had no experience of Korea.[11] Hodge's civil affairs team (an important part of any military occupation) was delayed for a month after Hodge's arrival on September 8, 1945. They reportedly received nine months of training for their original posting to the Philippines, and only a one-hour briefing on Korea. The Truman administration simply had higher priorities. The postwar disposition of Germany, the reconstruction of Western Europe, the occupation of Japan, and the civil conflict in China dominated the agenda. Korea was an afterthought. The assembly of such an unprepared team ensured difficulties in the US occupation of Korea, and these difficulties reflected once again how external forces would impinge on Korea's fate at such a critical moment.

American unpreparedness for the occupation was profound. Hodge received no detailed instructions from Washington for nine months after arriving in September 1945.[12] This absence of guidance led to a number of controversial policies. Hodge initially directed Japanese colonial authorities to help administer affairs, but this met with such Korean outrage that the order was promptly reversed. The US also kept the colonial police system in place to maintain order, retaining hated Japanese and Korean officers. Fears of communist infiltration led US authorities to permit brutal suppression of labor demonstrations or expressions of public dissent in places like Jeju, Daegu, and Cholla province during the three-year occupation. During the Jeju Uprising of 1948–9, the Korean military waged a bloody counterinsurgency campaign that killed 30,000 locals, according to one authoritative account.[13] At least some of these demonstrations were legitimately over dire economic conditions in the country. The absence of trade between the American- and Soviet-occupied sectors created immediate shortages on both sides that were exacerbated by the departure of Japanese capital, technology, and management. But Americans and South Koreans treated these disturbances as core threats to security entirely orchestrated by Moscow.

US occupation forces had neither the desire nor the capacity to comprehend the complex political situation emerging after liberation. As noted earlier, part of this stemmed from a latent racism that led Americans to believe that Koreans were not capable of self-governance even though indigenous forms of governance had emerged in the immediate aftermath of liberation. According to Japanese accounts intercepted by US intelligence at the time, the Koreans sought to organize themselves from the very day after liberation.[14] They disarmed the colonial police and took over local government offices. Thousands of released political prisoners returned home to become leaders of a proliferation of people's committees that declared self-rule at local and provincial levels These committees sought out and punished Japanese collaborators among their own populations, and tried to maintain law and order. But the dismissive attitude of the US was partly due to this cacophony of voices. When Hodge asked to meet with two representatives of the political parties in Korea, 1,200 people showed up. As one author noted, this caused the Americans to "dismiss Koreans as inferior—a blind, emotional, and stubborn people."[15] In reality, a spectrum of voices emerged in Korea, ranging from revolutionaries who wanted to overturn everything inherited from Japan, to moderates, to conservatives who had benefited from the Japanese order, to rabid anti-communists.

With the Soviets operating just north of the border, Hodge's simplest political filter was anti-communism. He chose not to distinguish between communists and progressive nationalists in the body politic. The calls for sweeping economic reforms, labor reform, land reform, wealth redistribution, and nationalization of Japanese assets by a cacophony of Korean political voices were all seen as communist-inspired, when many of these demands simply manifested the wishes of a population whose freedom had been suppressed for nearly four decades. Even for those advisers more sympathetic to understanding the complex situation, the growing Cold War competition with the Soviet Union on the peninsula posed a dilemma: if the US occupation forces could not guarantee that tolerating the moderates would not lead to communist takeover, then they would have to side with the far right.

For these reasons, propertied, educated Koreans who could speak English and who did well during the occupation found favor with the US while progressive nationalists like Yo Un-hyong, who advocated revolutionary reforms, were viewed with suspicion and marginalized. As noted, the American occupation authorities did not recognize the various grassroots "people's committees" that emerged as a form of self-governance, and would not meet with Yo until early October 1945. Instead, the US contributed to political polarization in the country by appointing indigenous political advisory bodies that were predominantly conservative. Eventually, Hodge brought back Syngman Rhee from the United States in October 1945, whose rabid anti-communist rhetoric and fluency in English suited US preferences. Kim Gu and Kim Kyu-sik from the Korean government-in-exile in China were also brought back for a conservative alliance with Rhee that never materialized. The US alienation of the left, the dismissal of indigenous political leaders, and Rhee's draconian efforts to usurp all power led to such internal dissatisfaction that Washington instructed Hodge to build a broader political governing coalition in July 1946, with Yo and Kim Kyu-sik, but this was unsuccessful. The assassination of Yo the following year, moreover, dashed any hopes of forming a moderate political coalition.

The American occupation, despite its flaws, did implement a number of positive reforms. It instituted an education system based on that of the US, which made schooling mandatory up to sixth grade; it doubled the number of students enrolled in elementary school and tripled those in secondary school. The US also helped to establish a national Korean university (Seoul National University), as well as encourage graduate educational opportunities. The land reform system created more property holders and reduced land tenancy compared with the colonial period. Koreans were also given the right to vote and the full range of civil liberties that were restricted under the Japanese, including the right of assembly and freedom of speech, press, and religion.

* * *

The Soviet Union was somewhat more prepared than the Americans for the occupation of their sector when the Red Army rolled into Pyongyang on August 22, 1945. They had already trained two divisions for deployment to Korea. In part, this stemmed from a deeper appreciation of Korea's value. As noted already, for FDR Korea's value was in not allowing others to hold it. Stalin followed a line of Russian leaders who saw not just Korea's strategic value, but its intrinsic worth as an important source of minerals and year-round warm-water ports for the Russian Pacific Fleet.

The Soviets initially demonstrated considerable political astuteness regarding the situation on the ground post-liberation. Unlike the Americans, they recognized the indigenous people's committees and sought out moderate political leadership in Cho Man-sik, a Korean independence fighter during the occupation period. They instituted a land reform program that expropriated all Japanese holdings without compensation and transferred them to Koreans. The Soviets nationalized all industry run under the Japanese and instituted a centrally planned economic model.

But Stalin's intolerance for any political leaders who would not support communism, as well as the abusive and criminal behavior of occupation troops, ended any short-lived welcoming of the Soviets as victors. In the latter case, the Red Army occupiers behaved atrociously by stealing food, plundering businesses, and raping local villagers. Red Army reports in November 1945 in Sinuiju described "violations of all manner of military laws, including those forbidding public drunkenness and robbery."[16] Inebriated soldiers frequented brothels, reportedly spreading venereal disease. In addition, the Soviets used schools as barracks, which upset teachers, parents, and students, who were impeded from creating a new education system separate from that of Japan. The undisciplined behavior of the soldiers so upset Koreans that ambushes and beatings of drunk Red Army conscripts late at night were not uncommon. The anger culminated in student riots in Sinuiju in 1945, which the Red Army suppressed with hundreds of casualties.

After the Sinuiju riots, the Russians started to tighten control of its sector. Civil rights for Koreans were restricted, as well as movement of people across the border to the southern sector. The Red Army targeted conservative nationalists and Christians, who constituted the heart of Korean resistance, burning down churches which served as gathering places for political action. It also restricted the return of Korean troops from Manchuria to avoid fueling the resistance. Moscow would not allow much-needed trade with the southern sector to relieve food shortages in return for northern Koreans' coal, electricity, and chemicals. It rejected US entreaties to set up a consulate in Pyongyang and shuttered its consulate in Seoul in July 1946.

When Cho Man-sik opposed Soviet plans, he was put under house arrest and likely executed, again demonstrating Moscow's iron-fisted rule. Stalin then chose Kim Il-sung to be his handpicked leader of North Korea. Kim was born near Pyongyang in 1912 and was raised in an unprivileged family with a mother and father who were devout Christians. After his family moved to China to escape the Japanese occupation, Kim joined the Chinese Communist Party and became an independence guerrilla fighter, who fought the Japanese in Manchuria. Kim was effective enough that he was targeted by Japanese forces, compelling him to escape to the Soviet Union, where he later joined the Russian military. Most important for Stalin, Kim's lack of ties to domestic groups in the north (he left the country in 1920) meant he could be counted on to be loyal to the Red Army. Kim's leadership was not accepted immediately, despite Soviet designs; competition among the Yanan faction (Koreans from China led by Kim Tu-bong), Gapsan faction (Koreans from Manchuria, including Kim Il-sung), Soviet Korean faction (other Koreans from the USSR like Pak Ch'angok), and domestic communist faction (led by Pak Hon-yong) continued until early 1948, when Kim gained control and was named head of the Communist Party and the functioning government installed by the occupation.

Establishment of Two Republics

The occupiers of the two Korean sectors continued to talk about executing the trusteeship formula agreed to between FDR, Stalin, and Churchill, but in reality, each was consolidating its sphere of influence. The December 1945 Moscow Conference resulted in an agreement between Washington and Moscow to maintain a trustee-ship of Korea for five years and to create a US–Soviet Joint Commission that would prepare for a unified provisional govern-ment. By the time the Joint Commission met in March 1946, however, George Kennan's Long Telegram and Churchill's Iron Curtain speech had set the Cold War context in which cooperation on Korea was all but impossible, despite the best hopes of the locals.[17] Successive meetings between the two superpowers proved fruitless, with each side's position informed by conservative and progressive Korean voices in each sector using support (or lack thereof) for trusteeship to gain political advantage.

In November 1947, the United States pressed successfully for UN Resolution 112 (II), stipulating elections in the spring 1948 for a unified Korean provisional government. A UN Temporary Commission on Korea (UNTCOK) was established to execute the UN directive. The elected pan-national Korean body would follow a proportional representation formula, which meant it would advan-tage the southern sector, with its larger population. In January 1948, the Soviets predictably denied UNTCOK access to the northern sector, and the US then called for elections only in the southern sector. With the writing on the wall that the forthcoming elections would permanently divide Korea, an eleventh-hour effort by Korean leaders in April 1948 tried to call for national unity. Kim Gu and Kim Kyu-sik from the south joined a delegation of leaders to meet with northern counterparts in Pyongyang. The two came back to the southern sector declaring that their northern brethren had agreed to nationwide elections. But their words were soon discredited by Pyongyang's threats to cut off electricity to the south if UNTCOK's work went forward as scheduled. In truth, no Korean could change the eventual outcome as external forces (the US and USSR) conspired with internal forces (Kim Il-sung in the north and Syngman Rhee in the south) to consolidate their half of the Korean Peninsula. The UN went ahead with elections in the south and the Republic of Korea (ROK) was established on August 15, 1948, with Rhee as its first president. The DPRK was established on September 9, 1948, with Kim Il-sung as the leader.

For the Truman administration, the end of its military occupation of Korea could not come soon enough. The priority was Western Europe where the dangers of economic collapse and communization threatened Poland, Greece, Turkey, France, and Italy among others. The US was ready to offer blanket security commitments (Truman Doctrine) and massive economic assistance (Marshall Plan) to the Europeans, but not to the Koreans. Having placed the burden on the UN to administer elections and oversee the establishment of an independent, albeit weak, South Korean government, Truman pressed for a prompt withdrawal from the peninsula that was completed by June 1949. US intelligence reports predicted the possibility of North Korean aggression following US withdrawal, but Truman hoped the South's inheritance of US military equipment left in the country, US economic assistance, US-trained South Korean forces numbering 45,000, and a residual US Military Advisory Group would deter conflict. This may have been wishful thinking, but the US government's focus was entirely on Western Europe where Washington policymakers believed nothing short of civilization as Americans knew it was at stake.

The Soviet Union ended its occupation of Korea in December 1948. However, rather than cutting his losses on the peninsula like Truman, Stalin committed to building a communist bulwark in Korea. In 1949, he concluded economic and military assistance agreements that substantially strengthened Kim's regime and enabled a rapid build-up of the North Korean military in the winter of 1949–50.

Moscow provided to Pyongyang capital, energy, medicines, transport, and munitions. It helped to beef up the country's transport infrastructure, in addition to sending technical expertise to compensate for the brain drain of the departed Japanese managers and experts. China also helped North Korea by returning 12,000 Korean soldiers who had served in China to help buoy the ranks of the North Korean military.[18] Indeed, there was almost nothing that Kim Il-sung requested that his two communist patrons did not provide, including support for Kim's plan to take the peninsula by military force.

On the eve of North Korea's invasion, the country had made reasonable strides in development after the end of the Japanese occupation. Land reform and the state-based distribution system had given the majority peasant population sustenance in material terms. Peasants strove to benefit from a Korean, as opposed to Imperial Japanese, education system. Soviet support had made the state and military stronger, relative to the South. A proliferation of *hanbok*, or traditional Korean attire, filled the streets of Pyongyang as Koreans happily dispensed with the *gukminbok*, or traditional Japanese military uniform. Ideologically, the people were subject to heavy Marxist-Leninist indoctrination, but always with a slant toward moving Korea toward a modern socialist identity. This frail yet blossoming peasant postcolonial society would be subject to the ravages of a war campaign brought on by the world's most powerful military as a result of fateful decisions made by the North Korean political leadership to try to unify the peninsula by force.

The Korean War

At 4 a.m. on Sunday, June 25, 1950, North Korean forces, supported by tanks, heavy artillery, and air power, rolled across the 38th parallel in an all-out mechanized military invasion. The North claimed that the military operation was in self-defense against South Korea and while there were indeed significant clashes between regiments as large as 2,000 on the two sides before June 25, none of this violence compared to the premeditated all-out military attack by the North. The mechanized campaign advanced along four corridors down the peninsula, and within three days, Korean People's Army forces took Seoul. In a desperate attempt to stop the invasion, the South Korean military blew up the bridges on the Han River stranding thousands of civilians and military in the wake of KPA forces.

A number of factors contributed to Kim Il-sung's decision to invade. First, he believed that the United States had written off Korea after ending the military occupation and withdrawing its forces. In January 1950, Dean Acheson's speech outlining US policy in Asia defined a defense perimeter that excluded the Korean Peninsula and Formosa. This speech reflected the results of an internal US government policy review, embodied in NSC 48/1 and NSC 48/2, in December 1949, that stipulated a maritime position in Asia built around Japan, the Philippines, Australia, New Zealand, and possibly Indonesia.[19] Acheson's speech raised abandonment fears for Syngman Rhee, who had also just learned that Congress had not passed the Korean aid bill for 1950. For Kim Il-sung, this all confirmed the US's lack of interest.

Second, Kim presided over a favorable balance of forces on the peninsula due to significant Soviet and Chinese assistance in the run-up to the war. Stalin provided military assistance secretly in the form of munitions, money, training, and equipment, and Chinese leader Mao Zedong sent several thousand Korean troops from China. This allowed for a significant build-up of the KPA in the winter of 1949–50. At the start of the conflict, the North enjoyed dominance over the South in every military aspect, including twice the number of troops, seven times the number of machine guns, six times the number of combat planes, and one hundred fifty times the number of tanks.[20]

Third, Kim convinced his two patrons to support his invasion plan. When he approached Stalin in March–April 1950, the Soviet leader worried about US intervention but consented nonetheless if Kim could promise a quick victory. Stalin was careful to avoid open involvement of the Red Army in the war, only providing experts and air support, with personnel dressed in the uniforms of the People's Liberation Army—the Chinese armed forces. Stalin instructed Kim to gain Mao's support, which he did in May 1950. Based on the lack of a US response to the ousting of Chiang Kai-shek from China, Mao did not believe the US would come to the aid of South Korea. He also believed a quick victory would further deter US intervention.

Finally, the North Korean leader viewed the poor economic conditions and popular resentment against Rhee's rule as an opportunity to activate revolutionary forces in the South. Kim assessed these forces to be much stronger than they really were; nevertheless, it gave him confidence that an invasion would be met with popular support among South Koreans.

The US Response

President Truman learned of the invasion while at his home in Missouri on June 24 and returned to Washington for emergency meetings. He saw the attack as clearly directed by Stalin. For Truman, the Korean conflict was either a distraction by the communists aimed to divert US attention from Europe, or it was a probe of US resolve to see what gains could be achieved militarily. In either case, the Korean Peninsula, assessed to be a strategic afterthought for US policy only months earlier, had now become the first place where the

Cold War turned hot. In a speech to the American public, Truman connected hostilities in this peripheral state to the core geostrategic conflict with the Soviet Union over Europe, and to the security of the American homeland:

> On Sunday, June 25th, Communist forces attacked the Republic of Korea. This attack has made it clear, beyond all doubt, that the international Communist movement is willing to use armed invasion to conquer independent nations. . . . The principal effort to help the Koreans preserve their independence, and to help the United Nations restore peace, has been made by the United States. We have sent land, sea, and air forces to assist in these operations. We have done this because we know that what is at stake here is nothing less than our own national security and the peace of the world.[21]

Truman also reacted emotionally to the nature of the invasion—an all-out mechanized invasion. He reportedly told Acheson, "We've got to stop the sons of bitches no matter what."[22] The attack drew for him lessons about the dangers of appeasement in the 1930s, except that this time it was the forces of fascism and communism threatening the new world order and the fledgling UN, which had taken on Korea as one of its first projects. In Blair House meetings, the president exclaimed, jumping up and down, "We can't let the UN down! We can't let the UN down!"[23]

Truman's decision to enter the war constituted one of the most dramatic reversals of US policy in history. Within a span of six months, the US reversed three core tenets of its Asia strategy laid out in NSC 48/1 and 48/2 in December 1949: (1) it would not get drawn into conflict on the Asian continent (the US would enter into a full-scale war); (2) it would not divert resources from the European theater (the Korean engagement would cost the US more than US $15 billion); and (3) it would leave open the possibility of rapprochement with the new regime in Beijing (the US would provide a defense treaty to Taiwan and would not have relations with China for the next two decades).

The United States supported a June 27 UN Security Council resolution (UNSCR 83) calling for member states to repel the North Korean invasion, constituting the first time that the young international institution would go to war to enforce the peace. There are several competing explanations for why the Soviets were absent from the Security Council vote for this resolution, but the most common is Moscow's protest to the UN for not recognizing the People's Republic of China (PRC) in the body. On July 7 a second UN Security Council resolution (UNSCR 84) established the UN Command with General MacArthur in charge of a fifteen-nation contingent that would fight for South Korea (Australia, Belgium, Canada, Colombia, Ethiopia, France, Great Britain, Greece, Luxembourg, the Netherlands, New Zealand, the Philippines, Thailand, Turkey, and South Africa). In a dramatic concession of sovereignty that would have ramifications for Korea for decades to come, Syngman Rhee, on July 14, handed over the operational command of the South Korean forces to MacArthur.

MacArthur had flown to the war front on June 29 and told Truman that US ground troops would be needed to stop the advance. From July 6 to July 20, an undermanned 9th Army engaged the advancing KPA in a slow retreat designed to buy time for the US to build up forces in Japan. By August 4, North Korean forces had pushed South Korean and US forces back to a foothold on the tip of the Korean Peninsula at Busan, then the South Korean capital. South Korea and the US held the 140-mile "Busan perimeter" for over one month until mid-September, when MacArthur launched Operation Chromite—a historic amphibious landing invasion at Incheon, a port city in western South Korea, behind advancing KPA troops. This created a two-front war that sandwiched enemy forces between South Korean and US/UN forces to the north and south while cutting their supply lines. The successful military operation crushed KPA forces enabling the recapture of Seoul on September 28.

Rollback

Korea entered the next phase of war in October 1950, when South Korean and US/UN forces, with momentum on their side, made the decision to advance north of the 38th parallel to roll back the communist advance and take the whole peninsula. US and South Korean forces advanced up the west and east coasts of the peninsula on the ground, coupled with a US amphibious assault at Wonsan. They succeeded in capturing the capital city of Pyongyang on October 19 and pushed defeated KPA forces up to the Amrok River, which separates the Korean Peninsula from Manchuria, forcing Kim to relocate his operations to Sinuiju on the border with China.

Chinese warnings that they would intervene on behalf of the North Koreans went unheard by MacArthur, who assured his president of this at a meeting at Wake Island on October 15. Moreover, if the Chinese did enter the war, MacArthur boasted that he could handle that. But Mao had already decided to intervene by early October and, on October 25, sent 120,000 troops into the North to stop advancing enemy forces. By mid-November, with numbers swelled to 300,000, the Chinese forces led by Peng Dehuai pushed the 8th Army and 2nd Infantry division into full retreat along the west coast and forced a naval evacuation on the east coast, with South Korean and US/UN forces taking heavy losses.

China and North Korea recaptured Seoul on January 4, 1951, and started to move south. A South Korea–US counterattack stopped this Chinese advance about 75 miles south of Seoul, cutting off Chinese supply lines and forcing their retreat. The city of Seoul changed hands for the fourth time in March 1951, at which point the war entered a military stalemate with all sides realizing victory was not possible. The exception was MacArthur, who again advocated for advancing north to the Chinese border, bombing the industrial base in Manchuria, blockading Chinese ports, and if necessary, using nuclear weapons. Truman relieved MacArthur in April 1951 and General Matthew B. Ridgway replaced the iconic American general.

Unproductive truce talks started at Kaesong in July 1951, as neither side was ready to make concessions on three issues—establishing an MDL, determining armistice guidelines, and returning POWs. Indeed, much of the early energy was devoted to disputes over the venue of the talks, which was eventually moved out of North Korean territory to Panmunjom, which sits on the North–South border. The two sides eventually agreed on establishing a 2.5-mile-wide DMZ on either side of the demarcation line.

Fighting in Korea continued for two years in the midst of ongoing armistice talks, together with repression of communist sympathizers in the South and pro-South Korean government individuals in the North. The key stumbling block remained POW repatriation. The death of Stalin in March 1953 provided an opening for a settlement, and Operation Little Switch, exchanging about 700 US, UN, and South Korean sick and wounded POWs in return for 6,700 Chinese and North Korean POWs and civilians provided confidence to all sides that an agreement was near. South Korean President Syngman Rhee, who vehemently opposed truce talks and advocated for retaking the whole peninsula, tried to sabotage the armistice negotiations in June 1953 by unilaterally releasing 27,000 POWs. Rhee's actions led to a temporary but bloody restart of hostilities, which meaninglessly took thousands of lives. To assuage Rhee's concerns and guarantee his good behavior, the United States provided the South with a mutual defense treaty. The armistice agreement of July 27, 1953, established a 155-mile MDL bisecting the peninsula not far from where the peninsula was originally divided in 1945. A military armistice commission was established to adjudicate compliance with the terms of the cease-fire. A Neutral Nations Supervisory Commission (NNSC), composed of Sweden, Switzerland, Poland, and Czechoslovakia, was also established to oversee the armistice.

After a little over three years, the fratricidal Korean War ended where it started, at the 38th parallel, but with no victory and at a tremendous cost. The capital cities of Seoul and Pyongyang changed hands in the course of the war a total of six times. The entire peninsula had been bombed or burned into oblivion. The military casualties in this conflict were heavy: 140,000 South Koreans, 34,000 Americans, more than 640,000 North Koreans, and over 1 million Chinese. But civilian casualties were even heavier, with some 3 million Koreans killed.[24]

In addition, there were dire economic effects. Well over half of industrial facilities, roads, railroads, power plants, and housing units were destroyed during the war. The total war damage for South Korea of KRW (Korean won) 41.23 billion (about US $6.9 billion) was equivalent to 83 percent of the country's gross national production (GNP) in 1953. South Korean foreign trade went down from US $208 million in 1948 to US $2.9 million in 1950. Food production decreased significantly, with rice crops down to 65 percent of the 1945–50 period. The result was hyperinflation. In the case of North Korea, the economic impact of the war was more difficult to ascertain due to the opacity of the ruling regime. But it is estimated that the total damage was KRW 420 billion, roughly four times its 1953 GNP.[25]

When it comes to politics, the end of the war reinforced Rhee's position as the leader of South Korea. His staunch anti-communism was now a clear asset, even if his unwillingness to support the negotiations to put an end to the war were seen as counterproductive by many South Koreans and Americans. In the case of North Korea, the war created divisions within the ruling Communist Party and strengthened opponents of Kim Il-sung, who looked foolish for launching a strike on the South. Yet this reinforced Kim's determination to eliminate his opponents as well as any attempt there may have been to have a debate about how to organize the politics of the North.

Rhee's attempt to sabotage the armistice talks constituted a last-ditch attempt to determine Korea's fate, but as at other points in the peninsula's history, Koreans had little control over the geopolitical forces swirling around them. Korean troops undeniably fought bravely against their brethren in the war, but the tragic nature of this conflict tarnished any sense of pride in shaping their destiny. The ultimate irony is that this localized conflict between Koreans had disproportionately larger effects on the world stage. The Korean War fundamentally changed the assumptions of US geostrategy as it led to the adoption of limited war doctrine and the domino theory. The conflict demonstrated that the Cold War would be fought through limited conflicts between proxies of the superpowers in peripheral areas of the world. But these conflicts in the periphery were connected to the core because allowing one of these small countries to fall to communism could set off a domino effect leading to others also becoming communist. The North Korean invasion, following closely on the heels of the Chinese Communist Party victory in China, looked like dominos to US security planners and therefore could not be ignored. In addition, the Korean War led to the militarization of the North Atlantic Treaty Organization (NATO) and the adoption of NSC 68, which laid out a new strategy of US rearmament and increased defense budgets for the Cold War. Prior to Korea, the US administration recognized the need to bolster defenses for the competition with the Soviet bloc but had a hard time convincing a war-weary American public just after World War II. Korea gave Cold War planners the justification they needed.

The war was particularly devastating for China, more so than the Soviet Union. Mao suffered more than 1.3 million casualties in the war, including the death of his son. Any hopes for US rapprochement with the new regime in Beijing would be dashed for the next two decades as the US supported Taiwan's defense by interposing the Seventh Fleet in the Taiwan Straits and finally giving Chiang Kai-shek a mutual defense treaty in 1954. On the positive side, China gained international stature in the world communist movement by fighting the world's most powerful country to a draw in Korea.

By highlighting the communist threat in Asia, the Korean War benefited Japan in ways that still enrage Koreans today. The US occupation of Japan turned from an operation to emasculate the Japanese state into a program to build it into a bulwark against communism in the region. This "reverse course" reinstated Japanese political leaders and *zaibatsu*, and initiated a project by George Kennan and others to turn Japan into the Great Britain of Asia. The Japanese economy benefited handsomely from the conflict as well as providing necessary supplies for the war effort.

The war was a major test of the new United Nations as an international institution. Given the role the UN played in Korea, the North Korean invasion amounted to a communist attack against the integrity of the young organization and the new world order it meant to produce. Going to war with the United States, and repelling the invasion, was a critical outcome for the UN, although it also revealed the specter of superpower deadlock on the UN Security Council.

Finally, Syngman Rhee and Kim Il-sung did not achieve their goal of reunification of Korea, but the war did produce a security treaty and alliance for South Korea with the United States and for North Korea with China and the Soviet Union. Given the blood spilled by China in the war, Kim would draw even closer to Beijing. Both Kim and Rhee would use these ties with their patron allies to obtain economic assistance and political support as the two Koreas sought to rebuild from the ruins of war.

3
THE KOREAS
1953 TO 1980

The MDL and DMZ separating the two Koreas should be a required visit for anyone traveling to South Korea for the first time.[1] This is the area that splits what used to be unified Korea into two separate countries. Ramon Pacheco Pardo first visited at a time when tensions were low and relations were cordial. The group tour was pleasant enough, with South Korean and American soldiers guiding the group amid a relaxed atmosphere. By the time they made it to the Joint Security Area, the situation changed. This is the only area where South and North Korean soldiers face each other. The group was told not to wave or make any other gestures at the North Korean guards keeping an eye on them. Everyone in the group had had to sign a waiver indicating that the visit could result in injury or death as a result of North Korea's actions. They all kept quiet. When the group was taken to one of the blue buildings where the two Koreas sometimes negotiate, they took the opportunity to cross over into the North, even if only briefly. A symbolic gesture—but one that South

Korea was comfortable in allowing. After all, South Korea was not poor anymore. This was no longer the aftermath of the Korean War, when people could still wonder which Korea faced a better future.

* * *

Poverty, and Laying the Foundations for the Future

There is no other way of putting it: North and South Korea were considered lost causes by the time they stopped shooting at each other across the DMZ in 1953. They were beyond poor, for in fact they were among the poorest countries in the world. Hunger, disease, and homelessness were rampant. Crops were few and far between. Millions suffered from cholera and other illnesses. Pyongyang, Seoul, and all other major cities lay in ruins. And to top it off, millions of Koreans from both North and South Korea had lost their parents, children, siblings, and other relatives. In two countries where women were secondary to men and literally married into their husband's families—being registered as part of their husband's household upon marriage and almost invariably moving into their family home—tens or perhaps hundreds of thousands of widows suddenly had to fend for themselves, even if they were not supposed to do so. In two countries where bloodline remained central to understanding one's position within society, tens if not hundreds of thousands of children—the future of North and South Korea—had lost their families and were reduced to begging on the streets. Koreans on both sides of the border were independent from colonialism, but separated as a result of external forces and dependent on foreigners' goodwill to feed themselves.

Perhaps good governance could solve the problem. But who could provide it? Kim Il-sung was a (self-anointed) independence war hero and had demonstrated remarkable skills in rising to the top in the North. But his lack of judgment had almost resulted in the end of his country at the hands of South Korean and American troops. Plus, rebuilding and managing a country was a whole different story compared to leading army units. Syngman Rhee, meanwhile, had shown his political chops by winning South Korea's first two presidential elections. But his government was extremely corrupt and only US President Dwight Eisenhower had been able to convince him not to try to take over North Korea by force. In fact, the US government and US advisers on the ground in South Korea had serious doubts that Rhee could rule the country effectively.[2]

Facing these circumstances, North and South Korea seemingly took similar economic paths but certainly went down different political trails. In the case of Pyongyang, early on Kim Il-sung started to openly develop a cult of personality that would lay the foundations for the Kim family to rule North Korea for its whole existence up to the time of writing (February 2023). In March 1953, Joseph Stalin passed away. With the leader of the communist camp for three decades gone, Kim felt emboldened to present his credentials as the undisputed guiding light of communism in (North) Korea. Already in 1949, Kim had started to adopt the title of *Sureong* or "Great Leader," a throwback to the title that leaders had used in ancient Korea. Until then, the title had been reserved to Stalin. But its use by Kim became more common and open in the 1950s, and Kim also received the titles of "Chairman" and "Hero" when he signed the armistice that put an end to the Korean War in 1953.[3] Thus, Kim felt emboldened to emphasize that he was the true leader of North Korea—and, by extension, of communists across the whole of the Korean Peninsula.

Certainly, not everyone in North Korea agreed that Kim was "great," or that he should be the leader of the country. In order to secure his position, Kim launched a brutal purge campaign. Kim had conducted purges already in the 1940s, when trying to secure his position as the leader of the Workers' Party of (North) Korea (WPK) and later of North Korea itself. But their frequency increased from 1953, as Kim moved to decisively consolidate his power. In 1953, Kim eliminated the military leaders who had fought against the South accused of plotting a coup—as well as WPK members who actually tried to remove Kim during the party plenum opening in September. Party members and other leaders tracing their roots to the South were also purged.[4] Yet opposition to Kim's rule and his growing cult of personality continued.

This created the conditions for the August Faction Incident. In August 1956, Kim purged Pak Ch'angok and Choi Chang-ik along with many of their followers. The former was the leader of the Soviet faction within the WPK, while the latter was the leader of the pro-China Yanan faction. When the party plenum opened on August 30, the two of them, along with other members of their factions, denounced Kim. However, by then a majority of party delegates had been appointed post-1950, supported Kim's rule, and had a more nationalistic ethos that made them suspicious of the intentions of the Soviet and Yanan factions. As a result, these two factions failed in their attempt to oust Kim. Purges continued following the August 1956 plenum, and by the end of the decade the two factions had essentially disappeared. Their members had been executed, sent to prison, or gone into exile.

It was also in the 1950s that Kim introduced the *seongbun* system to control the North Korean population, based on the political, economic, and social background of each North Korean's family members, as well as their behavior and actions. For while purges helped Kim to take control of the country's government, he could not be assured of the support of the North Korean population, particularly considering that many North Koreans had family in the South, or could trace their roots there. Plus, Koreans on both sides of the 38th parallel longed for reunification. This seemed a realistic prospect less than a decade removed from the de jure division of their country. Kim, therefore, had to ensure that he could control the North Korean population.

Under *seongbun*, every North Korean is classified into one of three main groups: core, wavering or basic, and hostile. There are subdivisions within each group, up to a total of around fifty categories. Each adult North Korean belongs to one of these categories, with around 30 percent of North Koreans belonging to the core, 40 percent to the wavering, and 30 percent to the hostile. What determines one's classification? Above all, family background for up to three generations. From the beginning, the core included pro-independence fighters, revolutionaries, or factory workers and peasants. The wavering included ordinary North Koreans. And the hostile included landowners, religious leaders, or North Koreans who supported the South during the war.[5] Also from the beginning, it became almost impossible to improve one's classification, which is maintained by security and party officials and updated regularly. But it certainly was possible to be demoted. This has acted as a form of social control for decades, for only those in the core can access the best education, jobs, healthcare—or even the possibility of living in Pyongyang. In fact, in the 1950s North Korea started to develop a sophisticated prison camp system, to which hundreds of thousands of those in the hostile class, or who were perceived to threaten the regime, would be sent over decades.[6]

In South Korea, Syngman Rhee also pursued an authoritarian approach to politics. However, the degree to which he was able to exercise control over South Korean politics and the population of the country certainly never came close to matching what Kim was eventually able to achieve in the North. To begin with, Rhee had to contest real elections. It is true that the South Korean president tried to rig the ballots that he and his party contested throughout the 1950s. But it is also true that there was a real even if imperfect contest. In May 1954, South Korea held its first National Assembly elections since the Korean War. Rhee's Liberal Party won a majority of the seats and proceeded to abolish the two-term presidential limit to allow the president to run a third time. Rhee duly won the May 1956 presidential election with 70 percent of the vote. But the Liberal Party's candidate lost the vice-presidential election to Chang Myon of the Democratic Party. This showed that Rhee and the Liberal Party—and by extension, the conservative movement—were not guaranteed a monopoly of power.

Rhee reacted by attempting to eliminate his opponents, much as Kim was successfully doing in North Korea. The 1948 National Security Law had made legal the arrest of those harboring pro-communist or pro-North Korean sympathies. Throughout the second half of the 1950s, the Rhee government used this law to silence the president's opponents. Well-liked former independence activist Cho Bong-am was arrested after losing the 1956 election to Rhee under this law, and would be executed in 1959. And Chang Myon was wounded in a shooting following his election as vice-president. He survived though, and led the opposition to the Rhee regime.

Opposition to Rhee indeed continued in parliament and in the streets, in the form of regular protests mainly held by students. This opposition eventually led to the president's downfall. In March 1960, Rhee was re-elected for a fourth time, after he ran unopposed following the death—one month before the election—of Chough Pyung-ok, his Democratic Party opponent. Chough died in a US hospital following an abdominal operation. Thus, there could be no suspicions that Rhee or his party were at fault. But there was a vice-presidential election scheduled for the same day as the presidential contest, and Chang Myon was running again. Chang lost the election, which was a credible outcome. But Lee Ki-poong, his opponent from the Liberal Party, received over 79 percent of the vote against Chang's 17.5 percent according to official results. This was inconceivable. The Democratic Party did not waste a single day in rejecting the result of the election.

Soon after, student-led protests erupted in Masan, a city in the Korean Peninsula's southeast. Protests quickly spread throughout the country. This was to be known as the April 19 Revolution. Supported by the Democratic Party, the protesters were able to force Rhee's hand. The South Korean president went into exile in May. South Korea held an indirect presidential election in August, following a direct election for a new parliament in July. The National Assembly voted for Yun Posun from the Democratic Party to become the new president. But under the new constitution that South Korea had adopted, the president was the head of state, while the prime minister was the head of government with real political power. And the new head of government was none other than Chang Myon.[7] Differently from the North, South Koreans could actually decide who their leader was going to be.

* * *

In the North, indeed, Kim staked his leadership on economic growth. Following the Korean War, most North Korean cities and infrastructure lay in ruins. Furthermore, arable land had also been depleted during the war, and the country had lost hundreds of thousands of workers, as the previous chapter recounted, as Koreans on both sides of the DMZ had killed each other in droves. North Korea, however, still had the advantages that had made it the preferred location for Japanese investment during the colonial era: its geographical location next to Manchuria and abundant mineral resources. Many

North Koreans also had the necessary skills to rebuild the country. Kim, therefore, had the foundations to try to develop the economy.

On December 28, 1955, Kim took to the podium in front of a group of WPK officials and delivered what can be described as the most consequential speech in North Korean history. Kim used his speech—titled "On Eliminating Dogmatism and Formalism and Establishing *Juche* in Ideological Work"—to introduce the idea of *Juche* or "self-reliance." In the context of competition with the South, de-Stalinization in the Soviet Union, and shifting relations within the communist camp, Kim introduced the idea that North Korea had to develop a distinct form of Korean socialism based on the traditional characteristics of the country and independent of foreign interference —in other words, socialism with (North) Korean characteristics.[8] North Korea had to develop its own way. And though *Juche* applied to both politics and economics, its impact on the former would take time to bear fruit—while its impact on economic policy was immediate.

Spurred by *Juche* and more traditional socialist economic ideas, the Kim regime launched the *Cheollima* industrialization movement in 1957. Land collectivization began in earnest in 1953, and North Korea had had a first three-year economic plan in 1954–6, for which it had relied heavily on Soviet economic support.[9] With the *Cheollima* movement, Kim wanted to rely on the willpower of the North Korean people to develop the economy. First presented by Kim himself in December 1956, the *Cheollima* movement sought to nationalize all industry and agriculture for North Korea to become economically self-sufficient (or "self-reliant") in a period of only a few years. After all, the *Cheollima* was a mythological flying horse able to travel up to 310 miles per day (a thousand *li*). North Koreans could emulate this flying horse in propelling the North Korean economy.

Initially, the *Cheollima* movement seemed to be working. North Korea's first five-year plan of 1957–61 led to much higher economic growth than in the South, with output in sectors such as steel, energy, or food production growing by double digits year on year.[10] North Korea seemed to be making adequate use of its still plentiful workforce, natural resources, and know-how. Even as the Soviet Union reduced its support to North Korea from 1957 onwards, the country's economic performance outpaced that of most other developing countries worldwide. Most impressive, North Korea was developing its heavy industry. Few other developing countries could match that feat.

In fact, *Cheollima* became so central to North Korea's economic growth, and by extension, *Juche,* that it was immortalized in posters, speeches, and even contests among working units. In August 1960, Kim delivered the speech "Riders of the *Cheollima*" in praise of those North Korean workers going the extra mile to produce more. The North Korean press and other propaganda organs went out of their way to praise these riders producing ever more.[11] More steel, more cement, more crops, or more home utensils. Anything that could drive North Korea to become a developed country. And yet, the *Cheollima* movement was not based on rational economic principles and left behind scores of exhausted workers. The movement would plant the seeds for North Korea's future poor economic performance.

Still, Kim at least had a plan to try to improve the North Korean economy. Below the 38th parallel, it was difficult to discern such a plan. The South Korean economy was battered following the Korean War, and the South did not have the natural resources that the North did. Certainly, Rhee understood that the circumstances in South Korea demanded a focus on something that the country still had, despite the death unleashed by the Korean War: human resources. Korea's real literacy rate remained relatively low in 1945, upon the independence of the country. As noted previously, universal education of Koreans improved somewhat during the Japanese imperial government and the US military occupation. By 1960, however, the

South Korean literacy rate stood at 85 percent for men. Women would only achieve the same rate in 1966.[12] The Rhee government also pressed ahead with a universal vaccination campaign and with a program to improve the housing stock. These were sensible measures to create the conditions for long-term growth. For South Korea would have to rely on its human capital to become rich.

But that was the future. Rhee failed to introduce any plan to boost short-term growth. In fact, the president's plan seemed to rely on US largesse to support his hopes for the (long-term) future, provide handouts to those whose support he needed, and drive growth in the near term. Indeed, the Eisenhower administration became increasingly impatient with Rhee. The US saw him as a corrupt leader with no long-term strategy. In the end, Washington encouraged Rhee to leave the country. In the meantime, South Koreans continued to be poor. And North Korea was building an incipient industry, which the South seemed unable to develop.

Once in power, the Chang government changed course and took a path similar to the North's. Chang announced the dawn of a "Miracle on the Han River" in his New Year's speech of 1961, a term making reference of the "Miracle on the Rhine River" unfolding in West Germany at the time. Soon after, the new government announced a new five-year plan. The plan actually seemed more rational than North Korea's, for it focused on the agricultural sector and light industries as a starting point. The Chang government may have assumed that the development of heavy industries would come later in time. The new prime minister would never have the chance to start to implement his plan though.

Survival with Allies' Support

As explained in chapter 2, the Korean War had made the Korean Peninsula the first "hot" battleground of the emerging Cold War.

Washington could not allow South Korea to fall into the hands of the Sino-Soviet communist camp. This would pose a threat to Japan, Taiwan, and other US allies and partners across Asia. Moscow and Beijing could not allow North Korea to become part of a unified, pro-US Korea. This would mean a US ally sharing an eastern border with them, potentially with American troops roaming freely around it. Simply put, the two Koreas were pawns in what would become the great geopolitical game of the second half of the twentieth century.

For North and South Korea, their "pawn" status brought some advantages throughout the 1950s if they played their cards well. Korea had long seen itself as a "shrimp among whales." In the 1950s, the whales were the US, the Soviet Union, and, to an extent, China. In the past, the shrimp had had its back crushed, as the saying goes. Most notably, Korea was colonized by Japan shortly after the latter had defeated China and Russia in its wars with them. The Korean War had laid bare that the Koreas could have their backs crushed again. They had to play their cards in the right way. And, to their credit, Syngman Rhee and Kim Il-sung did know how to play the great power game.

In the case of Seoul, support from the US was sealed with the United States–Republic of Korea Mutual Defense Treaty signed on October 1, 1953. Barely two months after the armistice agreement putting an end to the Korean War was signed, Rhee was able to extract from Eisenhower an agreement whereby US troops would remain in South Korea indefinitely. And indeed, stay they did. Tens of thousands of American soldiers remained in the country following the Korean War, or were deployed there. By the time that Rhee was forced to leave office in 1960, 50,000 US troops were stationed in South Korea.[13] Some South Koreans resented the presence of US troops, particularly many left-leaning liberals. They felt that they had not fought for liberation from Japan only to be "occupied" by a new foreign power. But most South Koreans were either neutral or outright happy to have American GIs in the country, providing the necessary protection against a potential new invasion.

And the Rhee government certainly took advantage of its alliance with the US and the threat that a communist North still posed. South Korea received US $3.6 billion in grants and loans from the US government between 1954 and 1960.[14] More than 60 percent of the South Korean population lived in extreme poverty, and foreign aid financed 90 percent of the budget and 70 percent of imports.[15] Without foreign aid flowing from across the Pacific, the South Korean economy would have collapsed. Seoul was also welcomed by the World Bank as its 58th member in 1955, opening the doors for technical expertise and—from the 1960s—huge aid flows. Dominated by the US, the World Bank would not have admitted South Korea without Washington's approval. Plus, the tens of thousands of American GIs stationed in South Korea brought much-needed cash. This was a mixed blessing, for readily available US cash created the conditions for a booming sex industry, in which tens of thousands of South Korean women worked.[16] But this cash also supported the restaurants, barber shops, bars, and the many other businesses that would have been unsustainable had they only relied on South Korean clients.

In the case of North Korea, its relationship with its two patrons proved to be more complex. Mao Zedong became critical of Kim Il-sung for his mismanagement of the Korean War. He thought of him as inexperienced and that he was the main reason why China had had to intervene to prevent South Korean and UN troops from reaching the Amrok River. Their relationship from then on, though, was marked by cordial relations between the two leaders coupled with a lingering mistrust despite a façade of communist solidarity. This would become a recurring theme in the history of Sino-North Korean relations. In fact, to this day the Kim family refuses to properly acknowledge China's role in helping North Korea to survive the Korean War. As visitors to the Victorious War Museum commemorating the Korean War, set up in August 1953, can attest, the Kim family presents the war as an epic struggle between the people of North Korea and US imperialists. There is little trace of China's role in the war. The same applies to North Korean textbooks and official books about the war. This reflects the paradoxical relationship between Pyongyang and Beijing, in that they need each other but North Korea cannot bear to acknowledge China's role in ensuring its very existence.

However, China had also learned a powerful lesson from the Korean War: the Korean Peninsula could become the road that US troops would transit to reach into Manchuria. This had been China's weakest link in the early 1930s, when Japan's Imperial Army had taken over the region. China could not repeat the same mistake a second time. It needed a buffer that would prevent another attack down its eastern flank. And North Korea provided this buffer, as it continues to do at the time of writing (February 2023). Therefore Mao did his best to prop up Kim's regime and prevent instability in North Korea. Or, worse, the collapse of the country. Throughout the 1950s, China provided an estimated US $500 million to its neighbor in grants and loans.[17] China also accounted for some 45 percent of North Korea's trade, with an annual value of US $100 million. Beijing understood that it needed to ensure the survival of North Korea.

Thankfully for the Kim regime, the Soviet Union did not want to be outdone by its communist ally. After all, Soviet troops had first entered the Korean Peninsula in 1945 on their way to attack Japan, as explained in chapter 2. The US could easily go in the other direction and use the Korean Peninsula as a launch pad to strike the Soviet Union's Far East. Plus, Moscow had seized the Kuril Islands, located in between the Kamchatka Peninsula and Hokkaido. Considering the troublesome history between Russia and Japan, and their membership of different Cold War camps, it was not unthinkable that Japan could regroup and one day seek to launch a strike against the Soviet Union to recover its territory. The Korean Peninsula could well serve as one of the places that Japan could use to attack the Soviets. In short and similarly to the case of China, geostrategic considerations as much as ideology drove the Soviet Union to provide North Korea with the necessary support for the country to rebuild its economy.

And help Moscow did. The Soviet Union provided North Korea with US $250 million in aid a few weeks after the formal end of the Korean War. Moscow also eased the repayment conditions for the debt that Pyongyang had accrued during the conflict. The Soviet Union continued to provide economic and technical support to North Korea even after Nikita Khrushchev's denunciation of Stalin and rejection of Stalinism in 1956 strained relations with North Korea. Kim purged the Soviet faction, but he did not break relations with Moscow. Quite the opposite. Kim went to visit Khrushchev four times between 1956 and 1959. What is more, North Korea made sure to maximize benefits of its membership of the Soviet-led communist camp. Throughout the second half of the 1950s, Kim received economic support and technical expertise from Central and Eastern European countries in areas such as agriculture, healthcare, or industry. In a 1956 tour of the region spanning seven countries, Kim cemented this support.

South Korea and the US were apprehensive about the support that North Korea enjoyed from its two communist benefactors. From an American perspective, South Korea probably would not be able to withstand a North Korean attack without the help of the US. Military leaders sitting both in the Pentagon and in the Korean Peninsula shared this view. But the Korean War had been costly, and Washington was looking at ways to reduce the price tag for defending Seoul. How could the US continue to protect South Korea in a way that was both cost-effective and agreeable to both sides?

The answer came from Europe. The US had started to deploy nuclear bombs and nuclear-armed missiles in the territories of NATO allies from the mid-1950s. These were the most powerful deterrent imaginable against a potential Soviet attack. East Asia came next, with Japan, South Korea, and Taiwan becoming hosts to US nuclear weapons. In the case of South Korea, the US deployed its first nuclear weapons in the country in January 1958. Hundreds of them would be deployed in the coming years, up to a peak of an estimated 950 warheads in the late 1960s.[18] This satisfied the Rhee government that the US was serious about its commitment to the protection of South Korea. After all, nuclear weapons were the ultimate deterrent against North Korea. Or, for that matter, against any thoughts that China or the Soviet Union might have had to support a new North Korean invasion of the South.

As the US deployed its nuclear warheads in South Korea to deter a potential strike from the North and its two allies, not everything was going smoothly in the communist camp. Khrushchev and Mao did not get along. The former thought that the latter was too inflexible, much like Stalin. The latter believed that the former was too willing to accommodate the US. After all, the Soviet leader had traveled to the US to meet with Eisenhower in 1959 as a way to reduce tensions between the two superpowers. In this context, the Sino-Soviet split seemed inevitable. And so it was. By the early 1960s, China and the Soviet Union were openly quarrelling against each other.

The politically astute Kim sensed an opening. His regime had the economic backing of Moscow and Beijing. North Korea also had an implicit security guarantee from the two of them that they would provide the necessary support in case of a new war in the Korean Peninsula. But South Korea had more. It had a formal alliance treaty with the US. Since the North was nominally following the *Juche* policy, it may have seemed difficult to host foreign troops, openly receive economic support, or sign a formal alliance like the South had. But, after all, it was obvious that North Korea was receiving the support of the Soviet Union and China anyway. Plus, Moscow and Beijing were seeking to lure fellow communist countries into their orbit. Herein lay the opening that Kim had spotted.

On July 6, 1961, North Korea signed a Treaty of Friendship, Cooperation and Mutual Assistance with the Soviet Union. Only five days later, Pyongyang signed a treaty with exactly the same name with China. Kim had traveled to Moscow and Beijing, respectively, to sign these two treaties. It might seem incongruous in relation to the idea of *Juche*, but Pyongyang was able to extract important concessions from the two communist powers. The agreements explicitly committed them to support North Korea in case of war, and implicitly guaranteed that Pyongyang would continue to receive their economic support. To an extent, North Korea had already been playing China and the Soviet Union against each other to ensure its economic survival in the aftermath of the Korean War. From the moment Pyongyang signed its treaties in 1961, this became an open policy underpinning North Korea's approach to foreign policy.

Park Chung-hee and the Start of the South–North Divergence

To understand where South Korea is today, and the different trajectories that South and North Korea have followed in recent decades, one needs to understand the figure of Park Chung-hee. South Korea's president from his coup in 1961 until his assassination in 1979 was the most consequential figure of the country in the twentieth century, and the key driver behind its transformation from rags to riches. Indeed, Park took a country that continued to be among the poorest in the world and dependent on US economic largesse, and guided it as it became a thriving export-led economy. To his critics, of course, Park was a key reason why South Korea moved away from the democratic experiment of the early 1960s and became a repressive dictatorship. His supporters, however, counter that South Korea was not ready for a democracy and needed a strongman to bring the prosperity that the country would eventually enjoy. Such is the mixed legacy of South Korea's best-known figure of the twentieth century.

Park led the coup that would usher a new era in South Korean history on May 16, 1961. A general in the ROK Armed Forces, Park had been alarmed by both the corruption of the Syngman Rhee years and, subsequently, what he saw as the weakness of Chang Myon as South Korea's new leader. And indeed, strikes and protests were rife, there was no real change in economic fortunes, and some student and left-wing groups were openly discussing immediate reunification with North Korea. Plus, the new prime minister was cracking down on corruption, including in the armed forces. Chang may have had a long-term plan to bring economic prosperity to South Korea in place, but Park believed that neither the country nor the military nor he himself had the time to wait. On the morning of the coup, Park harangued his troops by pointing out to their mission to make South Korea a great country.[19]

The reaction to Park's coup was muted, which signaled that most South Koreans did not particularly care for democracy itself nor, in particular, for a government that had not changed their economic situation. In fact, many of the first public demonstrations that day were in support of the coup.[20] The US, meanwhile, initially harbored some doubts about Park, who had expressed communist sympathies as a young military officer and had in fact been sentenced to death as a result of them. His sentence had later been commuted, and Park commanded the respect of his fellow military men by the time of his coup. The US would also quickly change its views about Park, who would be invited to the White House only five months after the coup. Many South Korean people also took to him. And those who tried to undermine the regime would have to face the Korean Central Intelligence Agency (KCIA). Launched less than a month after Park's coup, the KCIA would spend the next few decades investigating, arresting, torturing, and sometimes assassinating South Koreans accused of being North Korea sympathizers, suspected of supporting communism, or simply being seen as threat to the Park and Chun Doo-hwan regimes.[21]

Self-appointed as head of a Supreme National Reconstruction Committee, Park launched the first of the five-year economic plans for which he would become famous in January 1962.[22] Born in poverty and obsessed with avoiding a takeover by North Korea, Park wanted to turbocharge the economic development of his country. Originally trained at the Imperial Japanese Army Academy while Korea still was a colony of Japan—a country for which Park fought during World War II—the new South Korean leader also had a deep admiration for the country's neighbor. In particular, Park was complimentary regarding Japan's militaristic ethos. In his view, this had made Japan the strongest country in Asia during the first half of the twentieth century. And Park had carried on this ethos throughout his subsequent training at the Korea Military Academy and career in the ROK Armed Forces. As a result, Park's original five-year economic plan put textiles and light industry at the core of the first stage in a long-term plan to develop the South Korean economy— with Park hoping that the country's labor could be disciplined in such a way as to take advantage of this cheap and abundant resource.

In the meantime, however, Park had to contend with the fact that a growing number of South Koreans were grumbling about the manner in which he had come to power. Was the new leader of their country simply going to rule a military dictatorship? Yun Posun had resigned from his post less than a year after Park's coup, unwilling to provide any further legitimacy to the dictator's rule. He was now one of the leaders demanding the return of democratic elections. And Park understood that his rule could be hobbled without the legitimacy conferred by a popular vote. Thus, Park formally resigned from the army and scheduled a presidential election for October 1963. None other than Yun would be his main opponent.

The election campaign and vote were fairly clean affairs. Certainly, there was some repression of Park's opponents. But by the time the vote closed, it was unclear who would win the election. In the end, Park won 46.6 percent of the vote against Yun's 45.1 percent, with an 85 percent turnout. Park now had the legitimacy that elections confer. And throughout the 1960s, his presidency became authoritarian but not the full-blown dictatorship of the 1970s. The opposition would be intimidated by the KCIA and some other government acolytes. The government also cracked down on freedom of speech. Elections were rigged. And Park exhorted the virtues of a militaristic ethos, even if he did not seek to impose it by force. But there was a degree of domestic public debate about the direction of the country as well.

In fact, Park had to confront domestic opposition to some of his signature policies. The year after his election, Park announced that South Korea would dispatch the ROK Armed Forces to South Vietnam in support of American troops fighting in the Vietnam War. The first South Korean troops would land in the Southeast Asian country in February 1965. For Park, this was a way to show his gratitude to US President Lyndon B. Johnson, who backed his regime. Intervention in the Vietnam War also served to show South Korea's commitment to fight against communism, always with an eye on the Korean Peninsula and the enemy across the 38th parallel.

Importantly, participation in the Vietnam War brought hard cash in the form of salaries paid to South Korean soldiers and contractors as well as military equipment being produced in South Korea. But many South Koreans disagreed with their country's participation in the war, leading to demonstrations and protests.

However, the policy that really drew students and other groups to the streets was Park's decision to normalize diplomatic relations with Japan. The government faced months of protests after it announced that it would move ahead with diplomatic normalization. Park did not give in, however. In June 1965, Seoul and Tokyo signed the Treaty on Basic Relations Between Japan and the Republic of Korea. In exchange, Japan provided South Korea with US $300 million in grants, US $200 million in loans, and US $300 million in commercial credits for its occupation of Korea and the use of comfort women and labor slaves. Japanese government officials and business executives also started to provide advice to their South Korean counterparts. In Park's mind, the economic benefits of establishing relations with Japan outweighed the negatives.

Propelled by the newly launched Economic Planning Board with Park at the helm, *chaebol* including Daewoo, Hyundai, LG, or Samsung, and the state-owned banking sector providing credit to favored industries and firms,[23] South Korea experienced an economic boom throughout Park's time in office. The government aptly transformed foreign investment, transfers, and sales into savings, which it then used to provide the necessary funding to the private sector to continue to maintain high rates of economic growth. The government ensured that *chaebol* leaders understood that support for Park's ambitious economic agenda would bring them wealth, while noncompliance could result in ruin, if not prison. *Chaebol* leaders complied, and in return they received not only bank credit but also tax exemptions, materials and natural resources, and repression of labor to ensure low wages. This made the South Korean economy internationally competitive, launching the export-led model that would one day make the country rich. And South Koreans noticed. In 1967, Park was re-elected as president with 51.4 percent of the vote against Yun Posun's 40.9 percent. Yes, there had been repression of the opposition. But annual gross domestic product (GDP) growth rates hovering around the 10 percent mark were the main reason behind Park's re-election.

The South Korean president certainly did not want his country to remain stuck producing cheap goods. In April 1967, the government opened the Guro Industrial Complex in the southwestern part of Seoul. It was a clear signal that Park wanted South Korea to become an industrial powerhouse, capable of competing with the US, Western Europe, and Japan. From his perspective, this would ensure that South Korea would become globally respected and withstand the challenge from North Korea. Ramon had the chance to visit the complex a few times in the 2010s, now transformed into a digital hub focusing on R&D and IT. The complex had, of course, become unrecognizable from the one that Park had opened five decades earlier. But the idea behind it remained the same: to make South Korea achieve high rates of economic growth to compete with the wealthiest countries in the world.

South Korea's rapid economic growth during the Park era was creating a big divide between the glitzy lights of Seoul, Busan, or Daegu and the countryside though. Droves of South Koreans were leaving smaller towns to work in the factories, offices, restaurants, and bars popping up in the bigger cities. To address this, Park started the New Village Movement (*Saemaeul Undong*).[24] Launched in 1970, this movement sought to modernize South Korea's rural economy by providing financial and raw material support to villages for their inhabitants to improve the local infrastructure in their preferred way. Better housing and roads reached villages that arguably had never seen better days. Agricultural production increased as peasants had access to modern equipment for the first time. And life in the villages improved overall. This did not stop the flow of people moving to bigger cities, but it did help to slow it down and improved the self-esteem of rural towns. Park won his third election in a row in 1971, taking 53.2 percent of the vote against Kim Dae-jung's 45.2 percent. Along with Kim Young-sam and Kim Jong-pil, Park's main opponent in the election was one of the "Three Kims" who would go on to oppose dictatorial rule in the 1970s and 1980s. The opposition always faced a formidable obstacle: smaller towns supported South Korean dictators. The *Saemaeul Undong* movement was instrumental in cementing this support by helping villagers to take pride in their towns, and their country.

It was in this context that South Koreans suffered two shocks. The first came on July 4, 1972. That day, the two Koreas signed the North–South Joint Communiqué. In the communiqué, they agreed to pursue independent and peaceful reunification based on national unity. Representatives from the two Koreas had held several meetings starting in May leading to the July communiqué. They had decided to do so after US President Richard Nixon had traveled to China and met with Chinese leader Mao Zedong, and the two leaders had agreed to normalize Sino-American diplomatic relations. The meeting had come after months of secret negotiations. It is no exaggeration to say that it was one of the most monumental geopolitical shifts of the twentieth century.

With their key patrons seemingly moving toward reconciliation, the two Koreas took the decision to try to settle their differences independently. From Park's perspective, the dialogue and agreement with North Korea held the promise of him going down in history as the president who had brought reunification to Korea. In fact, the two Koreas had been holding lower-level meetings in 1971.[25] The meetings, however, seemed to be going nowhere until Nixon's visit to China made the two Koreas realize that it could be possible to take matters into their own hands. Yet talks between the two Koreas on the implementation of the joint communiqué quickly broke down. And any momentum to press ahead with reconciliation soon disappeared.

The second shock came in October 1972. Park's popularity seemed to be declining. In fact, Kim Dae-jung had beaten Park in Seoul and the surrounding area in the 1971 presidential election, and the New Democratic Party had substantially increased the opposition's share of the vote in the May legislative election of the same year at the expense of Park's Democratic Republican Party. As a result, there were doubts that Park could retain power in future elections. Plus, international geopolitics were in flux, not only because Nixon had met with Mao, but also because the US was looking for a negotiated resolution to the Vietnam War. In other words, by the second half of 1972 Park felt his position threatened.

In October 1972, therefore, Park launched a self-coup, and established a more authoritarian and repressive regime. He dissolved the National Assembly, declared martial law, and instated draconian censorship rules. His government then drafted the *Yusin* Constitution, which essentially allowed Park to govern for life if elected by an electoral college rather than a direct popular vote.[26] The new constitution was approved in a referendum the following month, with 92.3 percent of the vote on a 91.9 percent turnout. Park was accused of manipulating the vote. But its result was clear: Park could rule as long as he wished. The KCIA became even more powerful, and repression of the opposition became commonplace. Most notably, the KCIA kidnapped Kim Dae-jung in August 1973. He was about to be thrown out of a boat sailing from Japan to South Korea. He was only saved at the last minute when a Japanese military jet flew over and sent a warning signal.[27] This intervention followed energetic protests to Park from US ambassador to South Korea Philip Habib, as well as by his Japanese counterpart, Torau Ushiroku.

Emboldened by his newfound power, Park focused on the upgrading of the South Korean economy. The 1972 and 1977 five-year plans focused on heavy industries such as electronics, machinery, petrochemicals, or shipping. The World Bank and international advisers warned Park that this would be counterproductive, since, in their view, South Korea could not compete in these industries. Some within the South Korean government also had their doubts. Park pressed ahead, and one day he would be vindicated. One needs only to visit South Korea's massive shipyards in Geoje or Ulsan to see this for oneself. But Park was increasingly taking these decisions almost unilaterally. This could be a problem.

At the same time, Park launched a secret nuclear weapons program. The South Korean president had doubts about the US's commitment to the protection of his country. Aside from Nixon's rapprochement with China and his quest to find a negotiated solution to the Vietnam War, the American president had also withdrawn over 10,000 troops from South Korea.[28] With North Korea still posing a security threat to Seoul, Park instructed South Korean scientists and ministers to acquire the technology to develop nuclear weapons. Visits to nuclear powers France and the UK ensued, as well as to other countries with their own nuclear programs, such as Israel or Norway. Park also invited around twenty nuclear scientists of Korean origin to help South Korea acquire nuclear technology. However, the US learned of South Korea's plans in 1975 and forced the country's government to cease development of the program. The plans would eventually be completely halted in the 1980s, once Chun Doo-hwan had replaced Park.[29]

Toward the second half of the 1970s, pressure on Park to reform or quit became unbearable. Yook Young-soo, the president's wife, was assassinated in 1974 when a bullet aimed at Park missed him but hit her. As the president wrote in his diary, he sorely missed his wife.[30] Those around him noticed that the president became more isolated and authoritarian. And it showed. Repression of any real or perceived opponent of the regime increased, with the KCIA running rampant and martial law being imposed several times over the years.

Yet this only emboldened the opposition. Students took to the streets to demand an end to dictatorship and a transition to democracy. Workers joined them, demanding better wages and working conditions too. Catholic and Buddhist groups secretly provided support to the pro-democratization movement. And following his election as US president in 1977, Jimmy Carter demanded that the Park regime improve its human rights record.[31] Politicians opposed to Park felt emboldened. In September, Kim Young-sam gave an interview to the *New York Times* demanding that Jimmy Carter cease its support for the Park regime.[32] He was expelled from the National Assembly, and Kim led the opposition in walking out of a parliament that long ago had lost any real power.

Something had to give. And what gave was Park's life, assassinated in 1979 as his wife had been some years before. But Park was assassinated not by an opponent of his regime. Nor by a North Korean agent. Park was killed by Kim Jae-gyu, director of the KCIA, born in the same town as Park, and a graduate of the Korea Military Academy as part of the same class as the South Korean president. To date, it is unclear whether Kim killed Park because he felt that he was being sidelined by his long-term friend or because he sought an end to his regime. After all, Kim Jae-gyu had tried to negotiate with Kim Young-sam and had argued that protests taking place up and down the country were not led by North Korean infiltrators—as the government tried to maintain.[33]

On October 26, 1979, Kim shot Park during dinner in the Blue House, then the official residence of the South Korean president. Park died shortly after. Kim would be quickly arrested and sentenced to death following a trial. Park, meanwhile, received South Korea's first-ever state funeral. Millions of people lined the streets to thank their president. For while it is true that millions of South Koreans had grown tired of the Park regime and demanded democratization, many other millions were thankful to a president that had brought prosperity to the country, helped prevent a new North Korean invasion, and restored a modicum of dignity following Japanese colonialism and the Korean War. Yes, South Korea was still poor compared to most of the US-led camp, and its alliance with Washington was the central component of its security policy. But the Park years had brought a degree of prosperity that perhaps could make South Korea the master of its own destiny.

A Sprawling Kim Il-sung Personality Cult, a Sputtering North Korean Economy

The 1960s and 1970s were the decades when Kim Il-sung consolidated power for himself and his family. Similarly to the case of Park Chung-hee, Kim was able to link the security and prosperity of the country he ruled to his own position as its leader. In this way, Kim amassed absolute power and governed North Korea as he saw fit. In sharp contrast to Park, however, Kim's rule of North Korea did not come with world-beating economic growth. By the 1960s, North Korea's economic growth was starting to slow as the catch-up phase was not followed by policies to promote further expansion of the economy. By the 1970s, it was becoming clear that the North could not keep up with the South and its economy was failing to move to the next level. In this context, Kim doubled down on a personality cult and all-encompassing propaganda to cement his position—along with ongoing repression.

Juche continued to be the main organizing principle behind North Korea's sociopolitical structure. Throughout the 1960s, Kim sought to develop and clarify the meaning of this concept on which he had staked his leadership. Most notably, Kim gave a speech in Indonesia in April 1965 to lay out the principles behind *Juche*.[34] The speech was significant because *Juche* had almost disappeared from public discourse. With the speech, Kim revived the idea that North Korea should be self-reliant and independent of foreign interference in the development of its political system, economic model, and military power and foreign policy. And indeed, North Korea's policies throughout the 1960s and 1970s strongly suggested that the regime wanted to follow through on this idea.

Starting with politics, the year 1967 marked a key turning point. In 1966, a group of independence heroes who had fought against Japanese colonizers sought to fight back against and limit Kim's personality cult, promote different economic policies, and find an alternative leader to rule North Korea. This group was known as the Gapsan Faction. Kim reacted by repeatedly accusing the group of disloyalty and purging around a hundred of its members in the spring of 1967. Members of the faction were either sent to prison or conscripted for forced labor in factories and the countryside.[35] Arguably, this was the last time that any North Korean faction came close to presenting a viable alternative to Kim's rule. More purges in 1968 of other individuals and groups thought to pose a challenge to the North Korean leader further cemented his position.

Furthermore, Kim's crackdown on the Gapsan Faction officially started the cult of the Kim family and, arguably, the start of the elevation of Kim's son to the position of heir apparent. Kim Yong-ju—Kim's younger brother—penned the "Ten Principles for the Establishment of a Monolithic Ideological System." The title of the publication was self-explanatory. From then on, North Korea would have a single, unquestioned ideology to rule the country. The principles demanded that North Koreans obey and follow Kim without questioning, and also instituted an obligation for all North Koreans to memorize the principles.[36] They would become the guiding document governing North Koreans' patterns of behavior for decades to come.

Focusing on economics, it was the year 1961 that marked a turning point. That year, the Kim regime announced a new seven-year plan that should have allowed for the continuing industrialization and modernization of the North Korean economy. Yet this plan resulted in the start of the unambiguous diversification of economic resources to support a strong, independent military. Light industry and agriculture were brushed aside, as North Korea focused its efforts on building weapons and providing the training that the Kim regime deemed necessary to protect the country without outside support.[37] At the same time, the public distribution system started to show its limits in feeding the North Korean population. The government was displaying its disregard for its own population in a way that made clear where its priorities lay.

And indeed, from the 1960s onwards the Kim regime focused on bolstering its independent military power as its top priority. In 1963, *Rodong Sinmun* had noted that "economic dependence on foreign forces entails political dependence on those forces. Economic subordination leads to political subordination."[38] But instead of developing a strong and truly independent economic system to prevent the much-maligned political dependence on foreign powers, Kim focused his efforts on military power to bolster independence of political action.

Most notably for the future of North Korea and global politics, North Korea launched its nuclear program in the 1960s. Kim learned that China was in the advanced stages of developing a nuclear program of its own. For sure, China conducted its first nuclear test in October 1964. Thus it became only the fifth country to join the nuclear weapons club. Serendipitously for North Korea, Leonid Brezhnev had replaced Khrushchev as the Soviet Union's leader that same month. This smoothed relations between Pyongyang and Moscow, particularly as the former became critical of China's brand of socialism. And the Soviet Union stood ready to support North Korea's nuclear program with technology transfers, and also by sending its own scientists to the country. Herein lay a paradox in North Korean security and foreign policy. Kim wanted to strengthen North Korea's independent capabilities, but he was not able to do so without external support.

Better relations with the Soviet Union seemed also to embolden Kim to become more confrontational with South Korea and the US. With the latter embroiled in a very public internal debate about its involvement in the Vietnam War, North Korea seemed to sense that it might be possible to plant some doubts in American heads regarding the need to continue to protect South Korea. Thus, North Korea secretly dispatched thirty-one commandos to kill Park Chung-hee. On January 21, 1968, the commandoes launched a raid to enter the Blue House and assassinate the South Korean president. They reached a checkpoint just 1 yard away from Park's residence, where they were repelled by South Korean police forces. Twenty-nine of the commandoes were killed, one was captured, and one escaped back to North Korea. The raid thus failed, but it could have made the US question its commitment to the protection of South Korea had it been successful.

Two days after the failed raid, North Korea targeted the US directly. Two Korean People's Army submarines, four boats, and two jets surrounded the USS spy ship *Pueblo* and seized it, together with eighty-two crew members, with another one being killed. The *Pueblo* was inside or near North Korean territorial waters, depending on one's version of the events. In any case, spy operations were routine in the waters of the East Sea and North Korea had not seized any of the ships in these waters previously. Following months of captivity and negotiations between Pyongyang and Washington, the eighty-two surviving crew members were allowed to cross the DMZ in December to make their way home via South Korea. Only a few weeks later, however, the Korean People's Army Air Force shot down a US spy aircraft flying over the East Sea. Its thirty-one crew members were killed. The US denounced the attack and resumed its reconnaissance flights a few days later. But no further action was taken.

The Kim regime continued its mismanagement of the economy, consolidation of Kim's cult of personality, and push for security and foreign policy independence into the 1970s. The living conditions of North Koreans did not improve. If anything, they went backwards. The 1970s arguably were the decade when differences in the quality of life and international recognition of North and South became obvious for anyone willing to look beyond Pyongyang's propaganda. But Kim and his regime only doubled down on their approach.

By the 1970s, North Korea's public distribution system had become unable to provide the North Korean population with the recommended daily calorie intake for an adult.[39] Self-sufficiency in the agricultural sector was unrealistic, and North Korea had to rely on food transfers from wealthier fellow communist countries to feed its own population—particularly from China. Arable land comprised only 20 percent of North Korea's whole territory, so self-sufficiency would have been hard to achieve in the best of times. With the Kim regime focusing on the heavy industry sector to support the North Korean army, human resources to fully utilize the existing arable land were lacking. Plus, the necessary equipment was also missing since the government was directing the North Korean industrial sector toward other priorities. The seeds of North Korea's future dependence on foreign countries for its population not to starve were being laid.

In spite of its claims of self-sufficiency, North Korea turned to foreign countries to address this situation. Pyongyang borrowed US $1.2 billion between 1970 and 1975 to build fertilizer and cement plants, and other materials necessary for its economy.[40] North Korea had been improving links with Western countries in the late 1960s and early 1970s as it sought to escape the constraints of East–West divisions. Therefore, France, Japan, and the UK were among the countries providing North Korea with the funding necessary to build its plants. Meanwhile, traditional communist friends such as China, the Soviet Union, and Central and Eastern European countries continued to offer goods and food to North Korea. Yet, this only exacerbated dependence on foreign countries in a country that continued to preach self-reliance.

In fact, North Korea sought to diversify its list of foreign partners in the context of Sino-American dissension and general East–West rapprochement. This started with South Korea itself. In May 1972, Kim expressed regret over the Blue House raid, which he blamed on a rogue commando.[41] Very unlikely, considering the nature of the North Korean regime and society. But a sign that Kim wanted to improve relations with the South.

And only two months later, North Korea signed the historic joint communiqué with the South whereby the two Koreas agreed to pursue reunification independently. From Kim's perspective, improving relations with South Korea had two main advantages. To begin with, the South was the richer of the two Koreas. Better inter-Korean relations could thus potentially involve the North receiving aid from the South. The example of Germany was instructive, with the West helping the East as relations between the two improved following Willy Brandt's launch of his *Ostpolitik* in 1969. Furthermore, Pyongyang would also be implementing its idea of *Juche* by pursuing better inter-Korean relations.

By improving relations with the South, the North could show that its foreign relations were not hostage to the vagaries of the Soviet Union's and China's relations with the US or with the South itself.

The Koreas' joint communiqué, however, did not result in better relations. Instead, Pyongyang doubled down on its claim to legitimacy over the whole of the Korean Peninsula. In December 1972, North Korea replaced the 1948 constitution with a new one. The preamble, which still applies at the time of writing, reads as follows: "The great Comrades Kim Il Sung and Kim Jong Il are the sun of the nation and the lodestar of national reunification. Regarding the reunification of the country as the supreme national task, they devoted all their efforts and care for its realization."[42]

Instead, Pyongyang decided to concentrate its efforts on seeking normalization with the US. This may have been a conceivable goal in the context of improving Sino-American ties. But it was also a way to split the ROK–US alliance, at a time when there were doubts about Washington's commitment to its Asian allies as it prepared to end the Vietnam War. Thus, the rubber-stamp Supreme People's Assembly of the Democratic People's Republic of Korea produced a letter for the US Senate in March 1974 asking for the establishment of diplomatic relations between the two countries.[43] The Nixon administration declined North Korea's request.

North Korea may have mistakenly believed that the US would give the same value to potential normalization with Pyongyang as it did to normalization with China. This was never the case. Nonetheless, Kim followed suit by asking Mao for support to stage a new invasion of South Korea around the time of the official end of the Vietnam War.[44] Mao declined. A few months later, North Korean soldiers hacked to death two US army officers who were cutting down a tree in the Joint Security Area along the DMZ. The murder did not reduce the Gerald Ford administration's commitment to the ROK–

US alliance, coming a little over a week after its official inauguration. But it showed that North Korea was willing to test Washington's resolve in the aftermath of its withdrawal from Vietnam and as it came closer to diplomatic normalization with China.

At the same time, the Kim family was busy consolidating power. The personality cult of Kim Il-sung reached new heights in 1972—literally. No one visiting Pyongyang can fail to see the 72-ft-high statue of Kim in the Mansu Hill Grand Monument. Most foreign tourists visiting the city are taken to see the statue. As no North Korean tour guide fails to mention, it was erected to celebrate the 60th anniversary of Kim's birth. It symbolized the trajectory that the Kim regime was taking in the 1970s: image over substance, propaganda over performance. As the economy faltered, Kim doubled down on the symbols that showed his power over the country and its people. He also pushed ahead with the development of an indigenous nuclear program, when it was unclear whether North Korea really needed to focus on this rather than bread-and-butter issues.

But Kim was aware of his frailty. So he prepared to make his son his heir, his brother Kim Yong-ju falling out of favor after an internal power struggle and being relegated to ceremonial positions for the rest of his life. In 1974, Kim Jong-il was designated as his father's successor at the young age by (North) Korean standards of 33. He codified the "Ten Principles for the Establishment of a Monolithic Ideological System."[45] The younger Kim was also given key posts in North Korea's main institutions, including the Secretariat of the WPK, and took more responsibilities from his father. By the end of the decade, it was clear that one day the younger Kim would inherit the country that his father had founded in 1948. This country, however, was not the behemoth that Kim Il-sung wanted to build. North Korea had no diplomatic relations with the US and was dependent on Chinese and Soviet largesse for the economy to continue to function.

4
CHANGE VS CONTINUITY
1980 TO 1990

There are two images that come to mind about Korea in the tumultuous 1980s. The first is the June 29, 1987, cover of *Time* magazine.
It was titled "Korea's Crisis," with an artist's rendering of military
general-turned-politician and president Chun Doo-hwan's anguished face, the capital city of Seoul ablaze, and rows of riot police
in their Darth Vader-looking gear fighting pitched battles against
students demanding democratic reforms. Reporters from Western
media like *Time*, the *New York Times*, and the *Washington Post*, nor-
mally based in Tokyo, were all stationed in Seoul following the story.
Pop stars like Michael Jackson included footage of democracy protests in Korea in music videos on MTV. No one knew how it would
turn out, but everyone sensed this was the biggest story in Asia, no
less because the world was soon to descend on South Korea for the
Summer Olympic Games. Would the Games be held behind barbed
wire by an illiberal regime? Would they have to be moved out of
South Korea for safety reasons?

As described later in this chapter, the other image is of a South Korean college student, Lee Han-yeol, being propped up on his feet by a fellow student protester embracing him in a bear hug from behind. Clad in a Yonsei University long-sleeved T-shirt, Lee's body is limp, head leaning over to his right side, with a stream of blood down the side of his face. Lee's skull has been shattered by a tear gas canister fired by riot police on students protesting for democracy in Korea. The photo became iconic, the equivalent of that of the anguished girl next to a dying student at the Kent State shootings over the Vietnam War, or the lone Chinese citizen standing in front of a row of tanks about to plow through democracy protests in Tiananmen Square.

As a graduate student who spent summers researching in Seoul at the time, Victor Cha felt the tension in the air. University campuses looked like war zones. Security forces would stop any group of college-age-looking students, demanding their IDs and their destination. Tear gas burned the eyes and throat on a daily basis. And a stroll to the local *dabang* (tea house) in front of Yonsei to meet friends could be dangerously derailed by violence on the streets. South Korea felt like a ticking time bomb about to explode in 1986–7. The government would either relent toward the nationwide protests, or it would impose bloody martial law. South Korea's fate was once again in question, this time driven by internal forces and a citizenry that wanted political freedoms to accompany their newfound affluence.

* * *

The South's Push for Democracy

The 1980s were nothing short of a watershed in South Korean history. It is the decade when the South Korean people and government became embroiled in a dispute that eventually transformed into an all-out confrontation. The South Korean people at first greeted Park Chung-hee's assassination with disbelief, but almost immediately saw it as an opportunity to achieve something that they longed for: democracy. With Park gone, many South Koreans believed that their country was ready to move away from decades of authoritarian and later dictatorial rule, and kick-start a democratization process leading to a change in political system. This, the South Korean people thought, would put the fate of their political leaders in the hands of voters. Which should lead to a more independent South Korea, with leaders implementing the wishes of the people and not dancing to the tune of foreign powers.

Indeed, there was talk of a Seoul Spring in South Korea in the aftermath of Park's death. This was a reference to the Prague Spring of Czechoslovakia in 1968, when reformist leader Alexander Dubček had sought to introduce reforms to make the country's communist regime more liberal. In the case of South Korea, it was Choi Kyu-hah, the president, on whom South Koreans rested their hopes. As prime minister, Choi had replaced Park as South Korean president. He had then won the (indirect) election to serve the remainder of Park's term, scheduled to end in 1984. But sensing the mood in the streets, Choi had promised the restoration of democracy including free elections as well as changes to the authoritarian *Yusin* Constitution.[1] South Koreans dared to dream that their own Seoul Spring would have a better end than its ill-fated Prague namesake.

Alas, that was not going to be the case. On December 12, 1979, Chun Doo-hwan led a *coup d'état*. The South Korean army general did not even wait for a week to pass following Choi's election to make his move. With the support of most of the military, he was able to seize power relatively easily and with little bloodshed.[2] He then went on to consolidate power relatively quickly, with Choi acting as a figurehead president while Chun ensured that he eliminated potential rivals for the presidency. In April, Chun was self-appointed as director of the still all-powerful KCIA, which he renamed Agency for National Security Planning (ANSP). It was becoming obvious that the Seoul Spring was about to fail and Chun would become South Korea's new dictator.

On May 18, 1980, however, the people of South Korea made a final attempt to prevent the seemingly inevitable. It all started when university students in the southern city of Gwangju refused to comply with the martial law imposed by the government, following a 100,000-strong demonstration in Seoul three days earlier. The students in Gwangju took the decision not to go home. Instead, they marched toward the city center to protest against the government's actions. On their way there, ordinary citizens joined them. By the time they reached Gwangju's main avenue, thousands of people were demanding a proper democratic transition.[3] This was the start of the Gwangju Uprising, the most iconic moment in South Korea's struggle for democracy.

The Gwangju Uprising would last until May 27. The Chun regime acted with unusual violence and cruelty. Paratroopers blockaded the city. Communication lines were cut off. The government virtually isolated the city from the rest of the country. Paratroopers and the military killed over 150 people, wounded over 4,000, and arrested thousands. This included both demonstrators and other citizens simply trying to make their way around the city. In the end, the government had to roll out tank units across the city to regain control. Once the uprising was under control, the government started a propaganda campaign to blame the incident on North Korean infiltrators and communist sympathizers.[4] After all, the Chun regime would go on to be as anti-communist as Park's. Chun would never acknowledge that it was ordinary South Koreans fighting for democracy who were behind the uprising. The Gwangju Uprising would severely strain Chun's relations with the South Korean people during his seven-year rule.

In August 1980, in any case, Chun was officially elected as South Korea's new president. Again, this was an indirect election with a single candidate. Thus, on September 1, 1980, Chun was inaugurated. This was in the midst of South Korea's first recession since the Korean War, as a result of the second oil crisis of 1979 and the hit that the US, Europe, and Japan took as a result. With South Korea's three biggest markets suffering from their own contractions, the Chun government had to contend with both a lack of legitimacy in the eyes of the South Korean population and a period of economic malaise.

The newly inaugurated Chun government also had to contend with another problem: a bout of anti-Americanism that threatened to shake the foundations of the ROK–US alliance, which continued to be the bedrock of South Korea's security policy. Many South Koreans associated the US with the crackdown in Gwangju, if not directly at least by omission. After all, many South Koreans thought, the Carter administration could have forced the Chun government to stop the carnage unfolding in the southern city. Plus, the US's new president, Ronald Reagan, implicitly supported Chun since he was not pressing for the restoration of democracy. Anti-Americanism flared up in March 1982, when a group of South Koreans set the Busan American Cultural Service on fire in protest at what they saw as Washington's unconditional support for Chun's dictatorship. Anti-Americanism would only once again reach similar heights in the early 2000s, and it marred Chun's years in power.

Chun also had to face foreign policy challenges early on in his presidency. In September 1983, Soviet jets shot down a Korean Air flight that had inadvertently crossed into the country's aerospace.

The Soviet military mistook the Korean Air plane for a US reconnaissance jet, and ordered it to be shot down. All 269 people on board were killed. South Koreans were in rage, but there was little that they could do as the incident took place in the context of Cold War competition between the US and the Soviet Union.

One month later, a North Korean bomb killed twenty-one South Koreans in Rangoon, including four cabinet members. The bomb was intended to assassinate Chun, who was on an official visit to Burma. However, Chun had had to delay his departure from his accommodation, and thus the North Korean terrorists set off the bomb before Chun arrived at his destination.[5] Uncertain of whether the North would try to target him again, and not confident in his own security services, Chun relied on US military help to exit the country safely and bring home the deceased. This "quiet alliance" cooperation, however, never became known to the anti-American protagonists demonstrating on South Korean streets. Chun vowed to take revenge against North Korea and Kim Il-sung, who would have had to have authorized the attack. After all, North Korea was not the Soviet Union. Reagan visited South Korea, however, and urged restraint. Arguably, this visit was the key reason that Seoul did not retaliate.

In spite of these problems, the South Korean economy resumed fast growth once the 1980 recession was over. What is more, the *chaebol* propelling this growth were moving into electronics, semiconductors, automobiles, shipbuilding, and other high-tech sectors that in the past were reserved for more developed economies. Certainly, Daewoo, Hyundai, or Samsung for the most part were copying what more advanced foreign firms were doing and finding ways of building products more cheaply. But it is also true that not many other developing countries were successfully moving into these high-tech sectors. In other words, the fast economic growth of the

1980s was also laying the foundations for the future South Korean economy.

Strong economic growth, however, did not bring legitimacy to the Chun regime while the memories of the Gwangju Uprising and general repression persisted. Chun, therefore, started to think about ways to bolster his domestic position. A solution came from above the 38th parallel: reconciliation with North Korea. In 1984, Seoul announced a plan to provide Pyongyang with food, goods, and materials to improve the North Korean economy. The Kim Il-sung regime rejected this offer. But shortly after, South Korea suffered floods killing over 200 people. This time, it was Pyongyang that offered help. And Seoul accepted. For the first time since the Korean War, over 1,300 North Koreans crossed the DMZ legally to bring food, medicine, and clothes to those suffering from the floods.[6]

A year later, something even more unimaginable happened. Red Cross talks related to Chun's announcement that the South would provide food to the North and the North's actual provision of aid to the South expanded to discussions about inter-Korean people-to-people exchanges. The talks made better progress than had been expected. Thus, within months, 150 South Koreans and the same number of North Koreans crossed the DMZ in opposite directions. The groups included people separated from their families during the Korean War, artists, and journalists, who spent four days in the other Korea.[7] However, the goodwill did not last long. The North abruptly halted cooperation, called on communist countries to boycott the 1986 Asian Games scheduled to be hosted in Seoul, and planted a bomb in the South Korean capital's Gimpo Airport a few days before the games, killing five people. Any hope of reconciliation between the two Koreas was over for the time being. From a domestic politics perspective, this could not be a path toward legitimacy for Chun either.

In fact, 1985–7 was the period in which South Koreans were able to successfully make a final push for democracy. In February 1985, South Korea held its National Assembly election. Even though the South Korean parliament continued to be powerless, as it had been during the Park years, at least the votes to elect its members were relatively free. Chun's Democratic Justice Party won the election with 35.2 percent of the vote. But the opposition pro-democracy New Korea and Democratic Party, unofficially led by Kim Dae-jung and Kim Young-sam—themselves barred from running for election—received a 29.3 percent share of the vote. Their key promise was to hold a direct presidential election. This was proof, if any was needed, that a sizable number of South Koreans wanted change.

And 1987 was a crucial year in South Korea's quest for freedom. Back in 1980, the new constitution replacing Park's *Yusin* had set a single seven-year term for presidents. Therefore, in theory, Chun would not be able to run for re-election as Park had done multiple times. And there were indications that, indeed, Chun would not try to amend the constitution or find a subterfuge to try for a second term as South Korean president. This meant that perhaps South Korea would be able to have a free election and vote for a president promising the restoration of democracy. However, as time went by, it was becoming clear that Chun was trying to position his protégé Roh Tae-woo as his successor, even floating the idea that the election would be indirect; that is, the National Assembly would decide who the new president would be. Roh had been one of the military leaders supporting Chun's coup, and had then become a cabinet minister and the leader of the Democratic Justice Party.

Aware of the situation, South Koreans doubled down on their protests to force the government's hand. They were buoyed by the violence displayed by the Chun regime, which only reinforced their commitment to launch a new dawn in South Korean history. In January 1987, Seoul National University student and pro-democracy activist Park Jong-cheol was arrested and tortured to death. The Chun regime tried to hide what had happened, but the truth eventually came out in May. Opponents of the regime then organized a demonstration in Park's honor for the following month.[8]

One day before the demonstration, students took over the Yonsei University campus to protest against the Chun regime. As usual, the police and paratroopers responded with violence. A tear gas grenade thrown at the demonstrators hit Lee Han-yeol, a student at the university. The grenade penetrated Lee's skull, leaving him unconscious. Lee was rushed to the hospital.[9] As noted at the beginning of this chapter, a picture of him lying motionless in the arms of one of his friends became a symbol of what was to come.

On June 10, the June Democratic Struggle broke out across the country. The Democratic Justice Party nominated Roh as its candidate for the next election. Demonstrations ensued. They continued on a daily basis. Students and workers led. White-collar workers, many of whom hitherto had been reluctant to fully commit to the democratization movement, also joined in. Many would go to their offices as usual in the morning only to join the protests after work. South Korea's feminist movement, emboldened after holding the first Women's Conference two years earlier, also joined the struggle. Religious groups became an active part of the protest movement as well, after years of support for the democratic movement. In the meantime, Lee Han-yeol remained motionless in a hospital bed. He continued to inspire the demonstrators.

The role of the feminist movement was particularly interesting. To many, women continued to be second-class citizens. But their role in society had been changing as South Korea industrialized. Many factories in sectors such as textiles had an overwhelmingly female workforce, with women taking over 90 percent of jobs. At the same time, a growing number of South Koreans were attending university and joining white-collar professions. The days when South Korean women were relegated to the house were increasingly a thing of the past. Two developments reflected these changes. In 1977, Ewha Womans University had launched South Korea's first women's studies course, to research and analyze the changing role of women in the country's economy and society. And in 1984, South Korea's fertility rate had slipped below the symbolic 2.1 births per woman mark needed for the population to replace itself.[10] This meant that most South Korean couples were happy to have less than two children. Tellingly, it also meant that a growing number of women were able to resist societal pressure to have larger families.

At the same time, however, there was an obvious glass ceiling for women. Most managers were men, in both blue-collar and white-collar professions. Furthermore, many women were still forced to leave their jobs once they married or had their first child. And many female university graduates did not get a job to begin with, or they expected their professional careers to be short. It was in this context that the South Korean feminist movement emerged. Concurrently, South Koreans were fighting for their democracy. Many women equated democracy with their rights. They could not be equal in a military dictatorship led by strongmen who not only oppressed South Koreans but also had a very traditional view of the role of women in society. As South Koreans fought for democracy, many women actively participated in this fight and led some of the groups at the forefront of South Koreans' struggle.

On June 29, the struggle came to an end. Unlike the Seoul Spring, it came to an end because it was successful. That day, Roh Tae-woo delivered the Special Declaration for Grand National Harmony and Progress Toward a Great Nation. Roh pledged that South Korea would have free, direct presidential elections. Anyone would be allowed to run, including opposition figure Kim Dae-jung. Other freedoms would ensue.[11] In short, South Korea would become a democracy. The Chun regime had given up. The South Korean people were clear in their demands. And Reagan was also pushing for South Korea to become a democracy. Roh understood that there was only one viable way forward. South Koreans celebrated all across the country. Lee Han-yeol, unfortunately, finally passed away on July 5. His funeral became another celebration of sorts, with over 1.5 million South Koreans taking to the streets to mourn his death yet hopeful that this would be the last time that a South Korean citizen would have to give his life for democracy.

In October, there was a democratic amendment to the South Korean constitution that stands as of February 2023. In December, South Koreans would vote in a truly free election for the first time since the early 1960s, before Park Chung-hee seized power. Roh Tae-woo won the election, as the opposition vote split among the "Three Kims." Yet Roh had won fair and square. There was no indication that the vote had been rigged. The day of the vote went by without any major incident. The opposition candidates accepted the result of the election, as did voters. For a country that had lived under authoritarianism for almost thirty years, it was as if democracy was the natural state of affairs. For South Korean voters, this brought the hope that their country would be able to determine its own policies and future with no outside interference. Certainly, the ROK–US alliance and the constraints of Cold War enmity put a limit to the extent to which South Korean policymakers could follow the wishes of their voters. But at least voters could push for their preferred policies at the ballot box, which they had not been able to do for decades.

The North's Impulse Not to Change

October 1980 was a crucial month in North Korean history. The WPK was holding its sixth congress, the first since 1970. This could only mean that a big announcement was coming. And a big announcement indeed came: Kim Il-sung communicated that his son Kim Jong-il had officially become his heir, including having the power to make appointments to the party's Politburo and other state organs.[12] North Korea would not hold another party congress until 2016, which suggests that the sixth congress was essentially conceived as the coronation ceremony of the younger Kim. This was a first for a communist regime, and closer to the practices of Joseon Korea than to the policies followed by other communist countries, including China and the Soviet Union. From then on, Kim Jong-il portraits and monuments began to be placed around the country and the new leader engaged in a busy public schedule to emphasize his leadership credentials. North Korea was effectively the Kim family's kingdom, The North Korean people had no power to determine the political direction of their country. Yet, at the same time, the 1980s were a decade when North Korea became even more dependent on Chinese and Soviet support to run its economy. The power of the Kim family to run North Korea as they wished weakened.

The official announcement that Kim Jong-il would one day become the leader of the country suggested that North Korea was unwilling to change. Who could better ensure that Kim Il-sung's legacy would be preserved than his own son? The appointment of the younger Kim indicated that the regime was not open to other ways of thinking. After all, Kim Jong-il had been groomed for many years prior to his appointment. It is easy to imagine that he would have been educated and socialized in the ideas espoused by his father, including *Juche*.

North Korea could point out that dictatorial rule was also the norm in the South at the time, even if not hereditary. However, there were two crucial differences between North and South. The first was the scale of opposition to Chun Doo-hwan's regime in the South, both in the streets and by opposition political parties. There was no hint that there was a viable opposition to the Kim family, or that North Koreans were demonstrating *en masse* to try to force change. Both North and South Korea were dictatorships in the 1980s, but people in the latter enjoyed freedoms that their counterparts in the North could not even dream of.

The other key difference between the North and the South was their economic performance. In line with other communist regimes, Pyongyang sought control over the whole economy. By the 1980s, it was becoming clear that this was a failed formula. Not only North Korea but communist regimes in general were suffering from an economic slowdown. In the case of North Korea, the poor economic performance was even starker because the South offered a simple point of comparison. The regime had nowhere to hide. So it tried to keep up with a South Korean economy that was once again booming following the recession triggered by the second oil crisis.

The problem was that North Korea could not keep up. Competition between the two Koreas was unaffordable for Pyongyang. Throughout the 1980s, the Kim regime launched mega-projects, including tide-land reclamation and hydrothermal energy production.[13] North Korea mobilized huge human and financial resources to complete these projects, but they often went unfinished. Simply put, North Korea lacked both the money and the skills that the South had been working on for decades.

The regime therefore turned its attention to ensuring that the Kim family would continue to rule North Korea into the future.[14] In 1981, the newspaper *Rodong Sinmun* wrote about the need for *Juche* as a way for North Korea to remain independent. And one year later, Kim Jong-il published *On the Juche Idea*. This was a treatise setting out the history and aims of *Juche*. Essentially, the idea of *Juche* was linked to Kim Il-sung's personal history—particularly his experience as a Korean independence fighter. And the future of *Juche* was linked to Kim Jong-il as the guarantor of its implementation. At the same time, *Juche* was presented as distinct from Marxism-Leninism.[15] Therefore, *Juche* was not an interpretation of canonical communist ideas but rather an ideology inherent to the history of (North) Korea and the Kim family.

In this context, the cult of personality of the Kim family continued. Rather than using precious scarce resources in improving the economy, the North Korean regime focused on building symbols of the power that the Kim family commanded. To celebrate the 70th birthday of Kim Il-sung, North Korea opened three impressive monuments. They were the Arch of Triumph, the Tower of the Juche Idea, and the Grand Study House of the People. The first of these three, perhaps unsurprisingly, was bigger than the original in Paris. The second celebrated the guiding ideology that underpinned life in North Korea. The third created a space for students and ordinary citizens alike to read officially sanctioned books. The Kims were celebrating themselves and the system that they had developed to control the officially sanctioned ideology and culture of North Korea. They were also putting away any notion that the interests of the North Korean people came first.

Unable to compete economically with South Korea, the North was in no mood to compromise with its neighbor. In October 1983, the regime dispatched an assassination squad to Burma to kill Chun Doo-hwan, as mentioned earlier. Even though it is likely that we will never find out the truth behind the story, there were indications that the assassination attempt was organized by Kim Jong-il.[16] This meant that North Korean ruler Kim Il-sung knew about the plans. In other words, he pushed to undermine and bring chaos to South Korea. Even if unsuccessful, the attempt on Chun's life indicated a degree of desperation from a North unable to compete with its neighbor below the 38th parallel.

Furthermore, Pyongyang turned its attention to military competition. The 1980s can be considered the decade when North Korea started its efforts to develop a fully independent nuclear weapons program in earnest. In 1980, North Korea began construction of a nuclear reactor in Yongbyon, around 60 miles away from the capital, Pyongyang. The reactor would be completed by 1986.[17] And even though North Korea received outside support to build its first-ever nuclear reactor, it is certainly true that most of the work was carried out by North Korean scientists, researchers, and construction workers.

In fact, the progress made by North Korea in a relatively short period of time raised the alarm among the existing nuclear powers. The Soviet Union led efforts for North Korea to join the Non-Proliferation Treaty (NPT). Under the terms of the treaty, North Korea and all other existing nuclear powers were barred from developing nuclear weapons or engaging in proliferation activities. In 1985, Pyongyang finally joined the NPT to the relief of the US, the Soviet Union, and other nuclear powers.

Having said that, North Korea did try to improve relations during a short period in the mid-1980s. The offer of food aid to South Korea and active participation in the first-ever inter-Korean family exchange, as described above, signaled an attempt to improve relations. Perhaps this was linked to an event due to take place in Seoul in 1988: the Olympic Games. South Korea had been awarded the Games in 1981 and was poised to become only the second country in Asia to host them, following Tokyo 1964. Aware that the Games would boost international recognition for South Korea—as the Tokyo Games had done for Japan—Pyongyang came up with a bold idea in 1985: to share the hosting of the Games even though North Korea had not been awarded the bid. The International Olympic Committee (IOC) and South Korea considered the idea, but rejected the proposal after maximalist demands by the North.[18]

North Korea, therefore, turned its attention to sabotaging the Games. Seoul was due to host the Asian Games in September–October 1986, which would serve to prepare for the hosting of the much bigger Olympic Games two years later. Pyongyang called on its fellow communist countries across Asia to boycott the 1986 Games. And it was very successful in its endeavor, for all communist countries bar one boycotted the Asian Games. The problem? The communist country that did attend the 1986 competition was none other than China. Tentative Sino-South Korean economic exchanges had started a few years earlier, and, more importantly, Beijing was due to host the 1990 Asian Games. Therefore, China decided to attend the 1986 Games. This was a major diplomatic blow for Pyongyang.

A few days before the Asian Games kicked off, a North Korean agent detonated a bomb in Gimpo Airport, as mentioned earlier. The blast killed five people, but North Korea was unable to stop South Korea from running the Games successfully. This was another diplomatic blow to Pyongyang. Its proposal to co-host the 1988 Olympic Games was going nowhere, its terrorist activities resulted in deaths but no political outcomes, and Chinese athletes were competing in Seoul.

The Kim regime sought to replicate the communist boycott of the Asian Games at the Olympic level. It failed miserably. The Soviet Union and China made it clear that they would attend the Games, their athletes visiting Seoul to check the facilities in which they were to compete. Central and Eastern European countries were having none of North Korean calls for a boycott. Asia's communist bloc may have agreed not to attend the Asian Games, but the Olympic Games were a completely different matter. As the Games approached, it seemed that only Cuba and Ethiopia would join North Korea in boycotting them. And then, in the former case, Havana only seemed to be motivated by Fidel Castro's anger at having lost the rights to host the 1987 Pan-American Games.

In this context, North Korea went back to its old playbook. On November 29, 1987, two North Korean agents planted a bomb on a Korean Air flight. The bomb exploded over the Andaman Sea, destroying the plane and killing its 115 occupants. One of the agents, Kim Hyon-hui, who planted the bomb and disembarked the plane at a layover in Bahrain, was arrested and taken to South Korea. Kim testified that Kim Jong-il had directly given the order to bomb a South Korean flight.

The bombing of the Korean Air flight did not have the intended effect of preventing the Seoul 1988 Olympic Games from going ahead. But it did have the effect of showcasing how little North Korea had changed, in sharp contrast with a South Korea that less than three months after the destruction of the flight held its first democratic election in three decades. South Korea was evolving; North Korea was stagnating.

Indeed, North Korea arguably became more authoritarian throughout the 1980s. There was no pretense of collective leadership, Kim Jong-il was assuming more powers previously held by his now-ageing father, and repression of those who opposed or were perceived to oppose the regime continued. There was no hint of organized internal opposition to the regime in any case, highlighting the degree of sophistication of North Korea's surveillance and imprisonment system. As a case in point, North Koreans were unable to leave their country freely, at a time when other communist regimes were tentatively easing travel restrictions.

On the economic front, North Korea continued to prioritize its military build-up and heavy industries. In the meantime, the central distribution system remained inadequate to feed the whole North Korean population. Throughout the 1980s, the problems associated with the North Korean economic model grew even more.[19] And while fellow communist countries such as China under Deng Xiaoping and the Soviet Union under Mikhail Gorbachev experimented with economic opening, North Korea still pressed ahead with the principle of *Juche*. In other words, it was not only that South Korea was leaving North Korea well behind, but that Pyongyang epitomized an unwillingness to change even compared to other communist countries.

South Korea's Coming-of-Age Parties

The year 1988 was crucial in South Korean history, for it set the tone for the country's politics and society for decades to come. South Korea had held its presidential election in December 1987, but it was not clear that it could successfully transition into a democracy. After all, the military could decide that it did not wish the country to go down a democratic path. Not far away from South Korea, the Philippines was witnessing a succession of coup attempts by the military and loyalists to former dictator Ferdinand Marcos, who had been forced to leave office in 1986 as his country transitioned into a democracy. It was not unthinkable that the same fate would befall South Korea.

Remarkably, however, South Korean political leaders and the population showed great maturity from the beginning. Roh Tae-woo was inaugurated on February 25, opening the Sixth Republic era.

While democratically elected, Roh had been a key figure in the Chun government that had ruled South Korea with an iron fist throughout the 1980s. In fact, his critics labelled Roh's time in office as the "Five-Point-Five" Republic.[20] In other words, a midway point between the (dictatorial) Fifth Republic with Chun at the helm and the promise of a (democratic) Sixth Republic that could only come with a new leader, untainted by their association to the former dictator.

Yet political opponents of Roh and his party competed in the political arena. There was no attempt to overturn the result of the election, no denunciation of a rigged vote, no call for the people to take to the streets. Led by the "Three Kims," the opposition to Roh and his policies came from within the National Assembly, respecting the democratic procedures set out in the constitution that South Koreans had voted for in the referendum held in October of the previous year. For sure, there was robust debate within and outside the National Assembly. But this could only be natural in a democracy.

Certainly, demonstrations continued up and down the country. In fact, 1988–9 saw record numbers of protests against the government.[21] But the frequency and goals of these demonstrations were an indication of the strength of the nascent South Korean democracy. For once, South Koreans were able to take to the streets without fear of the violent response of the Park and Chun decades in power. This emboldened not only students and workers to conduct protests, but also judges, prosecutors, and other groups demanding changes. And the changes that they demanded were linked to better pay, the dismantling of some of the remnants of the Chun regime, or reform of the police, judiciary, or intelligence services to make them more accountable.

The Roh government responded to these demonstrations with maturity. It engaged with the demands coming from the protesters, taking some on board, ignoring others, but generally seeking to make the effort to consider them on their merits. Likewise, the Roh government allowed the first commemoration of the 1948–9 Jeju Uprising to take place in 1989.[22] South Koreans had been forbidden from even talking about the uprising for over forty years. Now they could commemorate the event without fear of retribution.

Particularly relevant, too, was the acquiescence of the government and the *chaebol* to demands for higher wages. Average salaries doubled in a period of only five years.[23] Conditions for workers generally improved, including the universalization of health insurance in 1989, despite the fact that South Koreans continued to work long hours and did not get the unemployment, pension, and other benefits that Europeans and workers in other developed countries had. But workers were getting more of the spoils of South Korea's rapid economic growth, and the government did not try to silence them as previous dictatorial regimes had done.

Moreover, Roh also reacted to his party becoming the opposition after the April 1988 National Assembly election in a democratic rather than authoritarian way—as his party lost its majority in the parliamentary election. This was the first time since 1950 that the president had to work together with a National Assembly dominated by the opposition—in this case, by the three different parties, each led by one of the "Three Kims." Roh sought to obtain the support of the opposition parties for his policy agenda, sometimes receiving their backing but often not. And instead of taking an authoritarian route, Roh played the democratic game. In January 1990, his party merged with Kim Young-sam's and Kim Jong-pil's, in an attempt to create a dominant right-leaning party similar to the decades-old Liberal Democratic Party in neighboring Japan.[24] Kim Dae-jung denounced the move. But, again, his party dealt with this blow in the National Assembly rather than asking South Koreans to take to the streets.

South Korea, therefore, had a political coming-of-age party in 1988 by launching the democratic Sixth Republic that survives as of 2023. Some of the features that would endure, such as the importance of charismatic leaders at the expense of the parties, the division into right-leaning and left-leaning blocs, or the role of public demonstrations in shaping policy were also settled fairly early on in the democratic years. Yet these were the features of system that was democratic, and that would allow South Korea's Sixth Republic to survive for longer than any previous one.

The world, in any case, noticed a different coming-out party. Olympic Games and other sports mega-events can be used for a country to announce that it has arrived. The 1964 Tokyo Olympic Games, the 1972 Munich Olympic Games, or the 1982 FIFA World Cup in Spain were used by the respective host governments to show that their countries had left their dictatorial pasts behind. They were celebrations of renewal, of pride in political and societal changes making the country and people freer.

On the other hand, these types of events can serve to show confidence in one's authoritarian regime. They serve dictatorial regimes to show both to their population and the outside world that they may not offer freedom, but they do offer competence. The 1936 Berlin Olympic Games, hosted by Germany while it was ruled by the Nazis, is arguably the best-known case. But there have been many others: the 1934 World Cup in Italy, the 1978 World Cup in Argentina, or the 1980 Moscow Olympic Games served, respectively, a Fascist regime in power for over a decade, a military junta that had recently taken over in a coup, and a decades-old communist regime to present the case for the superiority of their political system.

The 1988 Seoul Olympic Games were originally meant to have fallen under this second category. In 1981, the IOC had selected the South Korean capital as the host of the 1988 Games. Seoul had decisively beaten its Japanese rival Nagoya,[25] making the decision even sweeter from a South Korean perspective. But the South Korean Olympic bid had not promised more freedoms, never mind democratization. The Games were to serve the Chun regime and, by extension, the South Korean military, to showcase the level of economic development achieved by their country. They were also to show North Korea which of the two Koreas was more globally recognized. And they were to serve to demonstrate the organizational skills of the South Korean dictatorial regime.

By the time the 1988 Games were due to open in September, the situation had, of course, completely changed. Roh had actually been the head of the Seoul Olympic Organizing Committee from 1983 to 1986. Thus, he had been committed to the idea of using the Games to showcase the strength of the Chun regime. Now the leader of a democratic country, Roh set about to use the Games to present an open, vibrant, free, and developed South Korea instead. Which he did, from the moment that he officially declared the Games open following the inauguration ceremony.

A democratic South Korea thus used the Seoul Games to present itself to the world as a new country, in which people could enjoy their newfound freedoms. The Games also served to show the rest of the world that South Korea was modern and economically developed. This mattered hugely to South Koreans. Throughout the 1970s and 1980s, the mega-hit TV series *M*A*S*H* had presented South Korea as the backward and poor country of the Korean War. This was the era in which the show was set. Few people outside of South Korea were really aware of how much the country had changed in the ensuing decades.

Seoul 1988 was also a coming-out party of sorts for (South) Korean culture. The country's modern and traditional culture were a great unknown for most foreigners. To reverse this, the opening ceremony of the Games featured the *hangeul* alphabet, women and men wearing *hanboks*, traditional *geobukseons* or turtle ships used during the Joseon dynasty, a taekwondo exhibition, and many other signifiers of Korean culture.

The year 1988 was also a foreign policy coming-out party for South Korea. In July of that year, Roh had presented his *Nordpolitik* or Northern Policy toward North Korea and the communist camp. Inspired by Brandt's *Ostpolitik*, Roh's *Nordpolitik* was a policy for South Korea to improve relations with North Korea, China, and the Soviet Union, and also for the US and Japan to reach out to North Korea.[26] The idea was for South Korea to establish diplomatic, economic, and people-to-people relations with the communist bloc to strengthen its own position, as well as to create a better environment for inter-Korean reconciliation.

Seoul 1988 served as a turning point for *Nordpolitik* as well. No communist country other than North Korea and Cuba officially boycotted the Games. In sharp contrast, the communist camp had boycotted Los Angeles 1984 in retaliation after the US had led a boycott of Moscow 1980. Most importantly from a South Korean perspective, both China and the Soviet Union sent sports delegations to the Games. This paved the way for all other communist countries to attend as well.

Equally relevant, the Games served South Korea to show the communist camp its real face, rather than the portrayal disseminated by North Korea. Not that the communist camp blindly believed the information fed by Pyongyang. But in the 1980s Kim Il-sung had made a number of trips to Central and Eastern Europe, as well as China and the Soviet Union, no doubt to strengthen North Korea's position within the communist camp, and prevent contacts with South Korea. The Seoul Olympic Games symbolized North Korea's failure in this respect, and showed how South Korea had become the most international of the two Koreas, even from the perspective of communist countries. And for many South Koreans, the Games also brought the hope that their country could have an independent domestic and foreign policy. Their country was becoming rich, could host the biggest event in the world, and other countries wanted to improve relations. Something to build on as the 1990s approached.

Is Kim Il-sung Open to Change?

South Korea's ascendancy in the later 1980s had a flip side: a wobbling North Korea moving in the opposite direction. There was no doubt that the South was more successful in economic and now diplomatic terms. With Seoul 1988, South Korea was also starting to become the purveyor of Korean culture, as the general public across the world started to take an interest thanks to what they watched on their TV screens coming out of the South Korean capital. Plus, South Korea was riding the trend of political change coming with the third wave of democratization, with countries across East Asia, Latin America, Southern Europe, and, shortly after, Central and Eastern Europe leaving behind authoritarianism for political liberalism.

Kim Il-sung and his successor, his son Kim Jong-il, had a decision to make. They could set North Korea on the path of fellow communist countries, liberalizing their economies and, in a small number of cases, their politics. Or they could decline to change course and continue to implement a (nominally) self-reliant economic policy while maintaining political repression. In East Asia, Deng Xiaoping had been implementing his Open Door Policy announced in 1978, and the Community Party of Vietnam had followed in Beijing's steps with its *Doi Moi* policy, launched in 1986. In the case of Vietnam, the reforms had been launched even in the absence of diplomatic relations with the US that could have guaranteed easier access to Western investment and markets.

Would Kim Il-sung be ready to follow the path set by his fellow communist leaders? Certainly, North Korea was in a worse geopolitical position than other communist countries. After all, any change in economic direction could easily make North Koreans question whether it would not be better to simply follow the South Korean model. And political change was unthinkable, for it could easily lead to the North becoming like the South. The chances of the Kim family continuing to rule a country becoming increasingly similar to the South were remote. At the same time, North Korea could not stand still. As part of its rapprochement with the West and also South Korea, the Soviet Union was reducing its support to Pyongyang. In 1987, 50 percent of the North's food imports came from the Soviet Union. One year later, the figure was down to 25 percent.[27] Similarly, oil imports from the Soviet Union, which North Korea could purchase at a discounted rate of 25 percent compared to market prices, also went down. Perhaps the worsening economic situation could convince Kim to enact some modest reforms.

However, this was not to be. In 1984, North Korea approved a Joint Venture Law. And in 1991, it started to establish special economic zones. But these efforts went nowhere. Instead, the Kim regime continued to opt for optics over substance. In 1987, North Korea started construction of the Ryugyong Hotel in Pyongyang. Standing at 1,080 ft tall, the hotel is the tallest building in North Korea by far and today dominates the landscape of the country's capital. The building was to be completed in 1992, to commemorate the 80th birthday of none other than Kim himself.[28] In other words, the main purpose of the hotel was not to support economic growth in North Korea but to join the string of symbols across Pyongyang commemorating Kim. But the Ryugyong would eventually become a glaring symbol of North Korea's failure, as we explain later.

In the meantime, North Korea aimed to upstage Seoul 1988 itself. In July 1989, around 22,000 delegates from 177 countries descended on Pyongyang to participate in the 13th World Festival of Youth and Students for eight days of discussions and activities.[29] For decades used by the Soviet Union and communist countries as a propaganda tool, the festival was certainly bigger than Seoul 1988 in terms of the number of participants. And Pyongyang even scored a propaganda coup as South Korean university student Lim Su-kyung made a ten-day, four-country trip to reach Pyongyang from Seoul to denounce the South Korean government "on behalf of the million students of South Korea" dissatisfied with conditions in their country.[30]

Yet the festival ended up being another big failure for the Kim regime. Certainly, the celebration was never going to attract the global attention that the Olympic Games do. More worryingly for North Korea, the festival bankrupted the country. North Korea spent anywhere between US $4 billion and US $9 billion hosting the festival, building around 260 major facilities in the span of only two years.[31] Furthermore, the presence of overseas visitors, including from the US and Western European countries, showed ordinary North Koreans that living conditions in these countries were certainly not so dire as depicted by their government's propaganda. Even Lim herself did not look like the undernourished, impoverished South Korean oppressed by American imperialism that North Korean propaganda used to depict Koreans below the 38th parallel.

Therefore, hosting the World Festival of Youth and Students had the opposite effect in North Korea to the hosting of the Olympic Games in the South. Rather than moving toward greater political openness, the North went down the path of growing political repression. Rather than an economic opportunity grasped with both hands, the North faced an enormous bill to pay with not much to show in return. And as the festival coincided with the initial stages of the start of the fall of communism across most of the world, North Koreans saw their travel opportunities dwindle rather than grow.

Certainly, several events in 1989 came together to convince Kim that reform and opening up could only bring problems for his regime. In mid-April, students and workers started to gather in Tiananmen Square. Located in the center of Beijing, the square is one of the most recognizable landmarks in the Chinese capital. For weeks, up to 1 million Chinese demonstrators demanded political freedoms. In the end, the Chinese government put a violent end to the protest on June 4, killing hundreds if not thousands of people.[32] This was a first lesson for Pyongyang. Market-led reforms and economic freedoms could lead people to also demand political rights.

Meanwhile, Hungary opened the border with Austria in May. In this way, Central and Eastern Europeans could cross over to Western Europe. Among the hundreds of thousands of people making the trip were tens of thousands of Eastern Germans eager to move to Western Germany. Few Western Germans even thought of traveling in the opposite direction. The opening of the border between Hungary and Austria set in motion a chain of events culminating in the fall of the Berlin Wall separating the two Germanies on November 9. Tens of thousands of Eastern Germans waiting by the border made their way through to the Western part of Berlin as soldiers let them through. By midnight, there was a full-blown party in Berlin, with Germans separated since the division of their country in 1945 rejoicing together. This was a second lesson for Pyongyang. Given the chance, people living in the communist part of their separated country would not hesitate to cross to the other side.

On Christmas day, in the meantime, Romanians deposed and killed Nicolae Ceauşescu. The Romanian leader had ruled his country with an iron first since 1965. In fact, by the 1970s the Ceauşescu regime was considered to be the most repressive in the whole of

Central and Eastern Europe. As in North Korea, mass surveillance and imprisonment were commonplace in Romania. So was a cult of personality that could rival that of Kim Il-sung, including media articles, propaganda posters, statues, and grandiose buildings that the North Korean leader also cultivated.[33] Yet protests against Ceauşescu spread across Romania in December 1989. The president had to leave Budapest, but was arrested within days, subjected to a quick trial, and summarily executed. Within a few hours, footage and images of the trial and execution were being shown across the world's media. Unsurprisingly, Kim and Ceauşescu had been on good terms. This was a third lesson for Pyongyang. People who in theory adored you could very well be hiding their true feelings, and kill you without hesitation given the chance.

As a result of all these developments in North Korea, South Korea, and across the globe, by the late 1980s Pyongyang was more isolated and repressive than it had been for years if not decades. Seemingly, Kim Il-sung and his family had a single goal in mind: to retain power and ensure that they would not suffer the same fate as other communist regimes. In particular, the mere existence of South Korea was a threat that the North had to contend with as best as it could. This reality continues at the time of writing, and explains why Pyongyang is more constrained than Seoul in both its domestic and foreign policy.

5
DIVERGING PATHS
THE KOREAS FROM 1990 TO 2010

Lotte World Tower makes for a great day out. At 1,821 ft tall, it is the sixth-tallest building in the world as of 2023. It stands within walking distance of the Seoul Olympic Stadium, home to the 1988 Games. Not far away lies the famous Gangnam district that Psy brought to international fame. Once inside the tower, one can visit any fashion, luxury, and beauty shop imaginable. Ramon Pacheco Pardo and his family were there one afternoon in the summer of 2022, not to shop but to visit South Korea's biggest aquarium. After marveling at the hundreds of species, they went on to Asia's largest cinema, where the latest South Korean and Hollywood blockbusters were showing. They ended the day at a restaurant near the building, enjoying the lights of South Korea's capital at night while eating Korean fusion food. Certainly, not everyone would relish this as their ideal day out. But the point is that South Koreans and foreigners who enjoy this type of experience only need to go south of the Han River to experience it.

The pyramidal Ryugyong Hotel, in contrast, sits unfinished close to the Pothong and Taedong rivers. Questions about when it will open are met with polite smiles and a change of subject by one government-appointed minder. Those allowed inside during the years before the Covid-19 pandemic reported that the building remains unused and unfinished, a mostly empty structure covered by glass to make it look better from the outside.[1] In the mid-2010s lighting was added, and it seems that the state of the building's interior has been improved. Light shows take place on special occasions, helping illuminate a city where many corners remain dark at night. For years the North Korean regime actually airbrushed the hotel out of official Pyongyang pictures. Had Kim Il-sung had his way in the late 1980s, the Ryugyong Hotel would have been Pyongyang's early competitor to Seoul's later Lotte World Tower. Now, the state of the two buildings only serves to underscore the contrast between the two Koreas.

* * *

The Koreas and the End of the Cold War

The case of the two tallest buildings in North and South Korea, respectively, indeed serves to illustrate the difference between the two Koreas as of 2023. To understand these differences, one needs to travel back to the early 1990s. Until then, the economic, political, and socio-cultural dynamics of the two Koreas were certainly diverging. But since that time the combination of a starkly different series of decisions by policymakers and rapidly changing geopolitical conditions has created a gulf between the domestic conditions and external position of the two countries. By the mid-1990s, South Korea was on course to join the rich world's club while experts and politicians alike were betting on a North Korean collapse. Arguably, South Korea represented the Korean—and the Koreas'—dream of having a seat at the world's table. North Korea represented the Korean nightmare of being dependent on outside forces.

Seemingly, the early 1990s were a period in which reconciliation between the two Koreas was at hand. Roh Tae-woo doubled down on his *Nordpolitik*, and the policy was working in the aftermath of Seoul 1988. Most amazingly, Roh and Mikhail Gorbachev held a summit in June 1990. By September, South Korea and the Soviet Union had established diplomatic relations. It should be remembered that the authoritarian governments that had ruled South Korea almost since it had been established as an independent country had put anti-communism at the center of their domestic and foreign policy. Certainly, South Korea had kick-started trade and investment with some communist countries during the 1980s. Seoul had also established diplomatic relations with a handful of communist countries in Central and Eastern Europe. And the Roh government had pledged to make South Korean textbooks free of the anti-communist rhetoric of decades past. But the summit between the leaders of South Korea and the Soviet Union, and the rapid normalization of relations between them, was a different story altogether. It symbolized Seoul's rapidly evolving diplomatic clout, as well as the strength of its firms that even Moscow was interested in courting.

By contrast, North Korea did not make any headway in its relationship with the US or Japan. US presidents Ronald Reagan and George Bush had allowed low-level US–North Korea diplomatic exchanges to take place, in the context of improving US–Soviet Union relations and also in support of *Nordpolitik*. But Washington and Pyongyang were nowhere near normalizing relations. Japan, meanwhile, had re-started diplomatic contacts with North Korea in the late 1980s, and indicated its willingness to rekindle bilateral trade and investment links as well. But progress was slow and, in any case, the prospects of full normalization between Tokyo and Pyongyang were distant at best. And, above all, the Soviet Union essentially abandoned North Korea—as Russia did following the dissolution of the Soviet Union in the early 1990s. Moscow dramatically reduced its oil and food shipments to North Korea and demanded to be paid market prices for the remaining exports. Pyongyang was unable to meet these conditions. Trade between the two countries collapsed subsequently, with imports by North Korea standing at 10 percent of their 1987–90 average in 1993.[2]

In the context of the end of communism across much of the world, the expectation was that the Kim regime would simply collapse. The thinking was that South Korea would have to pick up the pieces and rebuild the North, in much the same way that West Germany was doing with East Germany. Therefore, there was no political incentive for the US, Japan, or any other Western countries to invest political capital in improving relations with the Kim regime. Similarly, the Soviet Union was in the process of discussing and agreeing to several deals with South Korea, including military technology transfers and arms sales.[3] China, meanwhile, was still recovering from the events in Tiananmen and had no incentive to step in and fill the void left by the USSR in North Korea in its entirety. All the more so since Seoul and Beijing were discussing normalization of bilateral relations, which they finally agreed on in August 1992. Kim Il-sung traveled to China in October 1991 to obtain Beijing's support, and Deng Xiaoping permitted an increase in the transfers of fuel and food to North Korea, but this was insufficient to prevent the economic crisis that the North would suffer in the mid-1990s. In fact, of the two Koreas, South Korea quickly became China's top economic partner following their diplomatic normalization.

The Kim regime certainly did not resign itself to its seemingly preordained fate. In September 1991, the two Koreas joined the UN at the same time. Seoul had long sought to join the institution. Pyongyang, in contrast, had been reluctant, for fear that this would facilitate recognition of South Korea as an important international actor without a similar benefit to the North. (As it turned out, North Korea was right about this.) Joint UN membership opened the possibility that tensions between the two Koreas would subside, particularly since Roh was still pursuing his *Nordpolitik* policy.

The two Koreas thus embarked on a diplomatic process to improve bilateral relations hitherto only rivalled by the 1972 effort. In December 1991, South Korean Prime Minister Chung Won-shik and North Korean Premier Yon Hyong-muk signed the Agreement on Reconciliation, Non-aggression and Exchanges and Cooperation between the South and the North. Known as the inter-Korean Basic Agreement, the text reaffirmed the commitment of the two Koreas to achieve "peaceful unification." At the same time, the agreement stated that "the South and the North shall recognize and respect each other's systems."[4] This was a lifeline for Kim Il-sung, since it had become obvious that any unification process would be on Seoul's terms. For the Roh government, the agreement served to reduce tensions in the Korean Peninsula, and to placate South Koreans wary of the potential costs of what would essentially have been the absorption of the North by the South. To reaffirm this commitment, in 1992 Pyongyang introduced an amendment to the 1972 constitution pledging "peaceful"—rather than "revolutionary"—reunification.[5]

Not only were relations between the two Koreas moving in the right direction, but improving relations was having positive, practical effects on the Korean Peninsula. In January 1992, the South and the North signed the Joint Declaration on the Denuclearization of the

Korean Peninsula. A few days later, North Korea finally signed a safeguards agreement with the International Atomic Energy Agency (IAEA), on which it had been dragging its feet for years. The agreement allowed IAEA inspectors to access North Korea's nuclear facilities. As for the South, Bush had announced that he would be withdrawing US nuclear weapons placed in different countries across the world. By December 1991, the last American nuclear weapons had been removed from the South.[6] A nuclear-free Korean Peninsula was within reach.

In this context, South Korea was also undergoing significant domestic changes. In the area of politics, Kim Young-sam was elected as the new South Korean president in December 1992. Two months later, he was inaugurated as the first civilian president since the early 1960s, and the first from the "Three Kims" who had opposed the Park Chung-hee dictatorship. No one could accuse Kim of being the leader of a "Five-Point-Five" Republic. For many South Koreans, his peaceful election and inauguration was the true moment when the country became a democracy.

In the area of economics, Samsung Chairman Lee Kun-hee launched the New Management Initiative in June 1993. Exhorting the firm's management and employees to "change everything, except your wife and children," Lee kick-started the revolution that would one day make Samsung one of the most innovative tech firms in the world.[7] From then on, Samsung's strict hierarchies were gradually loosened up and, more importantly for the world economy, the South Korean firm would start to focus on innovation as the driver of its growth. Other South Korean firms would follow suit, with the 1990s marking the start of the transition of the South Korean economy into a powerhouse, competing on the tech frontier stage.

In the area of culture, March 1992 saw the release of "Nan Arayo" ("I Know") by Seo Taiji and Boys. This was a new type of song, mixing the traditional South Korean ballad that still dominated the country's charts with new sounds and beats from the US such as hip hop and R&B. The music video was similarly innovative, with breathtaking dance moves and impossible camera angles. The song was a hit with younger South Koreans first, and eventually with South Koreans of different generations as it spent a record seventeen consecutive weeks at number one in the country's music charts.[8] Arguably not even Seo Taiji knew it back then, but "Nan Arayo" would eventually be considered the song that inaugurated K-pop.

Contrast this with the situation in North Korea. The *Washington Times* published an interview with Kim Il-sung in June 1992 in which the North Korean leader expressed his hope that Pyongyang and Washington would normalize diplomatic relations.[9] Only two months later, however, the IAEA reported discrepancies in the initial report that North Korea provided to the agency.[10] Tensions between the North Korean government and the agency escalated in the following months, until the former came up with a bombshell in February: Pyongyang would withdraw from the NPT in three months, as per the treaty's provisions.[11]

North Korea's announcement that it would withdraw from the NPT precipitated the first North Korean nuclear crisis. In June 1993, the newly elected Bill Clinton government and Kim's delegation met in New York. North Korea announced that it would not withdraw from the NPT after all. Months of negotiations would ensue, with Pyongyang seemingly willing to mend relations with the IAEA and terminate its nuclear activities in exchange for diplomatic and economic relations with the US, as well as heavy fuel oil transfers. The US, meanwhile, negotiated with North Korea while also considering a possible strike on its Yongbyon nuclear facility. South Korea, for its part, felt excluded from the process, and was especially alarmed at Washington's apparent willingness to strike North Korea.[12] Kim

Young-sam also expressed his willingness to meet with Kim Il-sung, to no avail. The IAEA, for its part, regularly made the case that Pyongyang was being uncooperative. For a while, negotiations looked like they were going nowhere.

In July 1994, Kim Il-sung passed away. This was a shock to North Koreans. News programs across the world carried footage of distressed North Koreans crying, wailing, screaming, and mourning. In future years, North Korean defectors would report that their feelings for the late Kim were real, unlike the mourning for his son in 2011.[13] North Koreans had only known one leader throughout their lives. They were not aware that living conditions in South Korea and many other countries across the world were much better than their own. Therefore, they mourned for a leader who they thought had protected them from becoming poor and subservient to the US. In their minds, this was the fate that had befallen their "brothers and sisters" in the South.

Kim Jong-il took over from his father, as expected. And in October, his regime signed the Agreed Framework between the United States of America and the Democratic People's Republic of Korea in Geneva. The Agreed Framework committed North Korea to give up its nuclear program in exchange for diplomatic relations with the US, the building of two light-water reactors in the North, and energy transfers. Arguably, this was a coup for a country that many still thought would collapse any time and that had negotiated this deal with the only remaining global superpower following the collapse of the Soviet Union.

Unfortunately for North Korea, many in the US agreed. The Republican Party won the 1994 mid-term US Congress and Senate elections and blocked funding to implement the Agreed Framework due to suspicions that North Korea was in violation of its denuclearization commitments. The Clinton administration had other domestic and foreign policy priorities and was not willing to spend political capital on the implementation of the agreement.[14] Unknown to the outside world at the time, North Korea secretly continued the development of its nuclear program. And with Kim Il-sung having passed away and Kim Jong-il still finding his feet as North Korean leader, there was no hope of a summit with Kim Young-sam. In short, implementation of the Agreed Framework stalled. Pyongyang, in any case, would soon be preoccupied with surviving the worst famine the country had ever seen (see below).

In the South, in the meantime, the Kim Young-sam government had other issues to focus on. To begin with, Chun Doo-hwan and Roh Tae-woo were on trial for their role in the 1979 military coup. Eventually, both would be convicted in August 1996.[15] They would be released not long after starting their prison terms. However, their conviction created a debate within society. On the one hand, critics argued that their trial, and eventual sentencing, was the by-product of an immature democracy with a "winner-takes-all" mentality, unable to solve disputes via negotiations and dialogue. On the other hand, many South Koreans argued that it was refreshing to see the powerful being held accountable for their past crimes, something that not even decades-old democracies were capable of doing. This debate would continue in decades to come, as other South Korean presidents would also go on trial.

Something that South Koreans of all stripes could agree on, however, was that they wanted their country to be recognized as developed and modern. The Kim government, therefore, embarked on an economic reform process along Washington Consensus lines with a single goal in mind: membership of the Organisation for Economic Co-operation and Development (OECD).[16] This rich-country club had only one other Asian member: Japan. Could South Korea become an equal to its former colonial master? The answer was yes. In December 1996, South Korea's ambassador to Paris deposited the necessary instruments for his country to join the OECD.[17] South Korean TV channels, newspapers, and radio stations opened the news with this story. Seoul had arrived in the world's elite economic league.

Famine in North Korea, Crisis in South Korea

The mid- to late 1990s were not the best of times for the Koreas. North Korean escapees who lived through those times vividly recalled, when the authors met with them, the "Arduous March" that they endured between 1995 and 1998, the physical effects still visible on their bodies. And any South Korean who had been through it would talk, when pressed, about the pains of the "IMF [International Monetary Fund] Crisis"; this was the name adopted by the country for the Asian financial crisis of 1997–8. These experiences and their effects continue to shape the politics, society, and economics of the two Koreas a quarter of a century later.

The "Arduous March" was the euphemism that the Kim Jong-il government and North Korea's propaganda machine adopted to hide one of the biggest policy failures in recent memory, anywhere in the world. Starting from 1992, serious cracks had started to show in the central government's public distribution system. The government had launched the "Let's Eat Two Meals per Day" campaign, since it had become unable to provide food to its own population for more than that.[18] Over the next two years, food and oil transfers from Russia almost ground to a halt, shipments from China were nowhere close to replacing Russia's, and North Korea's much-touted self-reliance was proving to be a mirage.

The killer hit to the government's ability to feed its own population came in the summer of 1995. Over the previous months, North Koreans had taken to the forests across the country to gather firewood. Winters in the Korean Peninsula can be very cold, and this was the only way that many North Koreans could survive the winter of 1994–95, as fuel shortages hit their country. The problem was that this made the country unable to cope with floods. And in August 1995, torrential rains led to massive floods across North Korea. It is estimated that up to 70 percent of the annual rice harvest and 50 percent of the maize harvest were lost. The country's outdated infrastructure crumbled, from roads and railroads to schools and hospitals. What followed was the "Arduous March," a term first coined by the authorities in 1993, but which became widely used only from 1995 as a euphemism to refer to the famine that North Koreans were enduring—and that the authorities could do nothing to stop.

In the period between 1995 and 1998, anywhere between half a million and 2 million North Koreans died of hunger or hunger-related diseases (out of a population estimated to be around 20 million).[19] Tens of thousands of North Koreans crossed the border with China in a desperate attempt to feed themselves and their families.[20] Everyone went hungry. City dwellers arguably suffered more, for they did not have access to the roots, grass, beans, and other natural "supplements" available in the countryside.[21] More floods, droughts, and even a typhoon further exacerbated the famine, to the extent that by 1998 there was no public distribution system to speak of. The Kim regime's system of repression continued to function though, with the number of public executions increasing from 1996 onwards as a way to continue to exercise control over a society that was falling apart before everyone's eyes.[22] On top of those opposed to the dictatorial North Korean regime per se, "ideological" enemies of the Kim family now included some of those caught stealing to feed themselves or their families, as well as those protesting against the economic conditions they had to endure. In this respect, Kim Jong-il proved to be no different from his father.

The situation was so grave that North Korea had no option but to ask for international help. Starting from September 1995, Pyongyang made repeated pleas to the international community for humanitarian aid. Led by the World Food Programme, the UN put together a coalition of donors providing millions of tons in food aid to the country in the coming years. Japan, the US, and many other countries offered food and other aid, in the case of South Korea and China bilaterally rather than through the World Food Programme.[23] Foreign food, medical and other support became a permanent feature of the North Korean economy, underscoring North Korea's position as a poor country in one of the richest regions in the world.

Considering the above, the Asian financial crisis that hit South Korea in late 1997 was certainly not so dramatic. But it was undoubtedly a shock to the country, threatening to tear apart the foundations of the economic model and social contract that had underpinned South Korea's growth for decades. The first signs of trouble came in January, when the *chaebol* Hanbo filed for bankruptcy once it realized that it would not be able to service its debt. Over the following months, more *chaebol* either filed for bankruptcy or had to ask for a government bailout. The situation escalated dramatically in July, when the Thai government realized that it could not defend the baht against speculative attacks and allowed the country's currency to float freely. In common with most other East Asian countries, Thailand had pegged the value of its currency to the US dollar for years, with the government and firms issuing debt in the American currency. Once the baht became a free-floating currency, its value against the US dollar decreased precipitously. Investors began to doubt the ability of the Thai government and the country's firms to service their debt, and capital flight ensued. The question now was whether there would be contagion affecting other East Asian economies—including South Korea.

The answer was yes. In common with other countries in the region, strong links between the government and the private sector were a feature of the South Korean economy. This had created a problem with corruption. As a case in point, Kim Young-sam's son had been arrested on corruption charges in May 1997.[24] The links between the government and private firms had allowed credit to flow almost unconditionally from banks to selected *chaebol*. This had allowed *chaebol*, among others, to issue debt denominated in US dollars throughout the 1990s. With foreign investment pouring into South Korea as successive governments liberalized the financial sector, in preparation for OECD membership as much as to attract new sources of financing, this had not been a major issue. But then corruption meant that credit had gone to *chaebol* units without sound business plans. And issuing debt in US dollars was fine as long as the Bank of Korea could maintain the peg of the won to the greenback. The whole system crumbled in fall 1997, as the capital flight that had extended to Indonesia and Malaysia reached South Korea too. The value of the won against the US dollar plunged.[25] South Korea had become another Thailand.

In December 1997, the Kim government had no option but to sign a US $57 billion bailout package with the IMF. This was the largest such package in the organization's history until then. Much like North Korea, South Korea's fate now seemed to be in foreign hands. In fact, the bailout package agreement had been signed only a few days before the upcoming presidential election. All candidates running for the presidency had had to agree to respect the terms of the agreement, including signing up to the well-known recipe of the Washington Consensus: privatization, deregulation, and liberalization. Yet this also meant that, from the perspective of South Koreans, the IMF would "own" the crisis from then on.

The year 1998 was the worst in the history of the South Korean economy since the Korean War era. The country's GDP shrank by

5.1 percent. The unemployment rate peaked at 8.6 percent. This was a drama in a country with no unemployment insurance system. Insolvent *chaebol* continued to crumble. Scores of family firms and shops had to shut their doors. Foreign banks and firms had their pick of undervalued South Korean counterparts to buy, made even cheaper as the value of the won nosedived. South Korea would recover from the crisis relatively quickly, with growth bouncing back by 11.5 percent in 1999 and unemployment falling below 4 percent of the working-age population by 2001. But the psychological scars lasted for decades to come, creating a collective trauma. Features such as the growth in temporary contracts and a relatively high youth unemployment rate—by South Korean standards—became entrenched.

Neither North Koreans nor South Koreans simply sat down and waited for their respective crises to go away. North Korea, in particular, underwent a dramatic change as a result of the famine that hit the country. In December 2017, the documentary *The Jangmadang Generation* made the news worldwide. Running at a little over 50 minutes, it showed the lives of young North Koreans, most of them in their 20s, who had made their way to South Korea and successfully adapted to life in their capitalist neighbor.[26] How could North Koreans who had supposedly grown up in a communist country with a command-and-control economy find success in a system that was the antithesis of that they had grown up in?

The answer lay in the *jangmadang*, the local markets that popped up in North Korea in response to the famine of the 1990s. With the public distribution system all but gone, no incentives to go on with government-assigned jobs—for which there was no pay or even work—and desperate to avoid starving to death, human ingenuity took hold. North Koreans started to launch their own markets to buy and sell food, handcrafts, home utensils and appliances, services such as hairdressing, and anything else that could be bought or sold. The state proved unable to put a stop to this clear threat to its authority. In fact, soldiers, government officials, and those with government jobs—in theory, all North Korean men of working age—started to work in markets as well, or to accept bribes to allow them to operate.[27]

But it was women who became the main traders in these markets. Often "free" from having to hold a government job, and with patriarchal family structures crumbling as the state and—as a result—men became unable to feed their families, women became central to the operation of the country's markets. As North Korean escapees to whom the authors have spoken over the years attest, this was the first time in North Korean history that many women became the main breadwinners. Most men were forced to continue to go to factories or government jobs, even if they were paid a pittance at best, and also had to do years of military service. Women, on the other hand, could go to markets to buy and sell food, clothes, and other items. They could also move more or less freely across the country, which men—having to attend to their daily jobs—could not. Thus, in many families women were the ones putting food on the table. In this context, many became more willing to challenge the "traditional" view that a man's place was at work and woman's place was at home: a seismic change for North Koreans.

Certainly, it is difficult to exaggerate the importance of these markets in changing the social fabric of North Korea. From the late 1990s onwards, North Koreans would go on to grow up and live in a market economy, the state lost its hold over society other than through repression, private cross-border trade with China began in earnest, and foreign goods not sanctioned by the state started to flow into the country. Ultimately, the supposed infallibility of the Kim family came into question. Neither Kim Jong-il nor his son Kim Jong-un would ever command anywhere close to the level of support that Kim Il-sung had in the past.

Below the 38th parallel, the South Korean people leaned in to help each other as well as the country as a whole. KBS, South Korea's state broadcasting company, launched a gold collection campaign to repay the country's debt to the IMF. Over 3.5 million people donated around 226 tons of gold, valued at US $2.2 billion.[28] Insufficient to pay off South Korea's debt, for sure, but a rallying cry that helped create the conditions for South Korea to repay its debt to the IMF in full by August 2001, three years ahead of schedule. Furthermore, the Kim Dae-jung government started to develop a more comprehensive welfare state, with stronger and more widespread unemployment insurance, public pensions, health insurance, sick leave pay, and other features similar to Europe's at that time. Future presidents would follow the same path, both liberal and conservatives.[29] Kim did not invent the South Korean welfare state, but was able to push through reforms that his predecessors had not been able to following the Asian financial crisis.

At the same time, the Kim government also introduced reforms more to the liking of the IMF. In particular, it became easier to hire and fire workers, and to employ them on temporary contracts. Facing a job market in which the *chaebol* offered fewer jobs and many firms were starting to make use of less secure contracts, a growing number of South Koreans decided to launch their own firms. Entrepreneurship certainly was not new to the country. But from the Asian financial crisis onwards, the government started to actively promote the creation of start-ups as a way both to drive innovation and create jobs.[30] And many young and not-so-young South Koreans decided to take advantage of this support. It was the time of the dotcom bubble, and, before the bubble burst—and even after—many South Koreans were inspired by the possibility of launching the next firm to hit it big. This feature of the South Korean economy continues as of 2023.

But the Kim government was also aware that South Korea needed to find as many growth engines as possible. Not only was it in the process of recovering from the biggest economic crisis in decades, but the threat of China joining the World Trade Organization loomed. South Korea's neighbor had the cheap labor and big market necessary to decimate its economy. Innovation could help South Korean firms stay at least one step ahead of their Chinese rivals. Thus, the South Korean government and firms, both big and small, started to substantially increase R&D spending as soon as their finances improved. South Korea went from spending an average amount in R&D as a percentage of GDP by OECD standards in the 1990s, to become one of the top two largest spenders by the 2010s.

However, the country also had to move away from its over-reliance on manufacturing. It needed to create a brand for itself that would allow it to sell other types of goods and services. This came from South Korean creatives. Where Seo Taiji led, many other followed. Savvy South Korean producers and businesspeople launched JYP, SM, and YG in the mid-1990s—three entertainment firms that would go on to dominate the market for K-pop soloists and, especially, bands. In the meantime, the South Korean film industry underwent a revival in the late 1990s, with blockbusters such as the action movie *Shiri* drawing millions of viewers to cinema screens. If *Jurassic Park* had made more money in 1993 than Hyundai with all its car sales that same year, could not the South Korean entertainment industry be that extra growth engine refueling the country's economy?

The Kim government thus launched a full-on campaign to support the entertainment industry via direct financing, tax credits, support for exports, deals with foreign TV networks, university courses, and, more generally, the necessary support to ensure that South Korean artists could thrive beyond the borders of their country. China, Japan, Taiwan, and Southeast Asia became the first countries and regions in which *Hallyu* became big. (In fact, the term *Hallyu* or "Korean Wave" was first coined by Chinese journalists.) Movies like

My Sassy Girl, dramas, including *Winter Sonata*, pop sensations such as the singer BoA, and bands, including H.O.T., were part of the first generation of *Hallyu* hits and stars that took East Asia by storm in the late 1990s and early 2000s. Younger South Koreans had new idols to look up to and new career options to pursue. The South Korean government had found a new sector to nurture in order to drive the country's economy.

In North Korea, Kim Jong-il took a very different lesson from the crisis of the mid-1990s. In 1995, Kim put the concept of *Seongun* or "military first" at the center of politics, economics, and society. Along with *Juche*, *Seongun* became the organizing principle of life in North Korea. It became the mechanism to pursue the dream of self-reliance. The armed forces would be central to running factories, plowing fields, repressing the North Korean population, and anything else that the state needed. And they would serve not only Kim Jong-il, but also, technically, his father Kim Il-sung, who was named "Eternal President" in an amendment to the constitution in 1998.[31]

At the same time, North Korea set the tone for its relations with the outside world in the late 1990s. On the one hand, the Kim regime tested a missile that flew over Japan in August 1998. North Korea was developing nuclear and missile programs in parallel, in a bid to not only boost its deterrence capabilities but also attract the attention of the outside world. This was *Seongun* applied to foreign policy, so to speak. In future decades, this became a feature of North Korean foreign policy.

On the other hand, the Kim regime would present a friendly face and show a readiness to negotiate. Most notably, US Secretary of State Madeleine Albright visited Pyongyang, and met and toasted with Kim in October 2000. She was the most senior American official to ever meet a North Korean leader. This was a return visit after First Vice Chairman of the National Defense Commission Jo Myong-rok had met with Clinton in the White House and delivered a letter from Kim asking for better North Korea–US relations. The North Korean leadership wanted to show that it could be reasonable and engage in diplomacy with the world's superpower. And in fact, Clinton entertained the idea of meeting with Kim during the last months of his presidency.[32]

Pyongyang seemed torn between military power and isolation on the one hand and diplomacy and becoming a normal member of international society on the other. Arguably, the Kim family has yet to take a final decision on this as of 2023. At the time of writing, we would argue that the former is the direction of travel, as the Kim regime seeks to retain power through oppression rather than by attraction. Probably the thinking is that this is the sole requirement for their country to remain independent de jure. But such is the secrecy around North Korea that it is possible that those holding the keys to its policy may be waiting for the right time to turn to the latter. After all, this is what has allowed the South more freedom to take its own decisions than the North.

Kim Dae-jung, Kim Jong-il, and Two Separate Koreas

The early 2000s was a time of hope for many in the Korean Peninsula. The worst of the Arduous March and the Asian financial crisis were over. But the biggest hope was for the future of the two Koreas. Events focused on inter-Korean reconciliation, and even unification abounded. So did signs that the two Koreans were getting closer to each other. At an event organized by his university, Hankuk University of Foreign Studies, Ramon saw passionate students debating the benefits of Korean unification. There would be costs, yes, particularly for the South, which after all would be the one paying to essentially absorb North Korea. But there would also be advantages that were not to be scoffed at. Some students talked about the possibility that eliminating tensions from the Korean Peninsula would reduce military spending and free money to increase welfare spending. Others simply wanted to roam freely around the North, including visiting Baekdu Mountain—the birthplace, according to Korean mythology, of Dangun, the founder of Gojoseon and therefore Korea. Another student pointedly argued that a unified Korea would be bigger, more populous, and therefore a force to be reckoned with in East Asia and beyond. A (male) student bluntly indicated that he hoped unification would result in the end of military conscription, which is compulsory for almost all able-bodied South Korean men. These dreams would not materialize, but were very much alive in the early 2000s if one took the time to listen to South Koreans.

Where did this hope come from? To put it in simple terms, Kim Dae-jung and his Sunshine Policy.[33] The Sunshine Policy built on the legacy of *Nordpolitik* and even earlier efforts to improve relations between the two Koreas. The policy put engagement between the two Koreas and inter-Korean reconciliation at the center of relations between South and North, with the former providing economic and diplomatic support to the latter to develop its economy and escape its international isolation. But Kim came to office at the right time and put his policy at the heart of his government. By the late 1990s, Kim Jong-il had consolidated his power, North Korea was in need of outside help, and South Koreans were very well reassured that any reconciliation would be on their terms. Plus, the Clinton administration had conducted a review of its North Korea policy. The Perry Process, led by North Korea Policy Coordinator William Perry, had concluded that it was beneficial for the US to support the Sunshine Policy, let Kim Dae-jung lead the engagement process with North

Korea, and find ways for Washington and Pyongyang to improve relations.[34]

The signs that relations between the two Koreas were getting better were everywhere. In 1998, South Korea agreed to provide aid to the North and Pyongyang allowed tourists from the South to cross the border and visit Mount Geumgang, considered to be one of the most beautiful mountains in the whole of the Korean Peninsula.[35] The opening of Mount Geumgang to South Korean tourism was particularly significant. For the first time since the Korean War, South Koreans were free to hop on a cruise ship or a coach and visit a tourist resort where they would be served by North Koreans. Hundreds of thousands of South Koreans took the opportunity to do so.

The defining moment of the Sunshine Policy was yet to arrive though. For the authors, watching this on TV overseas, it was the most moving of times. Imagine how it felt for the tens of millions of Koreans living in what many felt remained a split country. On July 13, 2000, Kim Dae-jung exited the Blue House and took a car to the airport, with his wife Lee Hee-ho sitting by his side. Thousands of South Koreans lined the streets of Seoul, all the way to Gimpo Airport. At the airport, Kim gave a speech, and took a plane together with his aides. Within an hour, the plane touched down in Pyongyang International Airport. Waiting on the tarmac was none other than Kim Jong-il. Kim Dae-jung exited the plane, walked down the steps, and went straight to the North Korean leader. The leaders of the two Koreas held hands and looked at each other.[36] Fifty-two years had passed since Korea had been divided into two. This was the first time that the leaders of the two countries had ever met.

The two Koreas had already announced the previous April that this moment would come. But that did not make the moment any less special. Kim Dae-jung and Kim Jong-il spent three days together, issuing the June 15 North–South Declaration, whereby they agreed to pursue reunification via a confederation of the two Koreas. In more material terms, the summit produced immediate results. In August, the two Koreans held the first of nineteen family reunions that were to take place between then and 2007.[37] The armed forces, different ministries, and cultural, student, and other organizations held multiple meetings in the coming months and years. In September, the two Koreas marched together during the opening ceremony of the Sydney Olympic Games. Tourism to Mount Geumgang increased. And in 2004, the two Koreas opened the Kaesong Industrial Complex, bringing together South Korean money and know-how with North Korean workers.[38] Kim Dae-jung was awarded the Nobel Peace Prize in 2000, mainly in recognition for his efforts in promoting inter-Korean reconciliation.

North Korea, indeed, seemed ready to open up to the outside world. Throughout the late 1990s and early 2000s, Pyongyang established diplomatic relations with the European Union (EU), most Western European countries, and other Western countries such as Australia. Some, like Germany or the UK, opened embassies in the North Korean capital, with North Korea also opening embassies across Western Europe. Even more significantly, Kim Jong-il received a visit from Japanese Prime Minister Koizumi Junichiro in September 2002. The two leaders issued the Pyongyang Declaration, bringing the promise of diplomatic normalization and economic assistance from Japan in exchange for a satisfactory resolution to the case of Japanese citizens abducted by North Korea over the decades.[39]

Yet this turned out to be an illusion. In 2003, the news came out that Hyundai had forked out the equivalent of US $0.5 billion in advance of the inter-Korean summit, money that had found its way into North Korean government coffers.[40] To many South Koreans, it looked as if Kim Dae-jung had essentially bribed Kim Jong-il to hold the summit. Whether this was true or not, the bribery scandal tarnished the reputation of the Sunshine Policy. And in any case, there had already been signs that North Korea was not exactly enthusiastic about any inter-Korean exchange that did not involve a payment from the South to the North. Family exchanges were few and far between compared to what South Koreans had expected. Plus, it seemed that Seoul had to constantly beg Pyongyang to allow the reunions to take place. Also, military talks, as well as talks to open other parts of North Korea to South Korean investment or tourism, were moving ahead painfully slowly from Seoul's perspective. Even the opening of the Kaesong Industrial Complex had to be delayed due to North Korean demands for more control over its business operations.[41]

More devastating for proponents of inter-Korean engagement was the realization that North Korea had cheated on its nuclear commitments. George W. Bush came to office in January 2001. His administration immediately announced that it would revise Clinton's approach toward North Korea. Kim Dae-jung could witness the change first-hand. When visiting Bush only two months after his inauguration, he realized that there would be no more support for this Sunshine Policy from the US.[42] By the time the review was finalized in the spring of 2002, it was clear that things had changed. Following the 9/11 terrorist attacks in New York and Washington, DC, the Bush administration focused its foreign policy on fighting terrorism. In January 2002, Bush delivered his first State of the Union address. The US president name-checked North Korea. Bush labelled the country "a regime arming with missiles and weapons of mass destruction, while starving its citizens." Bush placed North Korea in an "axis of evil," along with Iran and Iraq: working together with terrorists they were arming to "threaten the peace of the world."[43] Bush's message to Kim Jong-il could hardly be clearer.

Still, perhaps Washington and Pyongyang could rekindle the dialogue initiated toward the end of the Clinton administration.

In October 2002, US Assistant Secretary of State Jim Kelly led a delegation to Pyongyang. The delegation messaged a willingness to continue diplomacy but also accused North Korea of developing and running a highly enriched uranium program that could be used to develop nuclear weapons, in contravention of the Agreed Framework and the inter-Korean Basic Agreement to keep the Korean Peninsula nuclear-free. One day later, First Deputy Foreign Minister Kang Sok-ju admitted the existence of the program and argued that North Korea was entitled to protect itself.[44] Within two months, the Bush administration had effectively terminated the Agreed Framework by halting oil shipments to North Korea.[45] In January 2003, Pyongyang announced that it was withdrawing from the NPT. Unlike in 1993, when it had made the same announcement, this time North Korea carried out its threat. By April 2003, North Korea had admitted running a nuclear program and abandoned the NPT. The Kim regime was free to develop its nuclear capabilities—yet another blow to the Sunshine Policy, which had not served to prevent the worst excesses of North Korea's foreign policy.

South Korea, in any case, had reasons of its own to celebrate irrespective of relations with North Korea. In September 2000, Seoul hosted its first-ever Queer Culture Festival. Many older South Koreans still rejected homosexuality. But a growing number of younger South Koreans had more in common with the peers in other parts of the world who saw homosexuality as natural. In fact, university students had been behind the launch of gay and lesbian societies promoting the rights of these groups.[46] These societies promoted the rights of people whose sexual orientation had hitherto led to marginalization, normalizing diversity, demanding legal recognition of these rights, and organizing events to promote visibility. As the years went by, a growing number of South Koreans came to accept homosexuality as younger generations became more open-minded.

In November 2001, meanwhile, the Kim Dae-jung government launched the National Human Rights Commission of Korea. The organization lacked legal powers, but it became an opinion leader and led the way in promoting respect for the human rights of marginalized groups.[47] Its education and awareness-raising campaigns helped to create a more open-minded society over the years, giving greater visibility to transgender people, disabled people, or migrants, among others. In a sense, the commission pressed ahead with ideas and plans that South Koreans were ready to accept—but that no one had dared to promote before.

Yet the celebration most associated with South Korea in the early 2000s is, undoubtedly, the country's second sports coming-of-age party. Visiting the Seoul World Cup Stadium in the northwestern part of the South Korean capital to see a match is a great experience. Tens of thousands of fans fill the stadium, most of them wearing red T-shirts to honor their national football team. There is singing, dancing, laughter, and, best of all, no insults hurled at the opposition: just good-spirited support for the "Reds," the nickname by which the team is known. In fact, it's possible Ramon may have one or more "Be the Reds" T-shirts, somewhere back home—"Be the Reds" being the slogan of the team's official supporters club.

The South Korean national football team and its supporters became well known in May–June 2002, when South Korea and its neighbor Japan hosted the 2002 FIFA World Cup. South Korea made it all the way to the semi-finals, becoming the first—and at the time of writing, only—Asian nation to reach this round and beating three European powerhouses in a row. But arguably what was most impressive was the way South Korean fans celebrated their team's success. The streets of the country were filled with a red wave, as millions of South Koreans took to the streets to watch the matches together with family, friends, neighbors, and total strangers. They were cheerful, simply happy to watch their team even when Germany knocked South Korea out of the World Cup at the semi-final stage. This was a display of patriotism and civic nationalism that many South Koreans rightly felt proud of.

Not that nationalism and patriotism always work for the good. The early 2000s were also a time of rising anti-Americanism in South Korea, a reminder that many South Koreans continued to believe that their country was too close to, or even too dependent on, its ally. In June 2002, two schoolgirls were tragically killed on a road near Yangju. The two girls were walking by the side of the road when a US Army armored vehicle struck and killed them.[48] Under the agreement governing the presence of American troops in South Korea, US Army troops fall under the jurisdiction of the US military when performing official duties. Given the gravity of the situation, however, the South Korean Ministry of Justice asked for the driver of the vehicle and its commander to be tried in the country's civilian courts. The US military refused, which led to protests by South Koreans opposed to the just-mentioned agreement. Furthermore, the two accused were acquitted by the US military authorities. This sparked bigger protests.[49] Many South Koreans felt that US troops could kill local people without facing any consequences.

The protests were certainly understandable. However, many South Koreans felt that the nationalistic fervor of the time led some of their compatriots to cross the line. The Yongsan Garrison in downtown Seoul, where most US troops were stationed at the time, suffered arson attacks. Some South Koreans attacked American soldiers off duty. Civilians who looked like US Army soldiers were insulted.[50] This continued well into 2003.

At least South Koreans could express themselves freely. North of the 38th parallel, the situation was very different. In July 2002, the Kim regime had implemented several market-oriented economic reforms. The rationing system was abolished and street markets were legalized; economic decision-making was decentralized and devolved to factories and farms; the value of the North Korean won went down, bringing it closer to its real value; and special economic zones were set up in Sinuiju—opposite Dandong at the Sino-North Korean border—Kaesong, and Mount Geumgang. These reforms were similar to those implemented by China and Vietnam at the start of their own opening-up processes. There was a crucial difference between North Korea and its two communist counterparts though. Beijing and Hanoi had implemented the reforms to launch an opening-up process. Pyongyang was reacting to facts on the ground.

And indeed, the Kim regime increased repression against its own population. A growing number of North Koreans started to be sent to prison for economic crimes,[51] rather than for political and ideological reasons, as had been the case historically. Yet economic crimes were deliberately left ambiguous. One person could be sent to prison for importing goods from China or exporting them, while another would not because they had bribed the right person, crossed the border in the right place, or simply because their family had no quarrel with the guard patrolling the border. Someone could be imprisoned for selling a particular product on a given day, which this same person could have sold almost openly the day before. As a case in point, *Hallyu* reached North Korea as smugglers brought DVDs with South Korean dramas and movies or the CDs of the latest South Korean K-pop band through the Sino-North Korean border.[52] Some days, guards and other regime acolytes would procure these for themselves. On other days, they would demand a bribe from their sellers. On yet others, they would arrest the smugglers of these precious goods. Such was the nature of the North Korean *jangmadang*.

South Korea Goes Modern

Living in South Korea in the 2000s provided a unique opportunity to witness the transformation of a country undergoing profound changes. With the worst of the Asian financial crisis definitely over, with entrepreneurship and innovation becoming central to the South Korean economy, with *Hallyu* in full swing across Southeast Asia, the Middle East, or Latin America, and with the 2002 World Cup having shown South Korea in all its glory, the country was changing in front of one's eyes. But the biggest changes were social and, more specifically, concerned the role of women in society.

Talking to, and especially listening to, female South Korean university students gave a glimpse of the type of changes that the country was about to witness. The idea that a woman had to give up her career the moment that she had a baby was definitely out. So was the perception that a woman could only be fulfilled if she got married. Many female South Korean students were clear: they themselves and their careers came first, a line of thinking that was becoming widespread across the whole of South Korean society. In a particularly interesting conversation that Ramon had with fellow classmates at a bar near our university, a female friend discussed how her grandmother had supported herself and raised her family all alone after her husband had been killed in the Korean War, and how her mother had had to give up a promising business career in the 1980s after becoming pregnant because that was what society expected back then. This friend went on to make it clear that she was not about to "betray" the sacrifices of her grandmother and mother by simply leaving her career if she got married or pregnant. From the nods of approval from everyone sitting around the table, both women and men, clearly this was a shared view.

Could this be dismissed as anecdotal evidence from "elite" university students who do not represent the whole population? Perhaps.

But in a country where over 60 percent of high school leavers attend university, the views of university students matter. And the data was unequivocal. In 1990, the average age at which women got married was 24.78 years old. By 2010, the average age had increased to 28.91—closer to the average age in other developed countries. Many South Korean women thought that marriage could be detrimental to their careers, since many employers were still pushing women to quit their jobs after marriage. Plus, many men still expected their wives to stay at home and take care of their children. Thus, many women wanted to make sure that if they married, their husband would be supportive of their career—and their employer would not start asking when would they leave the workplace. During the same time period, the fertility rate went down, from 1.57 children per woman to 1.23.[53] This was toward the lower end of the range among developed countries. In common with other OECD members, South Korea's fertility rate was firmly below the replacement rate. As mentioned, for many women, having children was a very consequential decision for their careers. Plus, women with children would often undertake the lion's share of household chores, including childcare. Many felt that having children essentially meant having two jobs. And raising children not only meant less time for oneself but also less disposable income, as most children attended one or more of the *hagwon* or private cramming schools that provide extra lessons on everything from English to math. Tellingly, however, by 2010 most women taking maternity leave went back to work after their time away to take care of their children.

Perhaps even more importantly for the future of the country, by 2007 the South Korea sex ratio at birth was the natural ratio for humans.[54] Up until the 1990s, the ratio had been skewed in favor of boys due to a preference for male descendants and the availability of abortion. But by the mid-2000s, polls showed that the preference for sons was no longer evident among younger South Koreans. In this sense, South Korea was similar to other developed countries, in which most parents did not particularly care about the gender of their children, and certainly did not abort a fetus simply because of the gender of the unborn child. In a sense, this reflected that parents were hopeful that their child would be judged based on their ability instead of their gender.

Also, in 2004 the number of female National Assembly members reached 10 percent.[55] Two years later, the number of female managers reached the same percentage.[56] Certainly, these last two figures were very low and very far away from the levels seen in other OECD countries. But they symbolized the beginning of a trend that other data also supported. This trend was the growing presence of women in positions of responsibility, of women in prominent roles that young girls could look up to, and of women who were clear that climbing the career ladder was central to their lives. The growing relevance and popularity of female K-pop idols, movie stars, or writers, as well as women in sports ranging from golf to volleyball to ice skating, reflected this change in the position of women in society.

Equally relevant, in 2008 the Constitutional Court declared the *hoju* system unconstitutional as it violated a 2005 revision of the Civil Code carried out by the National Assembly.[57] Formally introduced in South Korea in 1953 but in practice in operation in Korea for centuries, the *hoju* system was a family register that placed a man as the head of a family. Thus, when a husband died the eldest son became the head. And when a woman married, she was transferred from her father's register to her husband's. If a woman got divorced and retained custody of her children, the children remained in their father's register unless he gave them permission to move. In short, women were not treated as individuals but as part of a man-led family unit. Certainly, the abolition of *hoju* or women becoming freer to behave in the way they wanted, according to the data introduced above, did not put an end to social discrimination against women. Yet South Korean women certainly welcomed the changes that society was undergoing.

If there is one change, however, associated with South Korea in the 2000s, it is the *Hallyu* boom. Ramon had the chance to live with three students who had come to South Korea from Japan. One of them was a Zainichi, a Japanese of Korean origin. He wanted to perfect his knowledge of the language of his grandparents, who had moved to Japan during the years of Korea's colonization. Another was a Korean-language major who wanted to improve his language skills to work in an export-import firm, doing business between South Korea and Japan. The third had simply fallen in love with Lee Hyori, a South Korean singer who took the country by storm in 2003, and was behind the eponymous "Hyori Syndrome"—and whom many Japanese students had heard of. Here you had a Japanese student who wanted to learn the language of the neighboring country in order to understand the lyrics sung by his favorite singer. This was new for South Korea.

As it turned out, plenty of Japanese, Chinese, Thai, Malay, and other students and tourists making their way to South Korea were first attracted to the country thanks to *Hallyu*. Jun Ji-hyun, the star of *My Sassy Girl*, became a sensation across East Asia and helped to promote South Korean cinema as much as anyone. Bae Yong-joon, the star of *Winter Sonata*, arguably became the first South Korean male heartthrob across East Asia and was a key reason behind the success of the K-drama industry. 2NE1, BIGBANG, Girls' Generation, Super Junior, TVXQ, or Wonder Girls were among the leading boy and girl bands to smash records and become big names across different parts of the world. Eventually, some of them started to make it in the US, particularly the West and East coasts with their large population of Asian Americans, and, slowly, in Europe as well. Yet it is fair to say that some Westerners did not take to K-pop and *Hallyu* in general, with some media articles suggesting that the bands were inauthentic and even calling them "manufactured" and "weird."[58] It would take a new generation of South Korean artists for *Hallyu* to achieve mainstream success and acceptance in the West years later.

Yet South Korea was clearly becoming more international. In 2000, the migrant population stood at 491,234 people or barely 1 percent of the total population. The figure was up to 1,261,415 or 2.5 percent of the total population by 2010.[59] This was below the percentage of other big, developed economies such as Australia, Canada, or the US. But it was a seismic change for a country long associated with emigration, rather than immigration. Most migrants moving into South Korea came from elsewhere in Asia, with countries including China, the Philippines, Uzbekistan, Vietnam, and Thailand emerging as the biggest sources of migrants into South Korea—along with the US and Russia.

Most migrants coming from the rest of Asia were moving to South Korea for two reasons: jobs and marriage. In terms of employment, most migrants were taking on so-called "3D jobs": dirty, dangerous, and difficult. In other words, jobs that South Koreans themselves no longer wanted in construction, food processing, certain manufacturing firms, and agriculture.[60] The second most common reason for migration into South Korea was marriage between a woman, usually from Southeast Asia, and a local man in a smaller city or town in the countryside. New generations of South Koreans had been leaving the countryside in droves, especially women, as explained in earlier. This had created a big gender imbalance, now being filled by foreign women.

Interestingly, many of the migrants moving to South Korea were themselves ethnic Koreans. This was particularly common for migrants from countries such as China, Kazakhstan, Russia, and

Uzbekistan.[61] They were retracing the steps taken by their parents or grandparents, who had abandoned a poor Korea to move back to a prosperous South Korea. And indeed, as South Korea's fertility rate was below the replacement rate, last achieved in the 1980s, policy-makers saw in migration a way to mitigate impending population decline. If the migrants were of Korean origin, policies would make it easier for them to move to South Korea—especially for those coming from developed countries such as the US.[62] South Koreans preferred migrants from Korean origin as well.[63]

Migration also involved North Korean refugees, who of course were treated differently since most were eligible for South Korean citizenship if they made their way to the country. Following the famine of the 1990s and North Koreans' greater exposure to the outside world thanks to goods smuggled into the *jangmadang*, the number of North Koreans entering South Korea annually increased from 1,043 in 2001 to a peak of 2,904 in 2009.[64] Some South Koreans felt ambivalent about the growing number of North Koreans moving into the South, but in general there was support for accepting them and helping them resettle in the country.[65] Unsurprisingly, younger North Korean refugees found it easier to integrate than older North Koreans, who sometimes struggled to adapt to life in a capitalist society.[66]

One other crucial transformation in South Korea concerned its foreign policy. Arguably, the 2000s was the decade when the country started to match its economic credentials with the actions necessary to be recognized as a significant foreign policy actor. In 2002, South Korea sent troops to Afghanistan to support efforts to rebuild the country following the removal of the Taliban from power by a US-led coalition. Over 3,900 South Korean troops would go on to serve in the country until the final withdrawal of international forces in 2021. From 2004 to 2008, South Korea also contributed 3,600 troops to the Coalition of the Willing put together by the US to invade Iraq.

This amounted to the third-largest ground contingent in Iraq, fighting insurgents while also providing humanitarian support, training, and security for coalition forces. In this multi-nation setting, the reputation and capabilities of the South Korean military were on full display, garnering respect from the international community. In spite of opposition to the war by a majority of South Koreans—in common with citizens in most developed countries—and even though Roh Moo-hyun, in office since 2003, was portrayed as anti-American, South Korea became one of the few Asian countries to commit troops to the coalition. By this decade, South Korea had also become one of the largest contributors to UN peacekeeping operations among OECD members. In short, the ROK Armed Forces were becoming a large contributor to international military missions.

Regarding trade, South Korea decided to follow the US and the EU and pursue a policy of bilateral free trade agreements (FTAs) as a way to boost its economy by making it easier for its exporters to sell to another country. And Seoul achieved some early successes precisely with these two markets, at that time the biggest in the world. In June 2007 the Roh government and George W. Bush administration signed a trade agreement that would become known as KORUS. This was a new prototype of a high-standard trade agreement that focused not only on reducing tariff barriers but also on eliminating non-tariff barriers and aligning labor and environmental standards. Following some renegotiations, KORUS finally entered into force in March 2012, during the Lee Myung-bak government. In this way, the ROK–US alliance gained a significant economic pillar. By then, South Korea had already signed a similar prototype FTA with the EU in October 2010 that had entered into force in July 2011. This was the EU's first-ever new generation FTA going beyond a reduction in tariffs, as well as its first FTA with an Asian country. Both liberal and conservative governments agreed that this trade policy was good for the South Korean economy as well as its international standing.

However, it was in the area of diplomacy that South Korea really came out of its shell in the 2000s. Above all, Ban Ki-moon became the eighth Secretary-General of the UN in January 2007. He was only the second East Asian to be selected to this post. As secretary-general, Ban was serving the international community. But he was also the flag carrier for South Korean diplomats and South Korea as a country.

Likewise, Lee Myung-bak represented all South Koreans when he traveled to Washington, DC, in November 2008 to sit at the table with the leaders of the world's most important economies and discuss how to put an end to the global financial crisis that had started in Wall Street and then spread to the rest of the US economy, followed by Europe. The G20 Head of Government Summit had been launched and South Korea—as a developed economy, one of the biggest economies in the world, and a voice for countries seeking to transition from developing to developed—had a seat at the table. Two years later, the leaders gathered again for their fifth summit. Their host? South Korea, as Seoul's Coex Convention & Innovation Center welcomed them to the Gangnam district. (This, of course, would not be the last time that the world would hear of Gangnam.) It is fair to say that South Korea had never hosted such an important meeting in its entire history. As the 2000s were giving way to the 2010s, South Korea had never achieved such recognition on the global stage. Arguably, for the first time in decades (a) Korea was not a shrimp but one of the whales with a voice that mattered in international affairs.

North Korea Goes Nuclear

On October 9, 2006, North Korea changed its own history and the history of the Korean Peninsula forever. Midway through the morning, the country's scientists conducted North Korea's first-ever nuclear test at the Punggye-ri nuclear site, located toward the north-east. The yield was small, reportedly under 2 kilotons compared to the 50,000 kilotons of the biggest nuclear test in history. Yet with its nuclear test North Korea entered a selective club of only eight other members: a significant achievement, capping over forty years of the Kim family's quest for nuclear weapons. Pyongyang's Korean Central News Agency (KCNA) celebrated accordingly:

> The field of scientific research in the DPRK successfully conducted an underground nuclear test under secure conditions on October 9, Juche 95 (2006), at a stirring time when all the people of the country are making a great leap forward in the building of a great prosperous powerful socialist nation.[67]

The report by KCNA went on to describe how North Korea had conducted its nuclear test "with indigenous wisdom and technology 100 percent." This, of course, was not true. While the extent to which North Korea's nuclear program had received foreign support was shrouded in secrecy, it was widely known that Chinese and Russian/Soviet technology and expertise had been instrumental in the development of the North Korean nuclear program. Furthermore, North Korea had been one of the clients of the A.Q. Khan network in the 1990s—a clandestine smuggling and information network run by one of Pakistan's top nuclear scientists.[68] In other words, the Kim family had not hesitated to leave *Juche* aside to reach out to third parties as a way to accelerate its nuclear program.

Regardless of North Korea's misleading boasting, it was undeniable that substantial parts of its nuclear program were homegrown, and the 2006 nuclear test did change perceptions of North Korea. Sitting at the White House at the time, Victor Cha lived through the test and its aftermath. Six days before the test, North Korea made an announcement that the test was coming. Days of urgent negotiations, calls, and exchanges between the US, North Korea, China, and South Korea followed. On this, Washington, Beijing, and Seoul were united: all were opposed to a North Korean nuclear test, which could have unpredictable consequences and might prompt South Korea and Japan to go nuclear as well. Officials in the three allied capitals believed that the Hu Jintao government might be able to prevent North Korea from conducting the test. As it turned out, it was not the case. Kim Jong-il had no interest in listening even to his country's only ally.

After learning about the test, an emergency meeting was convened. It was followed by dozens of meetings, calls, and exchanges in the following days and weeks, including at the highest levels. The US sought to coordinate a UN Security Council resolution closely with South Korea and Japan, its two allies. But China and Russia were also involved in trying to work out a unified response to the test. Chinese officials, in particular, were aghast and, it has to be said, embarrassed. North Korea's nuclear test had shown that China's "little brother" was not interested in listening to them. The Chinese insisted that Kim was feeling remorseful for having conducted the test. But North Korea did not transmit this message directly to the US or South Korea, so it was difficult to know the truth. In the end, Beijing and Moscow signed on for the first time to a UN Security Council resolution on North Korea condemning the test and imposing multilateral sanctions. All the relevant parties eventually settled for a dual approach, involving negotiations—through the Six-Party Talks already launched in 2003 and involving the US, China, Japan, South Korea, and Russia with Pyongyang—and sanctions on the Kim regime. This strategy led to three sets of denuclearization agreements in 2005 and 2007 that froze and dismantled parts of North Korea's nuclear programs. These diplomatic agreements during the Bush administration, like those of the Clinton administration, eventually were rendered null and void by North Korea's proliferation activities (further discussed below).

How did it come about that North Korea was able to "go nuclear"? Arguably, this was inevitable. Kim Il-sung had spent decades seeking to develop nuclear weapons as a way to gain prestige by joining the nuclear club, in order to be in possession of an independent deterrent against the US and South Korea, regardless of Pyongyang's relations with Beijing and Moscow. Upon inheriting the country's leadership, Kim Jong-il had set about fulfilling his father's goal. Pyongyang had continued to develop its nuclear program secretly, and in spite of several pledges to denuclearize, until its fateful test in October 2006.

Development of a nuclear program fitted with Kim's *Seongun* policy. By the mid-1990s, references to Marxism-Leninism were disappearing from North Korea's public discourse.[69] In fact, a 2009 revision to the North Korean constitution completely removed any mention to this Soviet-inspired ideology. *Seongun*, meanwhile, was included in the constitution for the first time in the 2009 revision.[70] This hugely symbolic change underscored the centrality of the military to North Korean policy, both at home and abroad.

Indeed, domestic life in North Korea had become more militarized. The Korean People's Army was employed not only for the protection of the country against external foes, but was also central to the repression of potential opponents to the regime, the building of new infrastructure, the running of factories, the growing of food, and any other activity imaginable.[71] Well-rehearsed and flashy military parades became central to public life, particularly in Pyongyang. The official media continuously extolled the virtues of the military, and the role it played in running the country. With universal conscription of men for a lengthy military service of up to ten years, all North

Korean families, except those officially marginalized due to their low *seongbun* status, were directly affected by this militarization of daily life.

In fact, the WPK became secondary to the organization of life in North Korea. Kim Il-sung had held his last party congress in 1980. Kim Jong-il did not bother to convene the congress even once. Officially, the younger Kim ruled as chairman of the National Defense Commission rather than as secretary-general of the party, the two main civilian titles that he held while leader of North Korea. In Kim's eyes, it was the army that could try to remove him from power since the party had been emasculated for decades. It made sense to emphasize the importance of the military to life in North Korea, and to keep the army happy in exchange for its support.

Unsurprisingly, this stance permeated North Korean foreign policy. The Six-Party Talks convened between 2003 and 2008 brought North Korea to a regular multilateral dialogue for the first time in its modern history. Indeed, the Six-Party Talks became the first multilateral security dialogue among the major powers of East Asia and the US. Victor was a member of the US delegation, and had a front row seat observing North Korean diplomacy and, more broadly, its foreign and security policy. Pyongyang's diplomats were skillful and agreeable, and proved to be knowledgeable. However, they were kneecapped by their leadership. North Korean diplomats could not make any significant decision, or even discuss a sensitive topic, without Pyongyang's explicit permission. This contrasted with the practice of the other delegations, and prevented progress.

More strikingly, however, it became clear that the North Korean Ministry of Foreign Affairs had limited power back home. North Korean diplomats were as shocked by the country's 2006 nuclear test as their foreign counterparts. Talking to them after the test, it seemed obvious that they had been blindsided and did not know the real state of the country's nuclear weapons program. It was not a case of North Korean diplomats trying to hide the truth; the distinct impression of the negotiating teams was that the North Koreans genuinely did not know what the Korean People's Army, the Ministry of Defense, and those responsible for North Korea's nuclear program were up to. In the eyes of Kim Jong-il, his diplomats came a distant second to his generals and soldiers.

Leaving aside the centrality of the military to North Korean life under Kim, markets continued to be the lifeline upon which the population relied to get on. A foreign resident in Pyongyang at the time explains how it was easy enough to buy any type of food, home appliance, or anything else one wished—as long as they had access to the markets. However, this same person also cautioned that life was not so easy in cities outside of the capital. People in the countryside could grow their own food, but those in urban centers couldn't always do so. Likewise, inhabitants of smaller cities did not have access to the range of foods and goods available in Pyongyang.[72] Defectors who left North Korea at the time corroborate this account. They were escaping their country not necessarily out of opposition to the regime, but simply to find a better life overseas or pursue the dreams that their country neglected.[73]

Certainly Kim sought to improve living conditions in the capital at the expense of the rest of the country. This made sense, since only those selected by his regime could live in Pyongyang and it was imperative to keep them happy. Most symbolically, North Korea resumed construction of the Ryugyong Hotel in 2008. Construction would not be finished, and Kim Jong-un would halt its development again in 2012.[74] But Kim Jong-il's priorities were clear. Hospital facilities and the breadth of medical services were noticeably better in Pyongyang compared to the rest of the country.[75] Yet another symbol of where Kim's main concerns lay.

Still, living conditions seemed to be improving across the country as a whole, with trade flowing almost unimpeded across the Sino-North Korean border, foreign firms looking to tap into the North Korean market, and private wealth growing. As a sign of the tentative changes that the North Korean economy was undergoing, the country's first mobile phone network launched in 2008. Koryolink was a joint venture between Egypt's Orascom and the North Korean state, and quickly grew its subscriber base into the hundreds of thousands.[76] It seemed that not even the Kim regime could prevent the tide of modernization that many other fellow developing countries across the world were undergoing.

However, there were signs that the North Korean leadership was unhappy with these changes to the country's economy. Most notably, the government announced a surprise currency reform in November 2009. The population was told that each person had one week to exchange their won notes for newer ones. The goal seems to have been to ensure the government's control over the activities of private markets, and the traders that had benefited the most from them. Thus the government set a cap of KRW 100,000 per individual, roughly US $40 at the unofficial exchange rate and enough for no more than a 110-pound sack of rice. The cap was lifted as a result of widespread panic. But the result of the reform was that private individuals who had accumulated previously unimaginable levels of wealth lost most of it within a week, unable to use their old notes anymore. A few months later, the architect of the reform was executed. But it was clear that the reform could only have been sanctioned by Kim himself. From then on, neither Kim Jong-il nor his son dared intervene in the market to the same extent.

By the late 2000s, in any case, there were rumors that Kim Jong-il's health was fragile and he might even have suffered one or more strokes.[77] Certainly, he looked thinner in pictures released by official state media. Unfortunately for South Korea, however, Kim would not leave quietly. Whether it was his swansong or, as some claim, a way for his son Kim Jong-un, who was then being groomed for power, to reassert himself, 2010 marked the lowest point in decades for inter-Korean relations.

In March 2010, a North Korean torpedo sank ROKS *Cheonan*, killing forty-six sailors while wounding a further fifty-eight in the largest loss of military lives since the Korean War. Pyongyang denied responsibility for the sinking, and at the time of writing maintains that it was not involved.[78] However, an international investigation involving South Korean and foreign experts concluded that a North Korean torpedo was responsible.[79] Relations between North and South Korea had taken a turn for the worse following the inauguration of Lee Myung-bak in the latter, which could have motivated Pyongyang's action. But regardless of the reasons, this was a military escalation on the part of the Kim regime.

Nine months later, in October, there was no doubt that North Korea was behind an artillery attack on South Korean civilians. North Korean forces shelled Yeonpyeong Island, a South Korean territory sitting near the Northern Limit Line separating the waters of the two Koreas in the West Sea. Two South Korean civilians and two soldiers were killed. KCNA issued a statement justifying the attack as a retaliation against South Korea,[80] as the ROK Armed Forces had been conducting military exercises in the area. However, the South Korean exercises were conducted regularly and had resulted in no casualties. Once again, North Korea's motivations were unclear.

In December 2011, the Kim Jong-il era came to an end. The North Korean leader died of a heart attack while traveling outside of Pyongyang. The official announcement of Kim's death was delayed by two days.[81] No reasons were given for this, but presumably it had to do with intra-governmental discussions about his successor. Unlike at the end of the Kim Il-sung era, the mourning for Kim Jong-il was not particularly sincere. Many North Koreans felt pressured both by the government and by their peers into showing sadness at the passing of their leader.[82]

Also unlike the end of the Kim Il-sung era, it was unclear who would take over power after Kim Jong-il. There was no obvious heir. But Kim Jong-un led the funeral procession for his father, a strong sign that he was in the running to take over from him.[83] The youngest Kim, however, was almost unknown. In fact, most North Koreans had never seen his face until he appeared in a group picture in late 2010, when he is believed to have been de facto appointed as his father's successor. However, many North Koreans, and almost all foreigners, did not really know about his exact role or precise family background, never mind that he was about to become the leader of a nuclear power. As a result, there was open speculation about the direction that North Korea would take. Arguably, nuclear weapons were what allowed the North to retain its independence. But the country was also dependent on foreign support to run its economy, and this could only change with an opening-up process.

1. Emperor Kojong (left) posing for a picture with his son, Crown Prince Sunjong (right), *c.* 1907. Kojong and Sunjong were the last two rulers of the Joseon dynasty that governed Korea from 1392 to 1910. The dynasty gives name to the longest-running period in Korean history.

2. Donuimun, one of the Eight Gates of Seoul in the fortress wall which surrounded the city in the Joseon dynasty, with a tram in front of it, in 1904. The arrival in Korea of modern forms of transportation reflected the efforts of the country to modernize in the late nineteenth and early twentieth century.

3. Seoul railway station, *c.* 1925. The station became the main arrival point to the Korean capital during the period of Japanese colonialism, reflecting the colonizer's investment in such matters as infrastructure to serve its own economic purposes.

4. A "righteous armies" (Uibyeong) militia pose for a picture, 1907. The "righteous armies" were groups of Korean volunteers fighting against Japan as it took over control of Korea, but they were outmatched by the Japanese army.

5. Ryu Gwan-sun, independence fighter, 1919. As a 16-year-old, Ryu was one of the leaders of the *Samil* (March 1st) Movement that sought to regain Korea's independence. Ryu was eventually arrested and tortured to death by the Japanese government.

6. "Comfort women" after being freed, 1944. Tens of thousands of Korean women were forced into sexual slavery, serving in brothels around the Japanese empire. It took decades for the first of them to decide to speak publicly about their suffering.

7. Korean citizens celebrate the independence of their country, August 15, 1945. Japan's surrender opened a new chapter in Korean history after thirty-five years of occupation, one in which Koreans hoped they would be able to determine their own future.

8. US soldiers taking down the Japanese flag from a building after the country's surrender, September 9, 1945. Japan's surrender to the US brought about Korean independence, but also illustrated that the fate of Korea seemed to remain in the hands of foreign powers.

9. South Korea's inauguration ceremony, August 15, 1948. Exactly three years after Korea's independence, the leaders in the South established their own country. This symbolized that the division of Korea into two countries would not be temporary.

10. Military trucks crossing the 38th parallel during the Korean War, 1950. Drawn by two US military officials, the parallel artificially divided Korea into two separate countries. The Korean War was the North's attempt to reunify Korea by force.

11. A row of refugees moving away from the battlefront crosses paths with soldiers marching towards it during the Korean War, August 1950. Over 2.5 million people died during the war, mostly Koreans but also foreign troops, with millions of Koreans being displaced by it.

12. A portrait of Syngman Rhee, *c.* 1939. Rhee was South Korea's first president from 1948 to 1960. He presided over an increasingly authoritarian regime and failed to address the South's economic backwardness, but he laid down the foundations for the country's future growth.

13. A portrait of Park Chung-hee in his military uniform, *c.* 1961. Following a coup in May 1961, Park would go on to rule South Korea until 1979. The Park government took a leading role in propelling the South's economic development, but also became a repressive dictatorship.

14. Kim Il-sung delivering a speech, 1946. A former independence fighter handpicked by Joseph Stalin, Kim manoeuvred to become North Korea's leader upon the establishment of the country in 1948. His family has ruled the North ever since, becoming the first hereditary communist regime in history.

15. Workers at a South Korean textile factory, 1970. South Korea's economic development started with the production of cheap goods by workers with long working hours, before the country moved up the chain to produce more technologically advanced products.

16. Kim Il-sung during an inspection visit with his son Kim Jong-il, mid-1960s. Following an internal power struggle, the Kim family were able to consolidate their rule over North Korea and pass on the leadership of the country from father to son, even as the economy stagnated.

17. South Koreans arrested during the Gwangju Uprising, May 27, 1980. Met with violence and repression, the uprising was one of several waves of protest against the dictatorial regime of Chun Doo-hwan, eventually leading to democratic elections in 1987.

18. Inauguration ceremony of the Seoul Olympic Games, September 17, 1988. The Seoul Games served to show a modern and dynamic face of South Korea to the rest of the world, boosting nationalism internally and recognition of the country externally.

19. Protest against IMF-mandated policies during the Asian financial crisis, December 2 1997. The crisis put a halt to decades of high economic growth, hitting South Koreans confidence in their own economy soon after accession to the OECD had brought pride to the country.

20. Kim Dae-jung (left) and Kim Jong-il (right) pose during the first-ever inter-Korean summit, June 13, 2000. Kim Dae-jung's "Sunshine Policy" combined with North Korea's economic problems brought the hope of reconciliation and even reunification between the two Koreas.

21. Park Geun-hye, February 26, 2013. The daughter of Park Chung-hee, she was the first female president of South Korea, ruling from 2013 to 2017. Initially popular, especially among voters who reminisced about her father, Park would eventually be impeached amid record-low approval ratings.

22. Coming to be known as the "Candlelight Revolution," this photo shows one of the protests demanding that Park Geun-hye be removed from power on November 26, 2016. South Korea has a vibrant civil society, and protests have become a popular way for citizens to express their views and peacefully request change in policy.

23. Propaganda posters in Pyongyang, 2008. The North Korean government has erected thousands of posters across the country praising the Kim family and their regime and denouncing the US and South Korea, in an attempt to control North Koreans' thoughts.

24. Agricultural workers in the North Korean countryside, 2018. Agriculture in general and rice-growing in particular continue to be an important part of the North Korean economy, particularly outside of the biggest cities. The growing methods, however, have failed to modernize.

25. Grand People's Study Hall in Pyongyang, 1989. One result of a construction spree in the 1980s, this magnificent building captures how the Kim family have prioritized grandiose propaganda projects over the well-being of the North Korean population.

26. Arirang Mass Games parade, September 11, 2019. The North Korean regime conducts several parades every year to glorify its rule. A portrait of Kim Jong-un, the third Kim to rule the North after replacing his deceased father Kim Jong-il, is displayed by participants in this parade.

27. A scene from *Parasite*, the 2019 movie. It became the first film not in English to win the Oscar for Best Picture, symbolizing the growing popularity and mainstream acceptance of South Korean cinema.

28. The Samsung Electronics headquarters in Seoul. The biggest South Korean company by size, Samsung was one of several South Korean conglomerates operating in high-tech sectors that became a hallmark of the country's economy in the twenty-first century.

29. Blackpink attending a video music award in Newark, New Jersey, August 28, 2022. This girl band became the biggest in the world by the 2020s, symbolizing the mainstream popularity of K-pop globally thanks to well produced and vibrant shows and songs.

30. A missile launch by North Korea, January 12, 2022. Following its first-ever nuclear test in 2006, the North Korean regime embarked on a campaign of nuclear and, especially, missile tests to improve its military capabilities and ensure regime survival.

31. Kim Jong-un and US President Donald Trump shaking hands before their summit in Singapore, June 12, 2018. For the Kim family, meeting with the US president symbolized international recognition.

32. The Pyongyang skyline is dominated by the pyramid-shaped Ryugyong Hotel, with mixture of taller skyscrapers and shorter office and residential buildings.

33. The Seoul skyline is dominated by office and residential skyscrapers and shorter building In the background, N Seoul Tower atop Namsan Mountain dominates.

6
AN OPEN SOUTH, A CLOSED NORTH
2010 TO 2023

The biggest girl band in the world, Blackpink, was coming to one of the most international and cosmopolitan cities of the twenty-first century, London. Tickets for their two shows had sold out within minutes. It was one of the most anticipated cultural events of the year, as the city was battling to leave the memories of the Covid-19 pandemic behind it. Ramon Pacheco Pardo did not hesitate. He wanted to see what this phenomenon was about. A growing number of friends and students were telling him that their interest in Korea had picked up thanks to its culture: K-pop, K-dramas, movies, sometimes even webtoons. So why had contemporary South Korean culture struck a chord with so many around the world?

As the underground train approached the concert venue stop, more and more Blinks—Blackpink fans—started to fill the carriages. Enjoying each other's company, singing along to their favorite tunes, comparing their colorful and imaginative clothes. The train stopped, and Ramon went to talk to some of the thousands of fans who had been queuing to see their idols hours, and in some cases days, in advance. After all, he was conducting research for this book, and that included talking to people from all walks of life. There were countless people of all genders, races, ages, and nationalities, many living in the UK but many others having flown in from elsewhere in Europe and beyond. And why were they there? In two words, community and happiness. Being part of the Blackpink community made them happy. Being a Blink brought meaning and joy to their lives. The band and its fans. All one. Korea and the divided Koreas had suffered so much throughout recent history; now South Korean art was uniting and bringing joy to the world. How times had changed.

* * *

Inward-Looking North Korea

Kim Jong-un was not yet 30 years old upon taking office and had spent part of his school years at a boarding school in Switzerland. At school, if not exactly popular, he certainly got along with his classmates, even if most thought of him as shy. His classmates vividly remember Kim's passion for basketball, which he loved to play and watch. NBA superstar Michael Jordan reportedly was among his idols. In short, Kim's formative school years had been spent in a very different environment compared to his father—who had grown up in North Korea—and his grandfather. This, some analysts speculated, could perhaps make Kim more willing to open North Korea in the way that China and Vietnam had done in the past. After all, China certainly, but also Vietnam arguably were more independent actors in international affairs and had more independence of action at the domestic level thanks to the riches brought by their opening-up processes.

Sure enough, North Korea signed an agreement with the US shortly after Kim took office. Agreed on the last day of February, the so-called "Leap Day" deal seemed to promise a return to the diplomacy of the Six-Party Talks years. Perhaps Kim was indeed willing to follow a different path from that of his father. But as the ink on the agreement had barely dried, and in spite of repeated warnings that it would be in contravention of international sanctions on Pyongyang, the young North Korean leader moved ahead with a satellite launch. And then Kim resumed missile tests after his father had paused them during the last two years of his life.[1] To top it off, North Korea conducted its third nuclear test in February 2013—its first since 2009. By then, the Obama administration had concluded that the youngest Kim had no interest in giving up the country's nuclear weapons program. Thus, it implemented a policy of "strategic patience" that essentially amounted to ramping up sanctions while ignoring diplomacy with North Korea and focusing on other, more pressing issues for the US.

Obama's policy seemed to be vindicated by Kim's approach to domestic politics. Kim engaged in the sort of purges the country had not seen since the late 1960s. He was a young leader who many doubted could survive the vicious politics concomitant to a dictatorial regime, even more so a regime where age mattered, since it was still imbued by a degree of Confucianism. Surely there would be those within the regime who would like to take Kim's place, perhaps leaving him as a puppet leader given his bloodline. In a sense, Kim's position was not so different from that of his grandfather, who had also pursued purge campaigns at a time when there was a debate in North Korea about the country's direction of travel.

Certainly, the speed and brutality with which Kim pursued his purge campaign indicated that he was in a hurry to consolidate his power. Dozens of older officials were pushed aside, whether from the

Korean People's Army, different ministries, embassies, or the party.[2] Above all, in December 2013 Kim had Jang Song-thaek publicly arrested during a Politburo meeting. His arrest was shown by the North Korean state broadcaster. This was the first time since at least the 1970s in which the arrest of a political figure had been shown on TV. A few days later, Jang had his trial. One day after the trial, he was executed.[3] Jang was none other than the vice chairman of the National Defense Commission—and the uncle of Kim Jong-un. He was said to be close to the Chinese leadership and to favor Chinese-style economic reform over the strengthening of the military. His very public removal and elimination sent a clear message: Kim would not hesitate to eliminate anyone who opposed his plans for North Korea.

Kim was determined not to be overshadowed by anybody else in the North Korean regime. He updated the "Ten Principles for the Establishment of a Monolithic Ideological System" to include his father's name. He did not pursue his own cult of personality at first, but doubled down on the cult of his grandfather and, crucially, his father, who had given him legitimacy by appointing him as the leader of North Korea.[4] Kim refused to meet with Chinese leader Xi Jinping, who himself had little time for North Korea. From a North Korean perspective, this was an indication of independence from what continued to be the country's main benefactor. In 2015, Kim introduced conscription for North Korean women as well as men.[5] This suggested a degree of continuity with the militarization of society introduced by Kim Jong-il.

At the same time, Kim also wanted to portray himself as a modern leader. North Korea's official media regularly carried his exhortations to modernize the economy. He was portrayed in "everyday" or relaxed situations, such as riding a roller coaster or at a beach resort. Ri Sol-ju, Kim's wife, was introduced as such by state media and had a public agenda of her own. This was unheard of in North Korea. Kim wanted to break with the staid image of his father and follow the style of political leaders in other countries who want to be seen as "man/woman of the people."

Furthermore, Kim officially introduced his *Byeongjin* or "parallel development" line at a Plenary Session of the party's Central Committee in March 2013.[6] This referred to the development of both the country's economy and the nuclear deterrent at the same time. Among other measures, North Korea would allow over 400 state-sanctioned markets to operate freely.[7] North Korean defectors reported that a growing number and variety of goods coming from or through China made their way to the markets.[8] Foreigners living in North Korea at the time—a tiny share of the country's population, but a valuable source of information—indicated that it was easy to buy all sort of products, including those in the sanctions list drawn up by the UN, the US, and the EU.[9] State media doubled down on reports about *Byeongjin*, new economic projects, and Kim's guidance up and down the country.

Furthermore, Kim convened the seventh WPK congress in May 2016. This was the first congress since 1980. It helped to shore up the pretense of group rule. And even if it was Kim who ruled North Korea, the congress was also a means to evaluate North Korea's progress in the intervening years.[10] In fact, foreign journalists were given access to parts of the congress for the first time. This was not as unusual as one might think when considering that Kim had allowed Associated Press to open a bureau in Pyongyang in January 2012—the first US organization to get permission to do so. Jean Lee, the news agency's correspondent, was relatively free to carry out her work even if acknowledging that there were restrictions and constant surveillance.[11] For Pyongyang, having foreign media served to present a more realistic view of the country.

Yet the degree of openness that Kim allowed should not be exaggerated. Two foreign residents in Pyongyang during the 2010s were in an enviable position to analyze this: both had spent years living in China in the past and were therefore well positioned to draw comparisons between two countries often lumped together when it comes to societal behavior and freedoms. Their verdict was strikingly similar: North Korea lagged well behind China when it came to access to regular people to strike up a conversation or simply interact with them. Chinese were generally free to speak their minds, while North Koreans were not. In fact, these two Pyongyang residents distinctly remembered the very few conversations they had had in North Korea that felt unscripted, given how rare these occasions were. They both agreed that North Koreans were much more conservative and guarded than the Chinese.[12]

And in fact, the years 2016 and 2017 were marked by a renewed challenge from North Korea to the international community that showed the limits of the differences between Kim and his father. Pyongyang conducted three more nuclear tests over those two years. In 2016, it conducted a record number of missile tests. One year later, it surpassed the record of the previous year and even conducted two ICBM (intercontinental ballistic missile) tests.[13] In theory, North Korea was now capable of mounting a nuclear warhead on a missile that could reach anywhere in the US. Kim triumphantly declared that North Korea had become a nuclear power.[14] At the same time, Kim engaged in a war of words with the new US president, Donald Trump. Trump threatened "fire and fury" against North Korea. Kim responded that he would retaliate against the US.[15] Kim accelerated the pace of missile testing and publicly threatened strike plans against US cities. Trump and his national security advisor, H.R. McMaster, authorized heightened military exercises in the waters off North Korea. Many journalists and experts, including the authors, speculated that the possibility of a war between North Korea and the US was about as real as it had ever been since the Korean War. Trump called for the Pentagon to provide military options for striking Kim. Among the plans produced was a limited US military strike, known as a "bloody nose," to target North Korean weapons facilities. How Kim would respond to a US military attack was unclear, but the assumption that North Korea would be rationally deterred from escalating to a nuclear confrontation was heroic, to say the least, given the country's history of belligerence and the public threats already levied by Kim. Trump didn't care—his advisors on the White House campus said it was "better for people to die over there than over here." Trump wanted to up the ante by drafting a tweet that called for families of US military stationed in South Korea to evacuate from the peninsula in order to scare Kim.[16] Trump's recklessness caused one of the authors, Victor Cha, to publicly oppose a renewal of conflict on the Korean Peninsula, ultimately leading to his losing the administration's nomination to serve as US ambassador to South Korea.[17]

In the meantime, Kim continued to purge his potential opponents. In the case of his half-brother Kim Jong-nam, he went a step further. Kim Jong-nam had been Kim Jong-il's heir apparent until 2001, when he was caught trying to get into Japan to visit Tokyo Disneyland using a fake passport. This prompted his fall from grace, and Kim went into exile from 2003.[18] Still, he was a Kim and had advocated regime reform. Some could see him as a potential challenge to Kim Jong-un. In February 2017, Kim Jong-un had his half-brother killed. Two women approached Kim Jong-nam in Kuala Lumpur International Airport and unknowingly exposed him to VX nerve agent. A few minutes after the attack, Kim passed away.[19]

Yet North Korea's relations with the outside world took an unexpected turn in 2018. South Korea was holding the PyeongChang Winter Olympic Games in February. The country's new president,

Moon Jae-in, saw this as an opportunity to reach out to North Korea and divert from the dangerous path that Trump and Kim were on. His gamble paid off, and Kim sent a sports team as well as a political delegation to the South, formally led by President of the Presidium of the Supreme People's Assembly Kim Yong-nam. But more importantly, Kim Yo-jong—Kim Jong-un's sister, who held several government positions—was a member of the North Korean delegation and was widely seen as its de facto leader. In crossing the 38th parallel, she became the first member of the Kim family to step onto South Korean soil since the Korean War. She delivered a personal letter from her brother to Moon. A whirlwind of diplomacy ensued.

Modern, Cool, Global South Korea

Immediately south of the Han River, Gangnam was home to farmers, cows, cabbage fields, and pear orchards in the 1960s. Some high-rise apartment buildings for public servants started to pop up in the 1970s, sharing the space with the fields. Even higher apartment buildings, and a variety of entertainment venues, started to take over the area in the 1980s, with the first subway line serving the district having just opened. Still, the area was nowhere as wealthy and desirable as other parts of Seoul. Gangnam's fortunes changed in the 1990s, with luxury apartments, new firms, trendy bars and clubs, and fashion retailers opening up in the district and sprawling into the surrounding areas. By the 2000s, Gangnam was arguably the most desirable district to live in, to party, to shop, or to launch your own start-up; the area was cool, hip, trendy . . . and very expensive. (Ramon can duly attest that Gangnam was no place for your average student to go out for the evening back then.) In 2012, the name of Gangnam took the world by storm. Showcasing a free and modern South Korea with a recognizable voice—and culture—with global appeal.

The transformation of Gangnam from the 1960s to the 2010s to a large extent symbolized the transformation that South Korea had undergone. Psy's "Gangnam Style" becoming the most danced-to song in the world and the most-watched video in the history of YouTube in 2012 symbolized something different. It symbolized, to many, that an outward-looking, cool South Korea had arrived on the global stage. And it had arrived with a bang. UN Secretary-General Ban Ki-moon, former Australian prime minister Kevin Rudd, pop megastar Britney Spears, International Space Station astronauts, and a Maori cultural troupe were among the many personalities and groups replicating Psy's famous horse-riding dance moves. As US President Barack Obama told his visiting counterpart, President Park Geun-hye, "people around the world [were] being swept up by Korean culture—the Korean Wave."[20] South Koreans rejoiced. Their country was now known for bringing joy and laughter to people everywhere. And yet, *Hallyu* was only starting to get ready to take over on a global level.

At the domestic level, however, the situation was different. Park, the daughter of former leader Park Chung-hee, had taken office as South Korea's first female president in February 2013. After meeting with Obama and delivering a speech to a joint session of the US Congress, Park's popularity had reached new heights. Her message of spreading hope and happiness,[21] particularly the latter, resonated with the many South Koreans who wanted something more from life than a well-paying job. In the 2000s, Park had been given the nickname "Queen of Elections" because of her knack for making the conservative party, regardless of its constantly changing name, connect with voters. In the initial months of her presidency, she seemed to retain that skill. Yet, one year into her presidency, many South Koreans started to grumble about her leadership style. Park refused to hold press conferences, and when she did, questions had to be submitted in advance. Not very democratic, many thought.

On April 16, 2014, tragedy engulfed South Korea. The MV *Sewol* ferry from Incheon to Jeju Island was carrying 476 passengers and crew. Midway through its journey, the ferry made a sudden turn and capsized. The captain and crew members ordered the passengers to stay put, while sending calls for rescue. The Korean Coast Guard, however, botched what should have been a routine rescue operation. The ferry sank, and a total of 304 people died—including around 250 high school students. More than half of the survivors were rescued by other boats, rather than the coast guard. The captain and several crew members were among the survivors. They had escaped the ferry before it sank.[22] Poor enforcement of existing regulation, overloading, and the crew's actions were all to blame for the disaster. But the government did not escape scrutiny. It was hours before Park attended the tragedy, which attracted strong criticism. Later on, it would emerge that she had been waiting for her hair to be done first.[23] The government also sought to downplay the tragedy and the government's role in it, further turning the public against the president. A growing number of South Koreans believed that their government was negligent and inattentive to the needs of the people. In May 2015, South Korea suffered an outbreak of MERS that killed 38 people—the largest number of deaths in the world after Saudi Arabia, where MERS had been reported initially in 2012.[24] To many South Koreans, this further reinforced the idea that the Park government could not manage the country.

On October 29, 2016, a series of weekly protests started in South Korea. For weeks, rumors had been circulating that Choi Soon-sil, the daughter of a shaman, had regularly been given access to government documents and advised Park on a range of issues. Choi had first met Park in 1974, when her father offered to give counsel to Park Chung-hee following the assassination of his wife—and Park's mother.[25] As the fall of 2016 passed, the weekly protests grew in number. They were labelled the "Candlelight Revolution," since protesters filled the streets of central Seoul and other cities in the country with candle lights to demand Park's removal from office. The protest of December 3 attracted an estimated 2.3 million people.[26] Six days later, the National Assembly voted to impeach Park for her links with Choi. The impeachment would be upheld by the Constitutional Court in 2017. Park would eventually be sentenced to prison on corruption charges in April 2018.

On a very different note, this was a period when South Korean attitudes changed and became more inclusive. Most notably, South Koreans' attitudes toward the LGBTQ+ community improved significantly. Young South Koreans, in particular, were as accepting of all types of sexual orientation as their peers in Europe, Japan, or the US.[27] (Older South Koreans, in contrast, lagged behind their peers, leading to the largest age gap in terms of acceptance of different sexual orientations in the world.) Reflecting this change in social mores, the Seoul Mayor's Office moved the city's Queer Festival to central Seoul in 2015. Similarly, South Koreans' views about migration also became more open and accepting. In this case, these positive views cut across all age groups.[28]

And the role of women in society also continued to evolve, with the number of female executives, National Assembly members, and entrepreneurs continuing to grow. Symbolic of this change was the appointment of Han Seong-sook as the CEO of Naver in 2017, and her replacement by Choi Soo-yeon in 2022. Naver was, and continues to be at the time of writing, South Korea's biggest online platform, with over half of South Koreans using it on a daily basis. Han was its first female CEO, and at 40, Choi was not only its second female CEO in a row but also one of the youngest business leaders in the country. South Korea's business world was certainly not as female-friendly as that of its OECD peers. But a growing number of women were showing that they could make it to the top.

As if to symbolize these changes and South Korea turning a page on the Park era, the Pyeongchang county hosted the PyeongChang Winter Olympic Games in February 2018.[29] (South Korea had won the rights to host the games in 2011, at the third time of asking.) The Winter Olympic Games are certainly not as big as their summer counterpart, or a football World Cup. But they did serve South Korea to show once again that it could organize a large-scale event, to demonstrate its latest technologies such as 5G or self-driving buses, and to present itself as a country happy with its global status.

Plus, all this was in sharp contrast to North Korea. International bodies such as the IOC were comfortable with awarding global sports competitions to South Korea because they believed that it could deliver well-organized events. This had also been the case with FIFA and its 2002 World Cup, or with the International University Sports Federation that had awarded its 2003 and 2015 Games to South Korea—as it would do with the 2027 edition. South Korea also wanted to host this type of events because its sportspeople were successful in a multitude of disciplines, for example regularly being one of the top countries in summer and winter Olympic game medal tables. In the case of North Korea, international bodies neither saw it as a viable host for their event, nor did North Korea regularly produce world-class athletes to showcase in events it might host.

In this case, the PyeongChang Winter Olympic Games also served to set in motion a process of inter-Korean rapprochement. On April 27, 2018, South and North Korea held their first bilateral summit in over a decade. Ramon was in Seoul on the day of the summit. It is fair to say that there was a sense of anticipation in the morning, when the motorcade taking Moon to meet with Kim was making its way to the Joint Security Area where the summit would be held. But there was also a sense that probably not much would change. After all, the two Koreas had already held summits in 2000 and 2007. And Kim Jong-un was, above all and before anything else, a Kim needing to ensure the continuation of his family's rule over North Korea. Shortly before the official start of the summit, however, things changed. Kim and Moon shook hands over the demarcation line separating the two Koreas. Kim then invited the South Korean president to briefly step over the line into North Korean territory. South Koreans smiled. A nice gesture. And then Kim crossed over the very same line to walk together with Moon toward the Peace House, sitting on the south side of the Joint Security Area. South Koreans gasped, and cheered. This was the first time since the Korean War that a North Korean leader had stepped onto South Korean soil. The word "historic" is sometimes overused. This time, it fitted the occasion.

The summit between the two leaders initially seemed to go well, raising the hopes of the South Korean people. Kim seemed humble, praising South Korea as a modern country. The two leaders signed the Panmunjom Declaration. Its contents were certainly not new. Above all, the Koreas committed to co-prosperity and independent reunification, boosting dialogue, military exchanges, and negotiations for a peace regime.[30] But Moon and Kim then held a joint press conference, with the North Korean leader talking to the South Korean press. This was yet another astonishing moment that few would have imagined that very same morning. It is fair to say that by the evening many South Koreans had become less skeptical of the North Korean leader. Ramon was having dinner with some friends at an outdoor restaurant close to Cheonggyecheon, the stream running through part of central Seoul. The weather was perfect to eat outside. The restaurant was completely packed. Diners at most of the tables, by the looks of it not your typical politics-obsessed crowd, were commenting on the summit. A TV screen showed a replay of the moment when Kim crossed into the South. The diners exploded into spontaneous applause and cheers. Perhaps the summit would lead nowhere. Perhaps Kim was just trying to fool their country, as his father had done. But that day, and that night, South Koreans could dream that inter-Korean reconciliation may beckon one day.

Ultimately, the inter-Korean process was not successful. More successful, in contrast, was South Korea's own #MeToo movement. Even though the situation of women in society was improving, it was far from ideal. For example, South Korea had one of the largest gender wage gaps in the developed world, even if it had been narrowing in recent years.[31] And there were still firms demanding that women quit their jobs after becoming pregnant or giving birth, one of the factors behind a decreasing birth rate. All in all, South Korea was in the bottom half in gender parity at the global level, above neighbors China or Japan but well behind other developed countries.[32]

In January 2018, Prosecutor Seo Ji-hyun posted a message on the internal network for prosecutors stating that she had been the victim of sexual harassment. She then gave a televised interview detailing the case, which resulted in a wave of denunciations of similar cases coming from artists, politicians, sportswomen, TV stars, and religious women, among others. Seo's sexual harasser was sentenced to prison, as were many of the other men accused of the same crime. In the past, they would have gone unpunished. In the meantime, the government passed a new Workplace Anti-Bullying Law, increasing the number of actions that fall under the scope of sexual harassment.[33] And in April 2019, the Supreme Court decriminalized abortion. Even though abortion was widespread and allowed under certain circumstances, there were still restrictions on this right. With the Supreme Court's decision, no woman or physician had to fear being prosecuted for having or practicing an abortion, respectively. South Korean women celebrated on the streets of the country. Their situation was improving, slowly but surely.

Tentative Opening, Decisive Closing

Following Kim Yo-jong's visit to South Korea, it seemed that North Korea was willing to consider opening up. With Kim having met with South Korean President Moon in April 2018, as we have just seen, the leaders of the two Koreas then went on to hold a second, impromptu summit one month later. This was also a first: all three previous inter-Korean summits had taken months of preparations and negotiations. This time, the leaders of the two Koreas met with only twenty-four hours' notice and only announced the meeting after it had taken place. This level of spontaneity was unheard of for a North Korean leader.

Kim went a step further in June. The North Korean leader took an international flight for the first time since taking over from his father. The plane carried him to Singapore, where Kim was due to hold the event of the year: the first-ever summit between a North Korean leader and his American counterpart. Kim and Trump held their summit on June 12. They first met one on one, followed by an expanded meeting including their teams, and issued a joint statement at the end of the meeting that called for denuclearization of the Korean Peninsula, normalization of political relations, a permanent peace regime, and the return of POW/MIA remains from North Korea to the US. The statement was seen as a "North Korean statement" in that it referred first to two North Korean demands: improving North Korea–US relations and achieving peace on the Korean Peninsula.[34]

Shortly after the summit, Ramon had the chance to have a lengthy discussion with a North Korean official over dinner. With the conversation being in Korean, and having been regaled with some wine, the North Korean interlocutor seemed to relax a little. This North Korean official peppered Ramon with questions about life in Seoul, South Koreans' perceptions of North Korea, Ramon's own views about North Korea, how the West in general felt about their country, and a myriad of similar topics. The North Korean official had an impressive and understandable thirst for knowledge. In the same way the outside world is curious about North Korea, this person was curious about the outside world. North Korean officials are very careful and adept at not crossing certain red lines. The Kim family, of course, was off limits. So were discussions about the North Korean economy. But this person did express their hope that the Kim–Trump summit would lead the US to remove sanctions on North Korea, allow their country to open up, and increase exchanges with the outside world. One could feel hope under the façade of hostility toward the West.

However, this was not to be. Instead, North Korea's impulse to turn inward took hold. In February 2019, Kim and Trump met in Hanoi for a second summit. The purpose of the meeting was to reach agreement on implementation of the principles laid out in Singapore because no progress had been made at the working-level pursuant to the first summit. In the pool spray before the start of the summit, David Nakamura of the *Washington Post* was the first American journalist to ever pose a question to the North Korean leader. Nakamura shouted out to Kim, asking whether he was confident he could get a deal with Trump. The North Korean leader answered in a matter-of-fact fashion, "It's too early to say. I would not say I'm pessimistic." Victor was covering the summit as an expert commentator for NBC News. Watching the two leaders at this pre-summit photo opportunity, he noticed Kim looking a bit like a deer in the headlights of the West's press, but more comfortable than he had been in Singapore eight months earlier. By contrast, Trump looked tired and stressed, probably because he had spent the entire flight to Hanoi watching the testimony of his former lawyer Michael Cohen revealing all of his misdeeds. Indeed, the investigations into Trump may have played a bigger role in US–North Korea relations than many think. Kim seemed to believe that Trump needed a "win" to take attention away from his domestic travails; and he may have been persuaded to think this way by the South Korean leader, Moon. Kim thus thought that he could get Trump to lift economic sanctions against his country for minimal concessions on denuclearization.

As it turned out, the meeting was a big embarrassment for the North Korean leader, with the American president leaving after only a few minutes when it became clear that the positions of their two countries were far apart.[35] The US wanted denuclearization from North Korea on a wider scale beyond the old plutonium production program at Yongbyon. North Korea was unwilling to provide this; Kim wanted major sanctions-lifting from the US in return for smaller denuclearization steps. The two leaders would go on to meet for a third time a few months later, in June, this time together with Moon and in the DMZ separating the two Koreas. True to Trump's style, the theatrics of this meeting were memorable. Trump briefly crossed into North Korea, becoming the first sitting US president to step inside the country. (Jimmy Carter and Bill Clinton had visited North Korea but only after leaving office.) But this meeting led nowhere. North Korea would spend the rest of 2019 conducting missile tests, hurling insults at South Korea, and eventually Moon personally, and waiting to see who would win the US election scheduled for the fall of 2020. Perhaps watching to see what the Biden administration's policies toward North Korea would be, the regime remained fairly quiet in 2021. Biden pursued a policy not unlike what he oversaw as vice-president under Obama, focused on sanctions and denuclearization without the promise of any up-front incentives to bring North Korea back to the negotiating table.

By 2020, in any case, the Covid-19 pandemic had taken hold across the world. North Korea was actually the first country to shut down its borders because of it. It did so in January, even before China—and at the time of writing, the North Korean borders essentially continue to be shut down. Almost all foreign residents left. Even the Sino-North Korean border remained almost completely sealed, in spite of food shortages even reaching Pyongyang.[36] In the meantime, Kim seemed to turn his attention to bolstering North Korea's nuclear and missile deterrent. At the eighth WPK congress, held in January 2021, the North Korean leadership emphasized that its priority would be to continue to develop the country's military power. With relations with the Biden administration essentially frozen, his regime then proceeded to conduct a record number of missile tests in 2022. In November, Kim Jong-un even used the latest ICBM test to present his daughter Kim Ju-ae to the outside world. The message was that the Kim family and the country's missile and nuclear deterrent were intrinsically linked. After all, North Korea's military program was Kim's top priority. Economic reform could wait. Arguably, so could a North Korea with a really independent domestic and foreign policy.

On Top of the World

For many South Koreans and foreigners alike, the 2020s were marked by two events: the rise of *Hallyu* to its peak in popularity and one of the world's best responses to the Covid-19 pandemic. With regard to *Hallyu*, the authors witnessed its growth themselves as professors specializing on Korea in the US and in Europe respectively. Over the years, the authors had seen the number of students interested in learning more about South Korea and taking Korean-language classes grow exponentially. In most cases, their interest in the country was spurred by consuming South Korean culture during their school years. *Hallyu*'s cultural ascendance was symbolized by *Parasite*

180

winning the Oscar for Best Picture in February 2020. Bong Joon-ho's masterpiece became the first movie in a foreign language to receive this honor. An honor that recognized both the artistry of South Korean filmmaking and its ability to speak to universal themes.

Similarly, the phenomenal success of Netflix's *Squid Game* became emblematic of the ability of South Korean dramas to bring together enthralling story-telling with topics that resonated well beyond the country. This drama became the most-watched in the history of Netflix. Equally astonishing, South Korean shows were the second most popular on the Netflix streaming platform in 2021—trailing only the cultural powerhouse of the US and placed above France, the UK, and other cultural powers.[37] Foreign firms paid big money to showcase their products in South Korean dramas, aware that they would be able to reach a global audience.

Yet, arguably, it was K-pop that really led the globalization of *Hallyu*. By the early 2020s, South Korea boasted the biggest boyband and girlband in the world: BTS and Blackpink, respectively. Singing predominantly in Korean, these bands had become global with tens of millions of fans from all corners of the world. The two of them also transcended the world of music. BTS were invited to deliver a speech at the UN General Assembly in September 2021; they became spokespeople against anti-Asian hatred, and used their lyrics to discuss the pressures that young people faced. Blackpink, mean-while, became known for their campaigning against climate change and support of environmental consciousness. K-pop fans even became well known for their social activism themselves. Most notably, BTS's ARMY disrupted a re-election rally by Trump.[38] In other words, K-pop was not only a cultural phenomenon but also helping to spark societal change. Again, the difference with North Korea was stark. South Korea's neighbor has neither globally recognized cultural icons, nor a culture that could spark change in society.

This did not cross the minds of most South Koreans proudly enjoying the success of their fellow citizens, but it was an interesting analytical point for those interested in the diverging fortunes of the two Koreas.

And as South Koreans celebrated the country's cultural success, along came Covid-19. South Korea had botched its response to MERS in 2015. And the Covid-19 pandemic had started in China, South Korea's neighbor. None of this boded well. Yet the Moon government quickly enacted a strategy in which government agencies, medical centers, and the private sector worked together to prevent the spread of the disease and, especially, severe cases leading to death.[39] As the world started to emerge from the worst of the pandemic in late 2021 and early 2022, South Korea had recorded one of the lowest death rates in the world, as well as one of the strongest economic recoveries from the pandemic.[40] Plus, South Korea had avoided the lockdowns that people in many other countries had to suffer. The way that the country dealt with the pandemic became representative of the confidence that South Korea had in itself.

This same confidence was also displayed in the global arena. Trump invited South Korea to attend the 2020 G7 summit. The summit was cancelled due to the pandemic. One year later, however, the UK once again invited South Korea to attend. This time, the summit went ahead. Moon flew to the picturesque county of Cornwall to attend the meeting with the leaders of other leading democratic economic powerhouses. As South Korea is a world leader in high tech, including semiconductors, electric batteries, or 5G, forward-looking countries in the G7 knew that it was necessary to confer with the country over the state of the world economy. One year later, South Korea was invited to attend the NATO summit held in Madrid. The recently inaugurated president, conservative Yoon Suk-yeol, flew to the Spanish capital. Over a dozen leaders of the alliance met with him to discuss the purchasing of South Korean advanced weapons systems and nuclear power plants. South Korea was the only Asian country both imposing sanctions on Russia and, crucially, supplying arms to Ukraine (via third countries, including Poland) to defend itself against Moscow's invasion.[41] As war ravaged Europe for the first time in decades, South Korea was standing together with fellow democracies in the NATO alliance. The contrast with North Korea, one of the few countries openly siding with Russia, could not be clearer.

Not everything was a cause for celebration. In October 2022, tragedy again struck South Korea. A crowd crush in Itaewon, a neighborhood in Seoul best known for its nightlife and foreigner- and LGBTQ+-friendly vibe, killed at least 158 people, mainly young partygoers celebrating Halloween. As in the case of the *Sewol* ferry disaster, many South Koreans felt that their government had been negligent; in this case, by not dispatching a sufficient number of police to control the crowds. Popular protests and a National Assembly probe into the crush ensued. South Korea having become a media haven in Asia, the tragedy was widely reported by international media. Expressions of condolence poured in from leaders across the world. Compared to the closed and repressive nature of North Korea, at least South Koreans could seek redress and open discussion of one of the darkest days in the country's contemporary history—and could take solace in the outpouring of international solidarity in the face of this new disaster.

A random day in early spring had starkly shown the differences between the two Koreas. In the morning of March 24, 2022, Kim Jong-un presided over North Korea's third ever long-range missile test from Pyongyang International Airport. In the afternoon of the same day, 64,000 South Koreans packed the Seoul World Cup Stadium to celebrate the national football team qualifying for the next World Cup. These two scenes played out a mere 120 miles apart. That is the distance between the capitals of North and South Korea. The two scenes vividly illustrate the contrast between the two Koreas as the world started to envision a post-Covid-19 pandemic era. A dictator and his military versus ordinary men and women. A celebration of the army and destruction in contrast to a celebration of the simple joy of attending a match of the world's most popular and global sport. It symbolized how much the lives of North and South Koreans had grown apart in the span of a mere seven decades.

7

UNIFICATION AND THE CHANGING REGIONAL CONTEXT

There are many academic conferences on Korean security issues for experts like the authors to attend. But this one in September 2010 was different. It was titled "Global Korea" and the topic of the conference was Korean unification, sponsored by the Ministry of Unification of South Korea. While the panels and speeches were taking place in the main hall of the glitzy Shilla Hotel in downtown Seoul, the organizers set up a 10 × 30 foot whiteboard in the coffee area adjacent to the hall, called the "Unification Board." The audience for this conference was not just your typical business types, scholars, officials, and press, but also included a healthy number of high school students. Participating students were invited to write their thoughts about unification on the whiteboard using multi-colored sticky notes. Inside the hall, luminaries such as the late Colin Powell and other global figures were asked to offer their opinions on Korean unification. Naturally, they said that they looked forward to the day that Koreans would be united rather than divided, living in freedom, peace, and prosperity, and not staring at each other across the most heavily militarized border in the world. Most of the younger Koreans in the audience were hearing these positive words about unification for the first time. After all, they were born after the Korean War and knew only one Korea—the South. For many, their defining moment was not the division of Korea in 1945 but South Korea's financial crisis in 1997. So, the discussion of unification usually elicited negative feelings about the economic burden of absorbing the much poorer North.

Victor Cha skipped an afternoon session of the conference because he was curious to read the hundreds of scribblings by the attending students on the rainbow of sticky notes that now filled the whiteboard. He was surprised by what he saw. Many stated that they had never really thought about unification positively, or that they had only viewed unification as dangerous, expensive, and difficult. They had believed that unification is a task that their generation should not be encumbered with. But with this conference, they felt as though their eyes were opened to the possibility that unification would benefit Korea, not hinder it, and that it was their generation's responsibility to think about how to prepare for it. This was fascinating, and was replicated in a similar conference in October 2022 sponsored by the Federation of Korean Industries. A process of socialization was taking place in which old negative views about unification were being uprooted and replaced by new positive ones.

* * *

The End of History

"Unification" has multiple meanings that reflect the complexities of Korea's modern history. Even the term itself is subject to debate. Some would argue that the appropriate word to use is "reunification" as this better reflects Korea's centuries of unity as a single nation and people before it was divided artificially by external forces in 1945. For thirteen centuries Korea was a unified country. From when the country was organized into three warring kingdoms (Baekje, Silla, Goguryeo) until its colonial occupation by Imperial Japan from 1910 to 1945, Korea and Koreans remained a single, unified entity. Only in the last century has Korea been robbed of its unity. The semantic debate underscores the deep scar that national division, now almost eight decades old, has left on the Korean psyche.

It is only against the backdrop of national division that we can appreciate how much the past eighty years have been an aberration in Korea's history. Unification is part of Korean identity. It is difficult to think of being Korean while not believing that those on both sides of the border are of the same stock, language, and family (literally, in the case of divided ones). Indeed, both Koreas claim to own the new era of unification in their national narratives. For South Korea, this would mean the liberation of the northern people from decades of repressive rule, poverty, and isolation under the cult of personality of the Kim family regime. South Korea's constitution has a provision that grants citizenship to those in North Korea. For North Korea, unification would mean removing the yoke of imperialism and foreign occupation from Korea (that is, the US troops on Korean soil), and the promise of nirvana under the rule of the Kim family, who represent the "true Koreans" unsoiled by the evils of external exploitation.

Are the two Koreas still truly the same nation given their vastly different development trajectories? Do younger Koreans in the North and South yearn for unification like their elders, or is the war and national division just something they have read about in history books? What would unification look like, and will it be a good outcome for Koreans? How do the regional powers view unification? As an opportunity? A threat?

As experts in the field, perhaps the most common question we, the authors, are asked at conferences and speeches in Europe, Asia, and America is: "When will unification happen?" Neither of us has a crystal ball to predict an answer, but we do know that unification will bring with it the "End of History" on the peninsula. It will mark the end of national division that saw South Korea become one of the most successful countries on the world stage by almost any metric, while North Korea languished in relative squalor and self-isolation. In this regard, unification would mark a "normalization" of Korean history as the nation becomes whole again, though one can hardly imagine that stitching the two systems and people back together would be anything resembling "normal." The start of this new history will not be easy, but then again, very little in history has come easy for Korea and for Koreans. But they have demonstrated time and again a remarkable resilience and ability to overcome all odds. Such will be the case with unification.

In an ideal world, Korean unification would boast the marriage of South Korean cutting-edge technology and capital with North Korean cheap labor and abundant mineral resources. The enfranchised democracy of a united Korea would have a total population of 80–90 million, putting it on par with Japan. The peninsula would become a throughway of commerce and energy connecting all of maritime Asia with continental East Asia and the Eurasian land mass. Unification would mean the end of a major security threat in the heart of East Asia and would produce peace dividends for all. Why is it so hard to achieve this vision?

The answer stems in part from the fact that a discussion of unification cannot be divorced from an understanding of inter-Korean relations. Each Korea's unification strategy historically has been refracted through the prism of its policies toward the rival regime across the border. These policies were far from uniform, ranging

from coercive regime change and containment measures, to cooperation and tension-reduction diplomacy.

Unification by Force

For decades, the dominant narrative on both sides of the Korean
Peninsula was about achieving unification as the overarching goal of
the Korean people. During the Cold War, this could only be achieved
through the victory of one side over the other. For North Koreans,
the discourse centered on liberating the Korean people from US
military occupation and from exploitation by a South Korean government that was a "puppet" of American imperialism. The phrase that
came to epitomize the view in the South was *bukjin tongil*, or *seong-
gong tongil*, which meant "march north" or "unification by force." This
discourse privileged unification as the immediate goal, but with
obvious differences in terms of who should predominate. Compromise
was alien to the relationship. On the contrary, *bukjin tongil* was the
ultimate zero-sum game between the two Koreas. One side's gain, no
matter how minor, was the other side's loss. The relationship was one
of mutual hostility with firefights a nearly daily occurrence along the
DMZ in the 1960s and 1970s, killing in aggregate over 900 soldiers
and civilians. The only channel of official dialogue was through the
military armistice commission (MAC). The purpose of the MAC
was purely armistice maintenance and armistice violations, and there
was no channel for peace talks or inter-Korean engagement or reconciliation. Any other channel, if it existed, was deemed not only ille-
gitimate but seditious.

The two Koreas were locked into what scholar Samuel S. Kim
once famously referred to as the "politics of competitive delegitima-
tion."[1] This mentality was evident in things like the Syngman Rhee
government's version of the "Hallstein Doctrine" (1955–70), which

stipulated that the South refused to have diplomatic relations with any country that recognized the rival North Korean regime. So when countries like the Republic of Congo sought to recognize both Koreas as legitimate in 1965, Seoul ejected the Congolese embassy and declared its diplomats personae non gratae.[2] This zero-sum mentality was also manifest in South Korea's infamous National Security Law. It was illegal to have contact with North Koreans, to listen to any North Korean radio or television broadcasts, or to possess any materials or information about the North. Indeed, any mention of engagement with the North was deemed treasonous, and grounds for torture and imprisonment.

North Korea practiced its own version of the Hallstein Doctrine, but scored major diplomatic victories over the South during this period in the context of the non-aligned movement. In 1975, North Korea applied to and became a member of the loosely organized movement. Not to be outdone, South Korea too felt compelled to apply, but was denied membership because of the stationing of US troops on its soil. When it came to UN membership, North Korea would not accept a dual-membership formula that would bring both countries into the international organization because it could not stand South Korea being accorded legitimacy in the UN, even if that meant North Korea would be accorded the same legitimacy as an independent nation-state. For Pyongyang, the only acceptable formula was a "one-Korea" formula, which meant only a unified Korea under its rule. For this reason, the two Koreas did not achieve permanent membership from 1948 until September 1991.

Even the periods of brief thaw in inter-Korean relations were not the result of a belief in mutual reconciliation but derived from cold balance-of-power calculations. North Korea, for example, made numerous proposals for improved relations with the South. These included a 1950 peace conference proposal (ironically on the eve of the Korean War),[3] a 1971 eight-point unification proposal, a 1973 five-point peace treaty proposal, and a 1974 letter to the US Congress proposing bilateral negotiations with the United States to replace the armistice with a peace treaty. All of these proposed the establishment of a Democratic Confederal Republic of Koryo, identified as one Nation (presumably with the North in charge) but operating with two systems. Each of these proposals, however, was designed to achieve one objective, which was the removal of US forces from South Korea, and indeed this troop withdrawal constituted the precondition for every proposal.

As detailed in chapter 3, the most significant interaction between the two Koreas during the Cold War period was a series of secret negotiations between Kim Il-sung's brother, Kim Yong-ju, and the chief of South Korean intelligence, Lee Hu-rak, that led to the July 1972 North–South Joint Communiqué. Both Koreas were somewhat paranoid about the emerging détente among their great power patrons, commencing with Nixon's trip to China in February 1972. The North hinted at an interest in starting talks and the South responded by proposing Red Cross talks, which were essentially covert official talks because both Red Cross delegations included as many intelligence officials as there were good Samaritans. Three months of Red Cross talks started in August 1971 and went nowhere until the decision was made to bump the dialogue to a higher level. This paved the way for a series of secret negotiations by the two intelligence agencies. The July 4 communiqué, signed by Lee Hu-rak and Kim Yong-ju, enunciated three principles of agreement between the two Koreas: (1) unification must be achieved through the independent efforts of the Koreans and without external interference; (2) unification must be achieved peacefully and not by force; and (3) the two governments commit to seek national unity as a homogenous people that transcends politics and ideology.

While the surprise agreement was widely heralded as an important breakthrough for peace on the peninsula, the motivations for Seoul and Pyongyang were less benign. Each suffered intense fears of abandonment as their superpower patrons, the US, China, and the USSR, entered into a period of détente with one another, and therefore the two Koreas sought a temporary reprieve in their otherwise contentious bilateral relations.

Moreover, the zero-sum nature of inter-Korean relations became evident shortly thereafter. In subsequent working-level meetings, the two sides could barely agree on an agenda for discussion, let alone reach any agreements. And only two years after the North–South Joint Communiqué, a North Korean sympathizer tried unsuccessfully to assassinate the South Korean president, but killed the country's first lady, Yook Young-soo, with a bullet through her head.

About a decade later, and as explained in chapter 4, another set of exchanges was prompted by heavy rains and landslides in South Korea that left 190 people dead and over 200,000 homeless.[4] Seeing even a natural calamity in the South as a zero-sum win for itself, Pyongyang ostentatiously offered to send relief supplies as a propaganda ploy. President Chun Doo-hwan (1980–88), who had survived a North Korean assassination attempt in Burma the previous year which killed half of his cabinet, unexpectedly accepted the assistance. The Red Cross used this as an opportunity to restart North–South talks, which spanned from September 1984 to September 1985, and these led to some small-scale family reunions. While this period is also seen as a thaw in relations, it too was deeply embedded in competition. Chun initiated secret talks with the North alongside the Red Cross negotiations through the KCIA channel, where some forty-two secret meetings took place between the two sides; but these meetings fell apart when North Korea demanded an end to the annual US–South Korea "Team Spirit" military exercises. Moreover, when the North's flood relief contributions arrived, South Korea ridiculed the poor quality of the clothing, rice, and building supplies. It afforded South Koreans unique insight at the time into how much better off they were than their counterparts, and thus proved embarrassing to Pyongyang.

Unification as "Too Dangerous, Too Difficult"

Views on unification changed after the end of the Cold War and contemporaneous with the unification of East and West Germany, as detailed in chapter 5. Koreans watched German unification with deep envy, but the realities of how difficult unification would be also started to be understood. As cathartic as witnessing the German unification process might have been, South Koreans saw the rampant inflation created by the union of the two currencies, and the social dislocation as East Germans tried to assimilate into a new, more fast-paced German lifestyle.

The newly evolving post-Cold War environment had catalyzed a change in perceptions about unification, especially in South Korea. While unification was previously seen as something desirable, for many it became something to be avoided because of the staggering costs and the terrible uncertainties. Prior to German unification, little attention had been paid to the process or mechanics of Korean unification. But watching the Germans contend with social, political, and economic integration caused some Koreans to believe that South Korea could "absorb" its northern counterpart. This was largely a far-right, conservative, hardline view based on a belief that the economy was strong enough and large enough to swallow up the North.[5] But the majority of South Koreans saw the challenges of unification more clearly. The theory that unification was "too difficult and too dangerous" emerged and took a prominent place in policymaking and scholarship.

During this period, there was an intense debate between two different schools of thought on the Korean unification process—the "hard landing" versus the "soft landing." The two different schools of thought were related to four different scenarios for unification: (1) North Korean regime collapse; (2) war; (3) gradual change in North Korea leading to peaceful integration; and (4) maintenance of the status quo or "muddling through."[6]

Scenarios one and two were associated with the hard landing school of thought. A hard landing would entail a process whereby "[t]he inability of the regime in power to maintain effective political, economic, social and military control, ultimately lead[s] to the dissolution of the regime and, in the extreme case, the state."[7] A soft landing, on the other hand—most often associated with scenarios three and four—was defined as "a process whereby gradual and controlled implementation of selective economic reforms enables a command economy to assume some characteristics of a market economy, although no regime change occurs."[8] Although different variations of these schools of thought existed in both policy and academic circles, the hard landing scenario predominated in South Korean thinking from the end of the Cold War in Europe until the Asian financial crisis in 1997.

There are several reasons why the hard landing theory prevailed at this time. A sequence of unprecedented events befell North Korea. As described in chapter 5, in 1990 the Soviet Union normalized political relations with South Korea, and with this decision, Moscow no longer provided patron aid and trade to Pyongyang. Within a year, North Korean imports of oil from the Soviet Union dropped by more than 50 percent.[9] In 1992, China followed suit and normalized relations with South Korea. Then, in July 1994, Kim Il-sung suffered a massive and fatal stroke, throwing the entire country into turmoil as a young, untested son took the reins of power. Shortly thereafter, severe flooding destroyed annual harvests, leading to a widespread famine in the country that killed perhaps up to 10 percent of the population (over 2 million people). These events led many officials and experts to predict an imminent collapse of North Korea.

In the late 1980s and early 1990s, the South Korean government itself was transitioning from a militaristic, right-wing authoritarian regime to a democratic one. The South Korean economy also emerged from the ranks of poor, underdeveloped countries to become one of the "Asian Tigers" with double-digit annual economic growth rates that left the stagnating North Korean economy permanently in the rear-view mirror. As described in chapter 4, South Korea showcased its development and democracy to the world when hosting the Summer Olympic Games in Seoul in 1988. The South Korean Ministry of Unification, as well as think tanks like the Korea Development Institute (KDI) and Korea Institute for National Unification (KINU), and private sector institutions like Goldman Sachs, all calculated the cost of unification, and the numbers were large and frightening to most South Koreans.[10] Having become a democracy, hosted the Olympic Games, and gained a seat in the United Nations, all between 1987 and 1991, South Koreans became not only increasingly proud of their newfound stature in the international community, but also feared that a costly and complicated unification process would hold them back from the glidepath toward the US $10,000 per capita income mark and eventual OECD membership.

During this time, there was also a perceived change in North Korean unification rhetoric. The retreat of communism caused an existential crisis for North Korea as its main sources of economic aid and ideological legitimacy started to dry up. Faced with a growing external threat, a failing economy, and a conventional military with deteriorating capabilities, North Korea seemingly shifted its strategy from "achieve unification at all costs" to "maintain regime survival at all costs."[11]

Given these developments, there was little domestic political will to push ahead with North–South dialogue and reconciliation efforts. Aside from a short, promising period of dialogue between 1988 and 1992, no lasting progress was made on inter-Korean relations throughout the 1990s. At that time, Roh Tae-woo, the president of the South, attempted to engage with North Korea under the banner of *Nordpolitik* or Northern Diplomacy, which aimed at pragmatic and non-ideological diplomatic outreach. The short period of engagement resulted in the signing of two accords, as mentioned in chapter 5: the Basic Agreement on Reconciliation, Non-Aggression, and Exchanges and Cooperation (1991) and the Joint Declaration on the Denuclearization of the Korean Peninsula (1992). While initially these accords seemed to signal progress on both sides by ending decades of mutual non-recognition, identifying areas of cooperation, and laying out an institutional roadmap for unification, there was a lot of rhetoric without substance. Unsurprisingly, the agreements ultimately failed to resolve the deep conflicts between the two Koreas. South Korea's normalization of diplomatic relations with the Soviet Union and China during President Roh Tae-woo's term also dealt a harsh blow to North Korea. After 1992, North Korea cut off contact with South Korea and refused all opportunities to engage in further inter-Korean dialogue. The subsequent South Korean president, Kim Young-sam, also attempted rapprochement with Pyongyang, but revelations about North Korea's suspected nuclear weapons program, and its announced withdrawal from the NPT in 1993, only added to the deepening distrust between North and South Korea.

Although North Korea later signed the 1994 Agreed Framework with the US and suspended its withdrawal from the NPT, Pyongyang's attempts to freeze South Korea out of the agreement's negotiations left many officials in the South with little inclination, or reason, to work with the North.

The result was that while the end of this period saw important political agreements among the two Koreas and its neighbors, these agreements neither individually nor collectively contributed to the unification process more than the earlier "winner-takes-all" or *bukjin tongil* period. What this period did show, however, was that through the study of German unification and its potential application to the Korean situation, new parameters were set regarding cost, caution, and prudence as to how the Koreans and the world thought about unification. These parameters, once set, would act as empirical blinders for the next decade.

Unification and the Sunshine Policy

In 1998, South Korea's new democratically elected president Kim Dae-jung put forward the idea of the Sunshine Policy, as laid out in chapter 5. Based on one of Aesop's fables, the policy's inspiration was the story of the Sun and Wind competing to see which could remove the coat of a weary traveler. The Wind went first and blew cold, fierce gale-force winds to pry the coat from the man, but this only caused the traveler to button up and grip the coat even more tightly around his neck to manage the elements. After the Wind failed, the Sun then tried. The Sun cast rays of sunlight and warmth on the traveler, which caused him to take off the coat.

The Sunshine Policy was in many ways that antithesis of the winner-take-all model of unification. Based in a progressive *minjung* ideology among the Korean body politic that sees the source of all of Korea's ills to be the externally imposed division of the country in 1945, the Sunshine Policy was a non-zero-sum strategy of uncondi-tional engagement designed to open North Korea to the forces of reform. The core assumption underlying the policy was that North Korean belligerence, pursuit of weapons of mass destruction (WMD), and otherwise deviant behavior stemmed from basic security deficits experienced by the state. According to this theory, promising mutual respect and conciliation to North Korea would lessen the regime's insecurities and reduce the threats posed by their military and WMD. The promise of economic cooperation, moreover, would promote North Korea's internal reforms and its opening to the outside world. This process of peaceful political reconciliation and economic cooperation would foster a prolonged period of mutual coexistence, followed by a "one country, two systems" format that would then be followed by gradual integration of the two systems, and eventually enable reunification through a process of mutual consultation and consensus.[12] The policy was tied to Kim Dae-jung's more liberal political ideology, and was subsequently carried forward by his successor, President Roh Moo-hyun (2003–8) and President Moon Jae-in (2017–22).

The emergence of this alternative school of thought was not just due to ideology, however. The Sunshine Policy, which aimed at promoting an "extended soft landing" when it comes to unification, was motivated by hard economic realities. South Korea experienced a sharp economic downturn in 1997–8 when a liquidity crisis meant that emergency assistance from the IMF was required to prevent the economy from collapsing. This crisis effectively made discussions of unification economically impossible, so engaging with the North Korean regime over the long term and paving the way for a gradual transition or a soft landing, seemed to be the best policy choice. In the context of this policy, the two Koreas held summit meetings on several occasions. South Korean President Kim Dae-jung and North Korean Supreme Leader Kim Jong-il held the first inter-Korean summit in 2000. The second inter-Korean summit was held in 2007 with Kim Jong-il and South Korean President Roh Moo-hyun. And South's president Moon Jae-in held a series of meetings with Kim Jong-un in 2018. The two iconic symbols of inter-Korean cooperation created by the policy are a joint industrial complex situated at the waist of the Korean Peninsula near North Korea's second-largest city of Kaesong; and a tourism complex (Mount Geumgang), also on the northern side of the DMZ. The former project spoke to the economic potential of inter-Korean cooperation, marrying up South Korean capital and technology with North Korean labor to produce light manufactured consumer products. The latter project appealed to the South Korean public who fancied the novelty of a trip across the border to the mountain generally considered the most beautiful in the whole of Korea, or who hailed from families still divided by the Korean War.

What was so distinct about the Sunshine Policy was the way it framed unification for the public. First, it propagated the view that unification should be pushed several generations into the distant future. In effect, Sunshine policies, informed by the practicalities of German unification and the Asian financial crisis, were meant to kick the "unification can" down the road. Second, and relatedly, the policies socialized an entire generation of Koreans and the world into viewing unification as a "bad thing"—too expensive, too impractical, and too inconvenient—and therefore it should not be a concern or goal of the current generation, or even its children or grandchildren. Instead, the focus should be on reconciliation, coexistence, and co-prosperity—leading to eventual unification. The difference between this view and its predecessors was that it assigned a negative normative value to immediate unification, perhaps in reaction to the decades of dominant conservative political ideology that strove for unification as a positive national goal. The prior two theories of unification—*bukjin tongil* ("march north") and "Too Dangerous, Too Difficult"—never denied that unification would be a formidable challenge for the Korean people, but maintained that the costs and pains associated with it would never diminish the positive identification of the goal with Korean identity. Sunshine Policy essentially carried the message that unification was not necessarily a normatively positive aspirational goal because it implied competition rather than reconciliation with the North, and that competition could drive the country into war, chaos, or bankruptcy. The disavowal of the pursuit of competition and the adversarial framing of North Korea was informed at its core by *minjung* ideology, which stressed the racial homogeneity of the Korean people and its exploitation by external powers. Thus, it viewed the northern neighbor as brethren rather than as a sovereign enemy, and any exercise of power aimed at unification or "winning" over the other was a client-state mentality originating from external competing powers (the US and the Soviet Union) that was ultimately self-destructive.[13] Thus, a decade of Sunshine Policy essentially told a generation of Koreans that a legitimate narrative existed in Korean identity that saw unification as something that should be avoided at all costs for the foreseeable future.

At certain times, the Sunshine Policy created friction between the US and South Korea, as Seoul argued for engaging the North Korean threat rather than greater containment of that threat. As it related to unification policy, there were many critics of the soft landing theories who argued they were flawed because they were based on a set of fragile and unproven assumptions. For example, the Sunshine Policy presumed that the only path to a soft landing was through engagement and reconciliation. Advocates assumed that there was a linear causal relationship between diplomatic incentives and positive opening and reform in North Korea's political system and economy. The Sunshine Policy also assumed that there would be no military conflict associated with a soft landing, while there would be an abundance of it in a hard landing. Finally, the theory assumed that neighboring powers would all naturally support the policy over tougher, containment-oriented approaches.

All three periods of Sunshine Policy under Kim Dae-jung, Roh Moo-hyun, and Moon Jae-in produced no real progress toward inter-Korean reconciliation, according to their critics. Of course, these periods saw economic cooperation between the two Koreas, and during Moon's tenure, an added emphasis on transport and energy infrastructure development. Moon's ownership of the policy will be remembered for its explicit rejection of unification as a national policy, replaced by a policy of coexistence and co-prosperity.[14]

Unification "Due Diligence"

The initial decade of the Sunshine Policy from 1998 to 2007 under the progressive presidencies of Kim Dae-jung and Roh Moo-hyun ended with the election of conservative South Korean president Lee Myung-bak in December 2007. Lee was a businessman, not an ideologue. He saw both inter-Korean policy and unification policy in pragmatic terms. What emerged during this period was a pushing back against the past decade of views on unification.

This new view of unification was a pragmatic one tied to Lee's own personal convictions. Many argue that this view also animates President Yoon Suk-yeol's views. That is, unification may be expensive, it may be difficult, and it may be dangerous, but Koreans cannot blindly stick their heads in the sand and hope the problem will go away. Instead, as traumatic as unification may be, it could very well come tomorrow, next month, or next year, so it is essential to carry out "due diligence" and prepare for the process.

This policy shift was likely informed by events unfolding in North Korea that indicated a high degree of both threat and instability to the region. Despite negotiated denuclearization agreements in 2005 and 2007, North Korea continued to pursue the development of nuclear weapons and ballistic missiles, conducting two nuclear bomb tests and eighteen missile provocations between 2008 and 2013. The massive stroke suffered by Kim Jong-il in 2008, and his eventual death in 2011, led many to predict, once again, that the North Korean regime was on the verge of collapse. In 2010, South Korean attitudes considerably hardened against the Sunshine Policy after a North Korean submersible torpedoed and sank the South Korean navy corvette *Cheonan,* killing 46 sailors in the largest loss of military life since the Korean War. Later that year, North Korea's shelling of a South Korean island, in broad daylight and captured on citizens' cell-phone cameras, raised concerns that North Korea's unstable domestic situation was manifesting itself in external provocations that threatened the entire region. Many officials and experts called for contingency planning to deal with the possibility of a North Korean regime collapse due to the threat posed by North Korea's nuclear weapons program and the growing instability of the Kim family regime.

What distinguished this "due diligence" view of unification from its predecessors was its call for prudence and preparation. This pragmatic view did not make heroic claims to defeat the enemy to the north like the winner-take-all view, nor did it make self-professed enlightened claims about cutting through Cold War barriers to engage distant brethren; instead, it argued that the time had come for Koreans and the other countries in Northeast Asia, given the uncertainties in the North, to start preparing for the unification process now.

As one expert close to Lee Myung-bak explained, if there were a bumper sticker for this theory, it would have read: "Prepare today, be lucky tomorrow." What this means is that the difficulties associated with unification require Koreans to benefit from a little bit of luck to manage all the challenges. But luck only comes to those who are prepared. Those who are not prepared are never in a position to be lucky. Thus, the "due diligence" concept was about pre-positioning oneself to be ready should the fateful day arrive. This view, its proponents argued, was eminently more practical and sensible than Sunshine era's simply wishing unification would go away forever. Moreover, the "due diligence" view made no normative assessment of unification—it was a view that could be espoused by hardliners or soft-liners alike. Though the conservative Lee presidency ended a decade of progressive rule in Korea, this view on unification did not fit easily on the ideological spectrum between Sunshine Policy on the left and "winner takes all" on the right. In sum, conservatives may want to take North Korea by force, progressives may want to engage the North, but this view worried that North Korea may just fall into the South Korean lap one day. And if South Koreans do not take the lead in preparing, it is hard to imagine that other countries would do the same.

This view differed from the Sunshine Policy in one important respect. Preparation for unification did not entail engagement with North Korea. Promises of President Lee Myung-bak's "Vision 3000: Denuclearization and Openness" proposal to bring North Korean income per capita to US $3,000 were political statements of interest in engagement, but these were highly conditional on North Korean security concessions rendering them impracticable. Instead, the focus was on preparing the South Korean people, not North Koreans. As the opening vignette of this chapter recounted, the Unification ministry took resources once used for inter-Korean economic cooperation by the previous administrations and focused it on large gatherings in major hotels attended by foreign policy luminaries to talk more openly about unification as a part of Korea's destiny. The political objective of these pragmatic efforts was to reverse a decade of "non-thinking" about unification, according to its proponents. Differently, critics would point out that the North had killed the largest number of South Koreans in decades during this period, while continuing to develop its nuclear program.

Unification "Jackpot"

A final version of unification was advanced under President Park Geun-hye and evolved from the earlier "due diligence" view proposed under Lee. Like her predecessor, Park also called for proactive preparation for unification, but supplemented this with a positive, normative framing of unification. The bumper sticker for this view, as laid out in her first presidential press conference in January 2014, was of unification as a "bonanza" or "jackpot" for Korea and her neighbors:

> Reunification is *daebak* [a jackpot]. Some Koreans oppose reunification for fear the costs would be too high. I believe reunification would be a chance for the economy to make a huge leap.[15]

According to this "jackpot" view, unification should be reimagined or envisioned as a process that could offer opportunities for growth, investment, and peace to both Koreas and to all Korean people. This view of unification does not see the process as a winner-takes-all one (unification by force), or something to be feared and delayed indefinitely (Sunshine Policy), or even something that we must reluctantly prepare for ("due diligence"). Instead, it conceptualizes unification as an opportunity for all Korean people and its neighbors:

> I believe that the Republic of Korea will similarly reach ever greater heights after unification. The northern half of the Korean Peninsula will also experience rapid development. A unified Korea that is free from the fear of war and nuclear weapons will

be well positioned to make larger contributions to dealing with a wide range of global issues like international peace-keeping, nuclear non-proliferation, environment and energy, and development. Furthermore, as a new distribution hub linking the Pacific and Eurasia, it is bound to benefit the economies of East Asia and the rest of the world.[16]

The jackpot theory of unification included elements of its predecessors. Though at the opposite end of the ideological spectrum from progressive *minjung* thinking, the jackpot theory of unification did share the normative framing of unification as a positive outcome—something that would help to rid Korea of its ills. For Park, this theme resonated with an overarching domestic political message (albeit unsuccessful) of a kinder and gentler brand of conservatism to bring more happiness to Korean society.

The jackpot theory was similar to the pragmatic view on unification in that it left space for engagement with North Korea to achieve a vision of unification, but in a highly conditional way that effectively rendered it impracticable. Park's unification policy was based on diplomacy she termed "Trustpolitik." This concept sees trust as existing in two interrelated forms. One form of trust is related to confidence-building measures—small steps taken over time that reassure each side that their actions are guided by specific rules and norms, and that they can expect the other party to abide by the same rules in the future. This type of trust is built up primarily through cooperation in areas covering non-traditional security or shared public goods like humanitarian assistance or environmental protection. The other side of trust is likened to "credible deterrence"—for instance, if you break the rules, then you will assuredly be punished. Rather than being something dark and negative, "Trustpolitik" and "jackpot" narratives aimed to paint unification as something bright and hopeful.

Confidence-building measures, cooperation, and transparency can pave the way for better inter-Korean relations and peaceful unification in the future. For the North, however, these messages from the South's president, and daughter of former military dictator Park Chung-hee, did not elicit any trust, or belief that she was serious.

The jackpot theory of unification shared similarities with its immediate predecessor in its efforts to socially re-engineer the negative discourse on unification that had taken root over the previous fifteen years. The government operationalized this concept in two ways. First, it produced reports quantifying the "jackpot"—for example, a 2014 National Assembly Budget Office report found that unification would cost KRW 4.65 quadrillion by 2060, but estimated the benefits to be three times greater, at KRW 14.5 quadrillion.[17]

Second, it spent the annual inter-Korean economic cooperation budgets not on economic projects with the North but on conferences and public relations campaigns in the South to help South Koreans think about unification in positive terms. Of note was the effort to reach out not just to college-age students, but to the very young. Pamphlets depicting cartoon figures following the rainbow to a jackpot (in other words, unification) at the end made obvious the desire to connect South Koreans of all ages to a positive identification with unification. Even the use of the colloquial term *daebak* was meant to appeal to a younger generation's slang usage. In 2014, KRW 14.3 billion from the inter-Korean economic cooperation budget was spent on the construction of the Center for the Future Unified Korean Peninsula, to educate the younger generation of South Koreans on the importance of unification. Other unification education activities undertaken by the government included organizing a cohort of teen reporters comprised of fifth- and sixth-grade students to participate in hands-on activities like posting articles about unification and publishing offline newsletters. The government also invested in producing and distributing music videos and animations to ensure that young people can more easily access and understand unification issues. Despite her eventual impeachment and imprisonment, according to her supporters, Park deserves credit for creating a paradigm for thinking positively about unification. Yet critics of Park (and Lee Myung-bak) would argue that inter-Korean relations had stalled during the almost ten years of conservative rule, while Pyongyang continued to make progress with its nuclear program.

Where Are We Today?

President Moon Jae-in's "peace diplomacy" was essentially a continuation of Sunshine Policy and *minjung* ideology. The Moon government felt especially motivated to pursue engagement with North Korea for three expedient reasons: (1) Lee Myung-bak and Park Geun-hye's successive terms in office led to neglect (in Moon's eyes) of inter-Korean relations for nearly a decade; thus, there was much lost ground to make up; (2) Obama's policy of "strategic patience" with North Korea exacerbated the damage done by South Korean conservative governments to the Sunshine project; and (3) Trump's threats to take the peninsula to war in 2017 had to be reversed.

The progressive Moon government saw inter-Korean reconciliation and peace as a coordination game, not a conflict game. The goal was to create institutions of communication and economic cooperation, and greater transparency and predictability across the DMZ. The Moon Jae-in presidency's policies largely fall within the framework of the Sunshine Policy, though it went under a more general name, "A Peaceful and Prosperous Korean Peninsula."[18] It made similar assumptions about the problem and viewed inter-Korean reconciliation and peace as the best path to a soft landing. Like its predecessor, the strategy explicitly framed unification in normatively negative terms; instead, it focused on reconciliation between the two

Korean peoples, while leaving formation of a unified state to the distant future. Moon laid this out clearly in a speech in Berlin, where he said:

> We do not wish for North Korea's collapse, and will not work towards any kind of unification through absorption. Neither will we pursue an artificial unification. Unification is a process where both sides seek coexistence and co-prosperity and restore its national community. When peace is established, unification will be realized naturally someday through the agreement between the South and the North. What my Government and I would like to realize is only peace.[19]

Moon's version of Sunshine Policy heavily emphasized race as a unifying element. This comports with traditional *minjung* ideology and was evident particularly in the 2018 summit meeting in Pyongyang. In Moon's speech at the May Day Stadium in Pyongyang to tens of thousands of North Koreans, he reemphasized that:

> Our people are outstanding. Our people are resilient. Our people love peace. And our people must live together. We had lived together for five thousand years but apart for just 70 years. Here, at this place today, I propose we move forward toward the big picture of peace in which the past 70-year-long hostility can be eradicated and we can become one again.[20]

For the three days of Moon's visit to the North, all of the ceremony and substance played heavily to racial unity as an element to transcend all political differences.

President Yoon Suk-yeol's administration, in power since May 2022, departs from Sunshine Policy, and most resembles the "due diligence" policies of the Lee Myung-bak government. This partly stems not only from personnel shared between the two administrations, but also from Yoon's "Global Pivotal State" (GPS) strategy, with South Korea playing a larger role on the global stage. This means less of a focus on promoting inter-Korean reconciliation as the main aim of the government. Yoon is not against providing economic assistance to the North. His "Audacious Initiative" offers to provide economic and infrastructure assistance, as well as humanitarian assistance (food, health), and to promote a "green détente" (environment) on the peninsula, which could be seen in the context of a "due diligence" policy to prepare for unification. Critics would argue, however, that the "due diligence" approach will again result in no inter-Korean engagement, and therefore will be counterproductive.

North Korea's Reaction to Sunshine Policy

North Korea has countered the Sunshine Policy with its own "Moonshine Policy," exploiting the South's generosity, while offering little in return. Pyongyang engaged in economic cooperation projects like the Mount Geumgang tourism complex and Kaesong industrial site, but only because these self-contained projects offered the regime hard currency without requiring a significant opening up of the system to outside influence. Both projects remained fenced off from the rest of the North Korean population, with only selected "loyalists" and young women (who were seen to be less prone to uprising) permitted to participate, and even these North Koreans were prohibited from interacting with South Korean managers.

The Moonshine Policy particularly exploited the Sunshine Policy's implicit assumption that the nuclear and missile programs of the North were not the main problem. Sunshine Policy generally played down the nuclear threat, seeing it largely as symptomatic of a deeper problem the regime had with insecurity and lack of reform. Sunshine Policy assumed that once this insecurity was rendered moot and reform took hold, the nuclear problem would take care of itself. Moonshine Policy's solution to this was to have its cake and eat it: Pyongyang would accept all that Sunshine Policy provided to encourage reform, and would shape it in a way that would be minimally invasive to the regime. At the same time, it would continue to pursue nuclear weapons.

At the end of the Moonshine period, the North had more nuclear weapons than before, had avoided a near-collapse of the regime, and had US $3 billion in cash from the South. At the end of the Sunshine period, the South had given political legitimacy to a progressive view on North Korea (in the past, such views were considered not only illegitimate but treasonous by law), had created two economic cooperation projects with the North, and had earned one South Korean president (Kim Dae-jung) a Nobel Peace Prize.

North Korean Views on Unification

We know virtually nothing about how North Korean people view unification outside of the official statements because of the government's tight control of information and suppression of speech. While a multitude of surveys document how South Koreans, particularly younger generations, remain fairly ambivalent about the economic burdens associated with unification, no comparable studies are available in the North. To the extent data exists, it is survey work on North Korean defectors. This does offer us some insights, although the sample of survey participants is obviously biased toward people who chose to leave the North.

A 2018 study by CSIS is one of the few efforts to understand how people *inside* North Korea think about unification.[21] Working through non-governmental organizations on the Sino-North Korean border, the study asked respondents in North Korean markets three questions about unification to gain a sense of their beliefs, hopes, and aspirations:

Will unification happen in your lifetime? / 평생 살아가는 동안 통일이 실현될 수 있다고 생각합니까?

Do you think unification is necessary? / 통일이 꼭 필요하다고 생각하십니까?

If yes, what is the main reason that unification should occur? / 질문에 '네'라고 답하셨으면 주된 이유가 무엇입니까?

a. Shared ethnicity (North and South are "one race") / 동일한 민족이기 때문에

b. Increase economic growth / 경제 성장을 위해서

c. Increase international influence / 국제적인 영향력 강화를 위해

d. Reduce costs related to division of peninsula / 한반도 분단 상태로 인한 비용 절감을 위해

e. To defend against outside threats / 외부의 위협을 막기 위해

f. Resolve issue of separated families / 이산가족 문제를 해결하기 위해

Although the sample size of the survey was small given concerns about preserving anonymity and the safety of the interviewees, the results of the study are quite novel and interesting.

North Koreans apparently deem unification to be quite important: 94 percent of the participants thought unification was necessary, and a majority (58 percent) said unification will happen in their lifetime. The average North Korean citizen defines the unification discourse in ethnic terms—that is, unification should happen because of Koreans' shared ethnicity. Only a small number define it in terms of national security.

These views are almost the opposite of how South Koreans look at unification. A 2017 KINU survey of South Koreans found just 138 of 1,000 respondents felt unification was "very necessary." Almost three times that number thought it was "not very necessary."[22] A 2019 survey by the Institute for Peace and Unification Studies at Seoul National University found only 3 percent thought unification was necessary in order to give North Koreans a better life.[23]

Shared ethnicity was cited by 44.1 percent of North Koreans as the main reason unification should occur. Almost 30 percent cited economic reasons for unification. Notably, a very small number saw the need for unification in terms of improving Korea's position against external threats, or in terms of increasing Korea's external influence.

On the question about the timing of unification, the majority of North Korean respondents said unification would happen in their life-time. Of those under 50, 71 percent said unification would happen during their lifetime. Of those over 50 years of age, 47 percent said it would happen during their lifetime while 32 percent said it would not. Again, this is the obverse of South Koreans: younger generations in South Korea are less interested in unification compared with their elders. The gap in opinions may stem from a romanticized view of unification still held among North Korean people learned from govern-ment propaganda. As noted earlier, however, views of unification in the South are contested and subject to political change, as well as affected by the economic realities of German unification—something about which the North Korean public probably has little information about.

What Would a United Korea Look Like?

In the aftermath of German unification, Victor hosted an event in 1997 at Georgetown University, bringing together officials from

South Korea's Unification ministry and German officials who had worked on unification. During the two days, the German officials explained many of the problems they encountered, ranging from currency union to unemployment. The South Korean officials furiously scribbled down everything that was said, much more than would be necessary for a report cable. When we asked at the coffee break what they found so important, they excitedly said that the discussion was extremely interesting to them. Victor's first thought was, "You mean, you have not studied all of these problems already?"

Victor left with an uncomfortable feeling that the South Korean government had not yet fully absorbed the lessons of German unification. South Koreans subsequently became acutely aware of the difficulties and complexities of uniting the two countries economically, politically, and socially. They learned quickly that these difficulties would be exponentially more acute given the even wider socio-economic gap between the two Koreas compared with those of the two Germanies.

What would unification look like? A lot depends on the way it comes about—through a "hard" or "soft" landing. Let us assume it will be somewhere along this spectrum, with the South leading the process. What is critically important when considering Korean unification is the size of the population, the economic gaps, and per capita GDP. Certainly, there are a great many other important factors, such as its technological base, natural resource endowment, and economic infrastructure. But when dealing with an economy as underdeveloped as that of the North, what policymakers will want to know immediately is how many new mouths there will be to feed. In the case of Germany, when the reunification of East and West took place in 1989, the West had a population about four times that of the East, the former sitting at 61.7 million and the latter at 16.4 million. The gap in average individual wealth, while great, wasn't drastic, with the average westerner making just under US $21,000 per year and the average easterner around US $7,300. Also, from the early 1970s, the two Germanies engaged in fairly extensive trade, with West Germany being the East's second-greatest trade partner (8 percent of total) behind the Soviet Union.[24] And through the 1970s and 1980s, millions of East and West German individuals would travel back and forth across the border, with tens of thousands even being allowed to resettle from East to West.[25] And among those who weren't able to travel, a significant number were at least able to watch West German television programs, establishing a degree of familiarity and comfort with daily life across the border.[26]

In the year 2023, North Korea's estimated 25.9 million people are half of the South's 51.8, with South Koreans, on average, being more than twenty-seven times more prosperous than their northern counterparts.[27] Further, since 1953, North Korea had been wholly isolated from the South, with no travel, trade, or social contact. Only the North Korean elite who live in Pyongyang have access to a wide range of Western (largely European, not American), Chinese, and Russian goods, but nothing along the lines of what the South enjoys as a globalized, cosmopolitan society. The elite in Pyongyang have access to cellphones, but these only work in North Korea. Access to the internet is limited to a North Korean "intranet" (not connected to the worldwide web). Outside Pyongyang, residents live in relative squalor, akin to the lives of their South Korean counterparts some forty or fifty years ago. Studies emerged that estimated the cost of unification to be extremely expensive. While there was a wide range of estimates, none looked particularly pleasing to the South Korean leaders. For instance, already in 1992, the Economist Intelligence Unit estimated it would cost US $1.09 trillion to bring North Korea's per capita GDP to within 70 percent of that of the South. The following year, the KDI estimated a figure of US $658.2 billion. In

1997, scholar Marcus Noland cited a figure of up to US $3.17 trillion to get the North Koreans to within 60 percent of their southern counterparts.[28] A 2005 RAND Corporation study cited a range of US $50 billion to US $667 billion over five years.[29] In 2009, Credit Suisse estimated unification costs at US $1.5 trillion. And a 2010 expert survey by the Federation of Korean Industries (FKI) came up with a cost of at least US $3 trillion.[30] In a 2015 report, the ROK's National Assembly Budget Office (NABO) estimated that it would take fifty years and more than US $4 trillion if unification were to occur peacefully from 2026 to 2076 without additional humanitarian aid or economic investment in the years prior to unification. In a different scenario, where there is an expansion of humanitarian aid to North Korea for ten years prior to unification, NABO estimated that a peaceful unification would take thirty-nine years and about US $2.6 trillion. If there was an expansion of economic investment for ten years prior, a peaceful unification was estimated to take thirty-four years and cost roughly US $2 trillion.[31]

The first and foremost challenge of unification will be taking care of the shorter-term, immediate needs of the North Korean people. The closer to a hard landing the unification scenario is, the more important this challenge will prove to be. It has been estimated that the initial emergency relief costs—of food, medical care, daily necessities, and in some cases, shelter—will at the very least total some US $250 million per month and could reach as much as US $1.25 billion.[32] This initial huge humanitarian relief effort targeted at the neediest—children, pregnant and breastfeeding mothers, the elderly, and orphans—will be an important first step in establishing legitimacy in the eyes of the North Korean people and potentially quelling any large-scale rebellion or unrest, and mass migration. The critical political message will be to demonstrate to the North Korean people that unification will bring them no harm, will not deprive them of their possessions, and will provide them with benefits. That will be the way to win hearts and minds.

One crucial prerequisite for the successful unification of the Korean Peninsula will be infrastructure and transportation. Despite being 20 percent larger (North Korea's territory is 74,898 square miles, while that of the South is 61,963 square miles), North Korea has less than a quarter of the total roadways of South Korea, and when paved roads alone are compared, North Korea actually has less than 1 percent (449 miles) of the South's total length (57,660 miles).[33] Furthermore, North Korea has just 39 airfields with paved runways, as compared to the South's 71, and has 264 merchant marine vessels, whereas South Korea has 1,904. North Korea's eight major ports—Chongjin, Haeju, Hungnam, Nampo, Rajin, Songnim, Sonbong, and Wonsan—too, will need refurbishment as they have fallen into great disrepair in recent years. One area where the North does have somewhat of a comparative advantage is in rail, with 4,620 miles of total length compared to 2,472 miles in the South. But the North's system is highly inefficient and, for the most part, has not been modernized since the Japanese occupation, and therefore its reconstruction will be another priority. An extensive road and rail network connecting North and South, and the necessary shipping and air infrastructure needed for northern Korea to connect to the global economy will be critical for the longer-term strength of a unified Korean economy.

Another infrastructure priority will be building up North Korea's communications network. Its sixty-year, self-imposed isolation has made it truly unmatched in this regard. For instance, in South Korea, when landlines and mobile phones are taken together, there are about 1.8 phones for each of the country's 51.8 million people. In North Korea, by contrast, there are a mere 7.18 million phones (fixed lines and mobile cellular combined) for its population of 25.9 million—

that's just one phone for every four people.[34] Furthermore, the near-complete absence of the internet in North Korea will need to be addressed. As a whole, South Korea currently has nearly 114 million IP addresses.[35] In the North, this number is only 1,657, and only a handful of people have experience of or exposure to the internet, with the majority only being allowed to access to the North Korean "intranet."[36]

A third crucial infrastructural priority will be power and energy. Currently, South Korea's installed electricity generating capacity (135.789 million kW) is sixteen times greater than that of the North (8.413 million kW), and this will greatly constrain northern growth.[37] South Korea also consumes 128 times more oil on daily basis (2.599 million barrels-per-day [bbl/day]) than does its northern neighbor (20,300 bbl/day), and has over 600 times more length in oil and gas pipelines in its territory.[38] Wholesale refurbishment of the electricity grid, as well as the use of nuclear energy, will be needed to supplement North Korea's hydropower network.

A fourth area of concern will be population control. The two issues here are migration and labor. The removal of restrictions on the North Korean people and opening of the border will create tremendous migration pressures. Years ago, it was estimated that the numbers of northerners heading south could number as many as 7 million—nearly one-third of the population.[39] Today, 2.6 million seems a more likely figure, but a substantial one all the same.[40] Northerners will migrate in search of opportunity. Southerners will press northward for land based on genealogical claims before Korea's division. There would likely have to be immigration-type check-points for north–south travel, and perhaps a visa system.

In the North, the group with the highest rate of unemployment after unification will be the military. North Korea currently has a standing active-duty military of 1.28 million—the third largest in the world—and an estimated 600,000 reserve personnel.[41] Some of this force (up to 200,000) might be retrained and incorporated into a future Korean military to make up for anticipated demographic shortfalls in the South, but most of it will no longer be needed.[42] Finding work for this ex-military population will be a high priority in terms of stabilization, to avoid large numbers of unemployed men who could be vulnerable to radicalization. One possibility for a great many of these individuals may be in a work program for the reconstruction of North Korean infrastructure outlined above. History has shown that large-scale public works projects are almost a requirement for dealing with unemployment and social security problems in transitional societies, and northern Korea would likely be no exception to this rule.

But the majority of the northern populace won't easily incorporate into a unified Korean society and government without massive educational reform and retraining. In spite of the fact that North Korea currently claims a 99 percent literacy rate and enrollment ratios of 96 percent for primary and secondary schooling, the content and quality of North Korean education is suspect. Comparatively, when East and West Germany reunified, some 80 percent of easterners had to undergo retraining to be able to function competitively in the unified German economy[43] and, as noted earlier, the gaps between East and West were not nearly as great as those between the two Koreas.

Much like the education system, the health sector of northern Korea will have to be basically rebuilt from the ground up as well. Past cases of broken health systems in Africa and Asia have shown that key priorities in reconstitution are targeted revitalization of hospitals and clinics, upgrading of skilled healthcare professionals, detailed surveys of existing health assets, and costing exercises with concrete targets for training. Therefore, the unified Korean government will, at least for a time, have to deal with a greatly stressed social services system, providing high levels of educational, unemployment, and healthcare subsidies, and will have to watch out for potential social disorder such as increased rates of alcoholism, drug addiction, gambling, or crime.

Another potentially problematic issue will be the monetary union of the North and South. While unification will almost certainly bring a unified economy monetized by the South Korean won, the unified Korean government will need to avoid some of the dislocating effects of the German experience of monetary union. Germany decided to convert East German marks at parity with those of the West, producing an artificial increase in East German incomes and leading to high inflation rates and about 40 percent unemployment in the initial transitional stages.[44] The monetary union will therefore need to occur in a way that accomplishes multiple, competing objectives simultaneously. The exchange rate must be set to avoid inflation and unemployment. Yet it must also be close enough to parity to allow northerners sufficient wealth to forestall a massive exodus to the south. Additionally, the North Korean won must be kept low enough to ensure that northern wages are still competitive enough to attract foreign investment and to take advantage of the combination of southern capital and technology and abundant, low-cost northern labor. This will most certainly be a hotly debated issue in a unified Korean government and will require policymakers to strike multiple, simultaneous fine balances between competing interests.

A final set of issues has to do with the social aspects of unifying the Korean Peninsula. One problem is that of transitional justice. How should a unified Korean government deal with the elites from the former North Korean regime? Should there be international tribunals, such as those for the former Yugoslavia, or truth and reconciliation commissions, as were undertaken in South Africa at the end of apartheid? How many of the former ruling elite should be tried and prosecuted and how many should be given a "golden parachute"? As controversial as it may seem, past cases show that stabilization requires consensus, including with stakeholders and pre-existing elements of the former regime. These issues could prove to be explosive in the context of a unified Korea.

A second social hurdle will be the problem of large-scale inter-Korean, regional political divisions. While most Koreans will welcome the marriage of northern labor and southern capital as beneficial to the united Korean economy as a whole, South Korean labor groups may be less enthusiastic. The downward pressure on South Korean wages resulting from the unification with the North could cause the working class in South Korea to look north with contempt. The wider southern population, too, while initially welcoming unification, may grow increasingly resentful at the costs they must bear in the form of taxes and social welfare burdens to assimilate the North. And in spite of Korea's vibrant nationalism, the more educated and affluent southerners could even come to have superiority complexes regarding their northern brethren. And the northerners, in turn, may see their southern counterparts as immoral, materialistic, money-crazed, and radically individualistic. The democratically elected politicians tasked with bridging these divisions and catering to their various interests will certainly have their hands full.

The third and perhaps most important and deep-seated social obstacle to overcome has to do with the North Korean people themselves. North Korea is *the* most isolated country on earth, and has been for most of the past eight decades. When unification happens, northerners will undoubtedly face a period of psychological dislocation as decades of indoctrination and brainwashing under the "Great Leader" lose all meaning. Many of the 33,000 North Koreans living in the South are living proof of this. The latest figures show that the primary, middle, and high school dropout rates are three times higher among North Koreans (3 percent) than for the South Korean population as a whole.[45] The unemployment rate among North Koreans in the South (around 7.5 percent) is double the South Korean national average (around 3.7 percent), and their monthly wages (US $1,902) are almost less than half of wages among average Seoulites (US $3,510).[46] Nearly one-third of North Korean defectors continue to identify themselves as "North Korean," as opposed to "Korean" or "South Korean," even after years of living in the South. Because of these integration challenges, the suicide rate among North Korean defectors was 10.1 percent in 2019, more than double that of the South Korean populace (4.5 percent).[47]

Some might argue that the challenges of unification are insurmountable. But pessimism of that nature underestimates the determination and sheer grit of the Korean people. As our history of Korea has demonstrated, this is a country that has made a regular habit of turning adversity into opportunity. Undeniably, the Koreans must approach the unification project with a will to succeed. Moreover, they will need help from the United States and other regional partners.

Unification in a Changing Regional Context

Our history of the Korean Peninsula in this book underscores how the swirl of external forces has often shaped the fate of Koreans. That would not be the case with unification. Whether unification comes through a hard or soft landing, it will be the pivotal event of the century for Asia. There is nothing more consequential in international relations than when borders change, old states die, and new states are born. Korean unification will shape—not be shaped by—the external environment. In this sense, regional powers will be reacting to Korean unification, rather than trying to shape it. They will, of course, all seek to influence it, but few would consider opposing it.

The United States' position has been clear—it supports a unified Korea that is whole and free. This stated position dates back to the George W. Bush administration and has been consistently applied since. The United States would be a major supporter of the unification process, providing economic assistance, political support, and security backing (for example, by removing nuclear weapons from northern Korea and providing external security guarantees). It would strongly support a united Korea's needs in the UN, World Bank, IMF, and other international institutions. The alliance would most likely remain intact after unification, though it could look different in the sense that US ground troops would probably leave Korea and be replaced by a largely air and naval presence. The US would want strong alliances with Japan and Korea—its two key allies—as the core of its position in Asia.

A united Korea would see advantage to maintaining the alliance given the geopolitical situation—a united Korea, presumably democratic, would share a land border with China and Russia, two illiberal regimes. Even as a country with a population approaching the size of Japan, Korea will still be dwarfed by its continental neighbors. Moreover, history has shown that states of different regime types that share a border often suffer from insecurity spirals. The future Sino-united Korean border may not look like the DMZ, but it would certainly be a more fortified border than that between the United States and Canada (for example). The same is likely for the border with Russia. It should be noted that the necessity of the US for Korea's future is generally a bipartisan view within the body politic of Koreans. In 2000, North Korean leader Kim Jong-il reportedly told Kim Dae-jung that the US presence would still be critical for Korea after unification.

It is often assumed that Japan would oppose Korean unification. Concerns about resurgent nationalism in a unified Korea directed against its former colonizer animates this view. But we think this is short-sighted thinking. First, it is in Japan's interest, as well as all the regional powers, that a united Korea is friendly to it. For Japan to oppose or impede unification would almost certainly ensure that a unified Korea would see Japan as hostile. Thus, Japan should seek to support and endear itself to the newly formed nation, not be antagonistic toward it. Second, the economic potential of a united Korea would provide great opportunities for Japan; like the US, Tokyo's voice in international financial institutions would be supportive of and positive regarding unification. Third, Japan would most likely be a supporter of humanitarian assistance for the unification process. Traditionally, Japan was one of the two largest donors of food to North Korea during the famine years in the 1990s through the World Food Program (the other was the US). Fourth, the costs for Tokyo of the status quo with North Korean nuclear tests and hundreds of ballistic missiles pointed at Japan are unacceptably high. Japanese officials in fact have been magnanimous in urging US and South Korean colleagues to have more serious discussions about unification contingencies, not even asking that they participate in this due to the South's sensitivities. Finally, it would be incumbent on a united Korean government to provide as much information as possible on the cases of North Korean abductions of Japanese citizens from the 1970s. Resolving this important political and human rights issue would go a long way to build good faith in bilateral relations.

Traditionally, Russia has been an ally of North Korea and President Vladimir Putin has made efforts to build personal trust with former leader Kim Jong-il. The relationship has become more estranged under Kim Jong-un after the barrage of missile and nuclear tests under his rule. Lately however, the war in Ukraine and bad state of relations with the West has caused Moscow to draw closer to a China–North Korea–Russia triangle of support. This has caused Russia to withhold support for UN Security Council resolutions against North Korean ballistic missile and nuclear tests when once it supported them. Perhaps in return, North Korea reportedly is helping to arm Russia with munitions for the Ukraine War and was one of the first to recognize Russia's gains in the Donbas region.

Nevertheless, it is likely that Russia would support unification of the peninsula under the South. Opposing or blocking unification would make no tactical sense for Russia as it would ensure a hostile relationship with a united Korea. There may be some in Russia who see a peace dividend in ending the burgeoning and unstoppable ballistic missile and nuclear weapons programs that they once helped to establish. However, the overwhelming reason Russia would support the process is that which has motivated Russia for over a century—the economic opportunities presented by the Korean Peninsula serving as a land bridge connecting Russian energy resources to East Asia. Russia would be a big supporter of refurbishing and expanding the railway infrastructure in North Korea. It would also likely support a standardization of the gauge systems between the two countries. Moscow might also seek cooperative warm-water port arrangements that provide them year-long maritime access to the Pacific. There would be strategic costs to a united Korea, with a US military presence adjacent to Russian territory once the North Korean buffer state has gone, but one lesson from the modern history of Russian interaction on the Korean Peninsula is the consistent pursuit of economic opportunity. Unification should provide this to Moscow in a way that trumps any security concerns.

The one party that may not support Korean unification is China. While China has seen vigorous internal debates about where its interests lie on the peninsula, Beijing does not appear to be in favor of active discussions with any party about how to prepare for sudden change there. China's net assessment is that the strategic costs of unification of the peninsula outweigh the potential benefits. The majority of China's Korea experts have always believed that North Korea, no matter how uncompromising and difficult the regime in Pyongyang may be, provides a strategic buffer against the US–Japan–South Korea "iron triangle," and they would be hard-pressed to accept its dissolution. For this reason, Beijing protected North Korean interests during both leadership transitions in 1994 and 2012, warning others not to intervene. While Xi Jinping was initially cool toward Kim Jong-un during Kim's first half-decade in office, Xi took a more proactive stance of building ties from 2018 in response to Trump's efforts at summit diplomacy with Kim. While Beijing responds to US entreaties for help with its junior ally with claims that it has no control over North Korea, clearly Beijing has more influence than others and it would like to keep it that way.

While there would be future economic opportunities presented by unification, China is the only country in the region that is benefiting economically from North Korea today. Since 2009, it has inked a series of agreements allowing it to extract minerals, coal, and other resources from the North at below-market prices to economically benefit two provinces, Jilin and Liaoning. It could lose these arrangements (or have them wholly renegotiated on less favorable terms) with a united Korea.

Regarding national security issues, China's reticence over North Korea's barrage of missile tests in 2022 and nuclear weapons development suggests that it does not see any major security threats, and thus a peace dividend from their removal is not a strong motivating factor. Moreover, the end of the North Korea threat would provide an opportunity for the United States to consolidate its position with its allies in East Asia, remove a North Korea contingency from its military planning, and allow it to focus on only one major regional contingency in Taiwan, presumably with a stronger air and naval presence on the Korean Peninsula.

These geostrategic risks to China are not inevitable and more cooperative security arrangements could be managed through increased regional dialogues before the unification process begins. But China has been unwilling to engage in such discussions at the official or expert levels for two decades now, despite numerous requests by the US and South Korea. Indeed, both conservative and progressive governments in South Korea have sought a US–China–South Korea trilateral strategic dialogue on unification, which China has not agreed to engage in. It is to be hoped that, with increased dialogue among South Korea, US, and China, Beijing's party stalwarts would not view a united Korea as a geostrategic risk.

The path to a reunified Korea would undoubtedly carry risks and is likely to experience setbacks, but in the end it would constitute a watershed in the politics, security, and economics of East Asia. In juxtaposition to its past, the reunified Korean Peninsula will be less impacted by external forces and will be more the shaper and generator of change. With a population assuredly growing past 100 million, it would be a state of significant size with considerable human capital. It will generate a security dividend for Koreans and for the region as tensions across a divided peninsula dissipate, and it will be a militarily stronger Korea. Through its economic integration, the two Koreas will boast capital, technology, labor, and drive that will generate growth and profit for all in the region. The external powers with an interest in Korea—the US, Japan, China, and Russia—which once determined Korea's fate, will seek to build good relations with the new entity, given its critical geostrategic position and economic promise. Indeed, a unified Korea will mark the beginning of a new history for Koreans and for all people of the region.

EPILOGUE

South and North Korea continue to occupy the world's attention as of 2023. A country that in 1945 was celebrating its independence, and was getting ready to start the next chapter in its history, has become two very different countries exactly seventy years after the end of the Korean War. The very fact that South Korea has become one of the most popular Asian destinations for tourists, while only a handful of tourists made their way to North Korea annually even pre-Covid-19, is telling in and of itself. In fact, "Korea" is today commonly used to refer to South Korea. For many, the South has become the representative of the whole of the Korean Peninsula. Seoul has "won" the battle for recognition against the North. The key question is whether this will remain the case in the future. Our assessment is that the answer is yes. North Korea will continue to attract the attention of policymakers, security officials, and human rights advocates across the world on account of the dangers and hazards it presents to the world and to its own people. After all, of the two Koreas it is the one that genuinely threatens regional stability, especially thanks to its nuclear weapons and missiles, and that has curtailed the civil liberties of its citizens. South Korea, however, will continue to draw the attention of most other people, whether economists studying the secrets of one of the biggest economies in the world, researchers and engineers seeking to develop new technologies, military leaders in search of security partners, or pop and film aficionados looking for the latest hit.

And what about Koreans themselves? What do they want for their future? When it comes to North Koreans, there is little trustworthy information we can rely on. But North Koreans free to speak, often refugees, report that their countrymen are no different from people elsewhere in the world. They want food on their table, a good education for their children, and to enjoy their lives. When Victor negotiated with North Koreans over their nuclear weapons, or when Ramon interacted with North Korean officials and researchers, they saw interlocutors not with horns on their heads, but normal people who liked to talk about their children, hobbies, and the challenges of work/life balance. But even in these conversations, there were things that could not be discussed simply because North Koreans had not had the opportunity to experience them; one had to tread carefully so as not to create an awkward silence that manifested the country's isolation. This basic lack of opportunity for the North Korean people is by far the biggest threat to the ruling Kim family, not the South or the US. We do not wish to venture whether North Korea will open up. There have been many false starts in the past, after all. Yet, at the very least, the Kim family will have to find ways to satisfy the needs of the country's population. Repression can only go so far.

If we had to pinpoint the most important variable for change in North Korea, it would have to be the marketization of the economy.

During the famine in the mid-1990s, markets in North Korea grew out of the breakdown of the government public distribution system or ration system. The government basically allowed the people to fend for themselves to avoid starvation. And they created markets—large and small, official and unofficial—that have flourished since as the alternative to the state's provision of goods. Most North Koreans get everything they could possibly want today through the markets, whether this is food, bicycles, designer clothing, or the latest smuggled South Korean music. According to a CSIS study by Victor, most North Koreans live within at most a day's bicycle ride from a market and, in many cases, in much closer proximity.

These markets have created more than material benefits for the North Korean people; they have uprooted the rigid social class structure. Market entrepreneurs, or *donju*, are now wealthy individuals who gain access to goods, services, and privilege in society outside of the state-based *seongbun* caste system that favors only party officials, the military, and those with hereditary ties with past revolutionaries. Markets have also created an independence of thought among North Koreans. The ubiquitous propaganda and ideological training of the Kim family's teachings leave little room for citizens to ponder anything else. But the material benefits provided by markets and the access to information about the outside world have created a space between state and society that was previously non-existent. In the CSIS survey mentioned in the previous chapter, for example, North Korean citizens admit that they know of people who criticize and ridicule the government in private for its incompetence.[1] Citizens get all of their goods from the market rather than from the state rations, and for that reason they trust information from the market more than they trust propaganda from the government.

Marketization of North Korea has uprooted the patriarchal social structure. The vast majority of citizens who operate in the markets as buyers or sellers are the women of the country. In that regard, they represent the leading edge of social change in the country. They are the breadwinners of the family. They are the entrepreneurial class of the country. They are arguably the most "cosmopolitan" and global of North Korea's citizenry. They are also those most resistant to any effort by the government to curb market forces. The government is wedded to these markets because they tax them and because the markets help to stabilize prices and prevent hyperinflation. But at times, the government will crack down on the markets in order to reduce the amount of personal savings and independence in the country. The anecdotal evidence of popular resistance to the state always centers on local officials trying to shut down a market or imposing extra tax burdens on the markets. A number of scholars have argued that these markets are creating a nascent civil society in North Korea, where people develop relationships, seek information, and build trust among themselves and beyond the reach of the long arm of the state.[2]

It is unlikely that the Kim family leadership would embrace these markets as a force for opening and liberalization of the country. The markets are a dual-edged sword—they benefit the state, but they are also a threat to state control over society. For this reason, if change were ever to come to the country, it is likely it would be generated from the bottom up rather than from the top down. And the nature of this change would most likely be sudden and violent rather than gradual and peaceful. The possibility of an enlightened and reform-minded leadership in North Korea has been posited with each leadership transition from Kim Il-sung to Kim Jong-il, and from Kim Jong-il to Kim Jong-un. The November 2022 unveiling of Kim Jong-un's school-aged daughter, Kim Ju-ae, will again give rise to speculation about a new generation of the Kim family that might be more enlightened. While the authors would very much welcome that, we have been around long enough to see these theories debunked time and time again.

As for South Koreans, they share the goals and aspirations of citizens in fellow developed countries: to maintain a good standard of living together with their loved ones, have fulfilling careers, and travel the world. Interestingly, a growing number of South Koreans think that being a good citizen and contributing to society is as or more important than being of Korean origin to be considered (South) Korean. Unafraid of the North, which many do not see as a real threat after all, aware that reunification will take time, increasingly proud of their country, and accustomed to traveling overseas, South Koreans' perception of themselves has evolved. This is something that politicians and other leaders have to grapple with.

But Korea, of course, remains divided. For many Koreans on both sides of the 38th parallel, their preferred future also includes unification. When this might happen is anyone's guess. Certainly, we as experts cannot hazard predictions. The reader of this book might pick up the newspaper tomorrow and read that the two Koreas are unifying because of the sudden collapse of the North and would not be especially surprised. Or, the reader might return to this book a little over two decades from now with the division of Korea now one century old and still not be surprised. That is how wide the range of probability— or lack of certainty—is regarding Korea's fate. The resilience of the North Korean regime after the collapse of the Soviet Union and its satellite states, and after the gut-wrenching famine of the mid-1990s, is admirable in a way. Against all odds, the small, isolated regime has survived while bigger counterparts have collapsed. In that sense, the story of North Korea resonates with the history of Korea. But at the same time, North Korea is resilient until the day that it is not. At that point, its demise will be less surprising to the world than its unexpected survival decades after the end of the Cold War.

Certainly, many Koreans and interested parties would like any process leading to the two Koreas becoming one to proceed slowly and follow a period of reconciliation and rapprochement. Others would like the process to move ahead more quickly, especially those who can still remember a single Korea and want to witness unification with their own eyes. Yes, there are also Koreans opposed to unification. But, of course, they express this view when the question is asked in the abstract. If, and when, the time for (re)unification comes, we suspect that most Koreans will rally behind the cause. And they will succeed, as they have done throughout history.

POSTSCRIPT
THE KOREAS CONTINUE TO DIVERGE

The year 2023 and the start of 2024 served to make clear the growing divergence between the two Koreas. South Korea continued down the path of greater economic, political, diplomatic, security, and cultural heft and engagement with the rest of the world. North Korea focused on the narrow path of military engagement with Russia, a country whose leader had decided to invade a neighbor.

South Korea's Pivotal Year

South Korea has only continued to go from strength to strength throughout 2023–4. Yoon Suk yeol's Global Pivotal State (GPS) strategy has been vindicated by the incipient emergence of a G7+ grouping in which G7 members, led by the United States, work together with other like-minded partners across multiple areas covering a wide range of economic, security, and political issues. South Korea was also invited to the G7 summit held in Hiroshima in May 2023.[1] More broadly, Yoon Suk-yeol had a particularly active foreign policy agenda which included the first-ever standalone trilateral summit with the United States and Japan in Camp David; arguably the most successful and comprehensive ever South Korea–EU summit; state visits to the Netherlands, Qatar, Saudi Arabia, the UAE, the UK, the United States, and Vietnam; and attending the NATO Summit for the second year in a row, this time hosted in Vilnius.[2]

Furthermore, South Korea became a strategic actor well beyond the Korean Peninsula. As Russia's invasion of Ukraine raged on, South Korea's transfer of artillery ammunition to the countries directly supporting Kyiv helped the Ukrainian armed forces to continue to defend their country. Credible media reports by the likes of the *Washington Post* and others noted that South Korea provided more artillery shells to Ukraine than all European countries combined throughout 2023.[3] In fact, arms sales became yet another tool in South Korea's kit to boost ties with multiple countries across different parts of the world.[4] And Seoul's Indo–Pacific Strategy, launched in late 2022, helped to bring growing ties with countries such as Australia, Canada, France, and Germany, which have a keen interest in the region. In the meantime, relations with India and across Southeast Asia also continued to strengthen.

At the same time, South Korea's cultural clout continued to grow. Blackpink, BTS's Suga, Ive, Seventeen, and Twice were among the many K-pop stars embarking in world tours. Perhaps even more tellingly, many of these stars were also the faces of American and European fashion, tech, and luxury brands, as they have become among the most recognizable stars worldwide. At the Milan and Paris fashion weeks, for many the pinnacles of the fashion world, it became difficult *not* to spot a K-pop star in the front row of the top designers' shows. As CNN explained, fashion industry insiders estimate that up to half of media exposure during fashion shows is related to K-pop artists, well above Hollywood actors or pop stars from elsewhere.[5] More bluntly, *GQ* wrote that "we're squarely in fashion's K-pop era."[6]

Beyond pop, Netflix announced an eye-watering US $2.5 billion investment in Korean dramas, movies, and unscripted shows over four years.[7] This deal made sense when considering that 16 of the platform's 100 most-watched series in the first half of 2023 were in Korean. Dramas such as *The Glory* and reality show *Physical: 100* became global hits.[8] The house of Mickey Mouse saw first-hand the importance of adding K-dramas to its offering. Superhero drama *Moving* became the most streamed international original Disney+ show globally in 2023, part of the platform's "gold rush" for Korean content.[9]

In the meantime, Korean food has gone mainstream. Growing up in New York, Victor remembered one Korean restaurant in Manhattan's garment district (now the teeming Koreatown section of the city). Growing up in Madrid, Ramon found it difficult to find proper Asian food, period. Yet, as of 2024, the United States, Spain and the rest of Europe, and almost every part of the world can boast of good-quality Korean restaurants, a Korean fried chicken outlet, and supermarkets selling kimchi. Even more humble Korean dishes such as corn dogs and *bunsik* snacks have become mainstream in the most fashionable cities across the world.

In the area of economics, South Korea continued its recovery from the Covid-19 pandemic as well as other external shocks such as the wars in Ukraine and Gaza and a sharp slowdown in China's economic growth. The resilience of the South Korean economy continued to be directly linked to its focus on innovation and new technologies. The likes of Samsung and SK continue to be among the manufacturers of the most advanced semiconductors, Hyundai has become one of the leaders in the electric vehicle market, LG is one of the biggest electric battery manufacturers, Doosan and Hanwha are among the leading firms in the "cobot" or collaborative robot sector, and South Korean shipbuilders account for three quarters of global green vessel orders. In fact, South Korea's Ministry of Trade, Industry and Energy reported that the country attracted US $32.72 billion in investment commitments in 2023—the highest amount ever.[10]

In the other direction, governments everywhere, from Europe to North America to the Middle East to South and Southeast Asia, competed to attract investment from South Korean firms. The Biden administration's Inflation Reduction Act helped make South Korean *chaebol* among the largest investors in the United States in areas such as clean energy and semiconductors.[11] Firms in the electric battery sector announced the opening of new facilities in the EU.[12] South Korean semiconductor firms also announced the opening of research facilities in Japan.[13] Indeed, Yoon's aforementioned busy international agenda was partly linked to foreign governments seeking to attract investment from South Korean firms. Thus, large business delegations traveled with the South Korean president during his state visits.

In short, South Korea is as globally popular, active, and impactful in 2024 as it has ever been. A question that we, the authors, often get is: "When will we see 'peak Korea'?" In other words, when will South Korea's influence in global affairs plateau, when will the "Korean Wave" reach its peak, and when, or if, will its tech-driven economy crash? We don't hold the answer to this question. The question has been around for decades already, a testament to the resilience of South Korea at the top of political, security, cultural, and economic developments. We are confident that South Korea will continue to thrive for years to come.

North Korea's Version of the Global Pivotal State

In North Korea, Kim Jong-un fashioned his own dangerous version of the "Global Pivotal State." He emerged from a three-year Covid-19 lockdown in 2023 with a desperate need for medical supplies, food, and fuel. Humanitarian organizations clamored about a grave situation on the ground not seen since the famine of the mid-1990s. At the elite level, Kim's last interaction with the world before the pandemic was the failure of summit diplomacy with Donald Trump. This not only caused a loss of face for the North Korean leader, but also cost him solicitations from Xi Jinping. Xi had refused to meet with Kim until Trump announced his intention to do so, after which Xi held five summits with the DPRK leader. Indeed, by the end of 2021, Kim had lost on his biggest diplomatic gambit ever, and his closest partner in the world, China, was nowhere to be found.

Then, the war in Ukraine changed everything.

In January 2023, the White House released satellite imagery of arms transfers from North Korea to the Wagner paramilitary group taking place at the Tumangang–Khasan railroad crossing in November 2022.[14] This was followed by the US Treasury Department's announcement of new sanctions in 2023 against Russian and North Korean entities connected to arms deals between the two countries.[15] Subsequent satellite imagery reports showed thousands of shipping containers of weapons moving from Najin port in North Korea to Dunay, Russia, and then by rail to the warfront via Tikhorestsk.[16]

In September 2023, Kim emerged from the pandemic lockdown and the personal embarrassment of the failed Trump diplomacy with a major summit trip to Russia, where Putin pledged to increase bilateral cooperation and Kim expressed outright support for Russia's war in Ukraine. North Korea expressly voted against all UN resolutions against Russia and quickly recognized the independence of the two Russian-occupied states—Donetsk People's Republic (DPR) and Luhansk People's Republic (LPR)—in eastern Ukraine.[17] Russia leveraged its position in the UN Security Council to block all UN-mandated punitive action in response to North Korean ballistic missile tests. Russia joined North Korea in condemning military exercises by the US, South Korea, and Japan, attesting that "Russia stands in the same trench with [DPRK]."[18] In a letter to Kim, Putin vowed to increase political, economic, and security ties with North Korea and said that North Korea's "firm support to the special military operation against Ukraine and its solidarity with Russia on key international issues highlight [their] common interests and determination to counter the policy of the Western group."[19]

Russia's need for munitions for the Ukraine war made it for the first time in history a supplicant of North Korea. Whereas in the past, North Korea's need for energy and debt relief defined the bilateral relationship, now Russia's need for ammunition and weapons put Kim Jong-un in the driver's seat.

Even more worrying is that the growing North Korea–Russia alignment likely extends beyond one-off arms-for-food deals to more robust high-end military technology transfer including military satellites, nuclear-power submarines, and ICBMs. First, there is a long history of bilateral missile cooperation dating back to as early as the 1960s when the Soviet Union provided the V-75 Dvina (SA-2a Guideline) surface-to-air missile to North Korea, which eventually became the latter's first missile system.[20] The Soviets also transferred other types of missiles, such as S-2 Sopka (SSC-2b SAMLET) coastal-defense cruise missile and P-20 (SS-N-2 STYX) anti-ship missile, and also gave technical training to North Korea on assembly and maintenance. Second, North Korea's ICBM and SLBM programs benefited significantly from the Soviet collapse in

1991, when North Korea recruited many Russian scientists and engineers who helped advance programs including the Hwasong-12 IRBM and Hwasong-14 ICBM which uses a modified North Korean version of the Soviet RD-250 engine.[21] Third, the three successful launches of the newest ICBM, the solid-fuel Hwasong-18, in 2023 are hard to explain certainly over such a short period of time, without outside help.

The implications of the growing military alignment between North Korea and Russia are vexing to say the least. The tactical advantage that each foe gains in expanding cooperation complicates the West's war efforts in Ukraine. It also complicates US efforts at shoring up extended deterrence on the Korean Peninsula with its South Korean ally as North Korea demonstrates increasingly more capable and potentially survivable ICBMs. In this regard, Putin may be trying to demonstrate that actions taken in Europe by the US will have consequences not just in that theater but also in the Indo-Pacific detrimental to US interests.

North Korea's post-pandemic version of its own "Global Pivotal State" engagement is not limited to Russia. Its relationship with Iran, Hezbollah, and Hamas has been manifested in its military wares showing up in the battlefield in the Gaza war in 2023–4 as well.[22] But its involvement in Ukraine has pulled the Korean Peninsula into the conflict as it has coincided with South Korea's role as one of the largest providers of materiel to Ukraine. All in all, Russia may be the biggest enabler of North Korea today, even more so than China. The latter has not been supportive of the denuclearization agenda and has not helped to bring Pyongyang back to the negotiating table, given the state of US–China relations. But Beijing reportedly has been opposed to more North Korean nuclear testing.[23] This stands in contrast to the burgeoning Russia–North Korea axis, which could accelerate North Korea's military satellite, nuclear submarine, and

ICBM programs. Such military cooperation could further embolden North Korea to employ nuclear coercion strategies as described in the National Intelligence Estimate on North Korea declassified towards the end of 2023.[24]

Will the Koreas continue to diverge?

In January 2024, Kim Jong-un announced that North Korea should consider the South as an "invariable principal enemy," to which the ideas of "reunification" and "reconciliation" do not apply.[25] Certainly, the two Koreas have grown apart over the decades. But as we show in our book, relations between the two countries ebb and flow. Even if they are far apart as we write these lines, there surely will be instances of rapprochement between the two in the future. As different as they are today, Korea's unified history will invariably bring them closer to each other.

ENDNOTES

1: Balance-of-Power Politics and the Occupation

1. Stephan Haggard and David C. Kang, eds., *East Asia in the World: Twelve Events that Shaped the Modern International Order* (Cambridge: Cambridge University Press, 2020).
2. Ch'oe Yŏng-ho, "The Kapsin Coup of 1884: A Reassessment," *Korean Studies* 6 (1982): 105–24.
3. S.C.M. Paine, *The Sino-Japanese War of 1894–1895: Perceptions, Power, and Primacy* (Cambridge: Cambridge University Press, 2002), Chapter 7.
4. Alfred Whitney Griswold, *The Far Eastern Policy of the United States* (New York: Harcourt Brace & Co., 1938), 125.
5. David P. Fields, *Foreign Friends: Syngman Rhee, American Exceptionalism, and the Division of Korea* (Lexington: University Press of Kentucky, 2019), 103.
6. Quoted in Arthur Judson Brown, *The Mastery of the Far East* (London: G. Bell and Sons, 1919), 202; emphasis added. Also see Theodore Roosevelt, "The World War: Its Tragedies and its Lessons," *Outlook (1893–1924)* 108, no. 4 (September 1914): 173–4.
7. Quoted in David Brudnoy, "Japan's Experiment in Korea," *Monumenta Nipponica* 25, nos. 1/2 (1970): 162.
8. Carter J. Eckert et al., *Korea, Old and New: A History* (Seoul: Ilchokak, 1990), 254–75.
9. Gregory Henderson, *Korea, the Politics of the Vortex* (Cambridge, MA: Harvard University Press, 1968).
10. Eckert et al., *Korea, Old and New.*
11. Ibid.
12. Ku Dae-yeol, *Korea under Colonialism: The March First Movement and Anglo-Japanese Relations* (Seoul: Royal Asiatic Society, 1985).
13. Ibid.

14. Lee Chong-Sik, *The Politics of Korean Nationalism* (Berkeley: University of California Press, 1963).
15. Ch'oe Yŏngho, Peter H. Lee, and Wm Theodore de Bary, eds., *Sources of Korean Tradition*, vol. 2 (New York: Columbia University Press, 2000).
16. Fields, *Foreign Friends*.
17. Kenneth M. Wells, "Background to the March First Movement: Koreans in Japan, 1905–1919," *Korean Studies* 13 (1989): 5–21.
18. Mark Clifford, *Troubled Tiger: Businessmen, Bureaucrats, and Generals in South Korea* (Armonk, NY: M. E. Sharpe, 1994), 26.
19. Eckert et al., *Korea, Old and New*, 281.
20. Today transliterated as *Dong-A Ilbo*.
21. Eckert et al., *Korea, Old and New*.
22. Mark E. Caprio, *Japanese Assimilation Policies in Colonial Korea, 1910–1945* (Seattle: University of Washington Press, 2009), 156.
23. Michael Breen, "Changing Identity: Koreans Told to Adopt Japanese Names," *Korea Times*, March 21, 2010, sec. National, https://www.koreatimes.co.kr/www/nation/2022/08/113_62759.html
24. Norman Pearlstine, "Commentary: Joshua Cooper Ramo's Korea Comments Contain Important Pieces of Truth," *Fortune*, February 12, 2018, https://fortune.com/2018/02/12/joshua-cooper-ramo-korea-nbc-winter-olympics/
25. Government General of Chosen, *Annual Report on Reforms and Progress in Chosen (Korea) 1938–39* (Keijo [Seoul]: Japanese Government General report, 1939), http://archive.org/details/annual-report-on-reforms-and-progress-in-chosen-korea-1938-39. Thanks to Hyewon Kang's research support for this data and citation.
26. Chung Young-Iob, *Korea Under Siege, 1876–1945: Capital Formation and Economic Transformation* (Oxford: Oxford University Press, 2006).
27. Sven Beckert, *Empire of Cotton: A Global History* (New York: Vintage, 2015), 311, 340–3.
28. Chung, *Korea Under Siege, 1876–1945*.
29. Eckert et al., *Korea, Old and New*.

2: Liberation, Division, and War

1. Emperor Hirohito's radio address, August 15, 1945.
2. Kim Jinwung, *A History of Korea: From "Land of the Morning Calm" to States in Conflict* (Bloomington: Indiana University Press, 2012), 387.
3. Peter Gatrell, *The Making of the Modern Refugee*, 1st edn (Oxford: Oxford University Press, 2013).
4. Wayne C. McWilliams, *Homeward Bound: Repatriation of Japanese from Korea After World War II* (Hong Kong: Asian Research Service, 1988).
5. J.L. Kaukonen, "The South Korean Wage Earner Since the Liberation," *Monthly Labor Review* 68, no. 4 (1949): 401–6.
6. "Final Text of the Communiqué," Department of State Office of the Historian: Foreign Relations of the United States: Diplomatic Papers, the Conferences at Cairo and Tehran, 1943, November 26, 1943, https://history.state.gov/historical-documents/frus1943CairoTehran/d343
7. Louis J. Halle, *The Cold War as History* (New York: Harper & Row, 1967), 202, note 1, as cited in Bok-ryong Shin, *The Politics of Separation of the Korean Peninsula, 1943–1953* (Seoul: Jimoondang, 2008), 43.
8. Arnold Toynbee, "Korea's Capacity of Independence January 31, 1945," Public Record Office, UKFO Research Department, Registry No. FO371/46468 X/PO5596, 1945, 1–4, as cited in Shin, *The Politics of Separation of the Korean Peninsula, 1943–1953*, 85.

9. William Stueck, "The United States, the Soviet Union, and the Division of Korea: A Comparative Approach," *Journal of American–East Asian Relations* 4, no. 1 (1995): 16.

10. Shannon McCune, "Physical Basis for Korean Boundaries," *Far Eastern Quarterly* 5, no. 3 (1946): 272–88.

11. James I. Matray, "Hodge Podge: American Occupation Policy in Korea, 1945–1948," *Korean Studies* 19 (1995): 17–38.

12. Bruce Cumings, *Origins of the Korean War*, vol. 1: *Liberation and the Emergence of Separate Regimes, 1945–1947* (Princeton, NJ: Princeton University Press, 1981), 128–9.

13. John Merrill, "The Cheju-Do Rebellion," *Journal of Korean Studies* 2 (1980): 139–97; Shin, *The Politics of Separation of the Korean Peninsula, 1943–1953*, chapter 17.

14. Suzy Kim, *Everyday Life in the North Korean Revolution, 1945–1950* (Ithaca, NY: Cornell University Press, 2013), chapter 2.

15. Matray, "Hodge Podge," 33.

16. Adam Cathcart and Charles Kraus, "Peripheral Influence: The Sinuiju Student Incident of 1945 and the Impact of Soviet Occupation in North Korea," *Journal of Korean Studies* 13, no. 1 (2008): 5.

17. Stueck, "The United States, the Soviet Union, and the Division of Korea," 24.

18. Kim, *A History of Korea*, 406.

19. Victor Cha, *Powerplay: The Origins of the American Alliance System in Asia* (Princeton, NJ: Princeton University Press, 2016), chapter 3.

20. Kim, *A History of Korea*, 407.

21. "Radio and Television Address to the American People on the Situation in Korea, July 19, 1950," The American Presidency Project, n.d., https://www.presidency.ucsb.edu/documents/radio-and-television-address-the-american-people-the-situation-korea

22. Robert L. Beisner, *Dean Acheson: A Life in the Cold War* (Oxford: Oxford University Press, 2006), 340. On the emotive nature of the U.S. reaction to the North Korean invasion, see Jonathan Mercer, "Emotion and Strategy in the Korean War," *International Organization* 67, no. 2 (April, 2013): 221–52.

23. Philip Caryl Jessup, *The Birth of Nations* (New York: Columbia University Press, 1974), 10.

24. Kim, *A History of Korea*, 419; "Host Nation—Republic of Korea," United Nations Command, accessed August 4, 2022, https://www.unc.mil/Organization/Contributors/; "American War and Military Operations Casualties: Lists and Statistics" (Washington, DC: Congressional Research Service, July 29, 2020); "6.25 전쟁 [Korean War]," National Museum of Korean Contemporary History: Ministry of Culture, Sports and Tourism, accessed August 4, 2022, http://www.much.go.kr/L/AQkhKt2MH3.do

25. Lee Jong Won, "The Impact of the Korean War on the Korean Economy," *International Journal of Korean Studies* V, no. 1 (Spring/Summer 2001): 98–9, 103–4.

3: The Koreas

1. North Korea restricts who can travel into and around the country, never mind who can visit the DMZ from its side of the border, and so it is not guaranteed that one will be able to visit the area.

2. Robert H. Ferrell, ed., "Eisenhower Diary Entry, 24 July 1953," in *The Eisenhower Diaries* (New York: Norton, 1981), 248.

3. "Kim Il-Sung Biography," KBS World Radio, 2020, https://world.kbs.co.kr/special/northkorea/index.htm?lang=e

4. James F. Person, "New Evidence on North Korea in 1956," in *Cold War International History Project Bulletin 16*, ed. Christian F. Ostermann (Washington, DC: Woodrow Wilson International Center for Scholars, 2007), 447–527, https://www.wilsoncenter.org/sites/default/files/media/documents/publication/CWIHP_Bulletin_16.pdf

5. Kongdan Oh and Ralph Hassig, *North Korea in a Nutshell: A Contemporary Overview* (Lanham, MD: Rowman & Littlefield, 2021), 71–5.

6. "Prisons of North Korea" (U.S. Department of State, 2016), https://www.state.gov/wp-content/uploads/2019/03/Prisons-of-North-Korea-English.pdf

7. Hong Yong-Pyo, *State Security and Regime Security: President Syngman Rhee and the Insecurity Dilemma in South Korea, 1953–60* (Basingstoke: Palgrave Macmillan, 2000), 138–41.

8. Kim Il-sung, "On Eliminating. Dogmatism and Formalism and Establishing Juche in Ideological Work," in *Kim Il Sung: Works*, vol. 9 (Pyongyang: Foreign Languages Publishing House, 1981), 402–25.

9. Victor Cha, *The Impossible State: North Korea, Past and Future*, updated edn (New York: HarperCollins, 2018), 114–15.

10. James Person (ed.), "New Evidence on North Korea's Chollima Movement and First Five-year Plan (1957–1961)," North Korea International Documentation Project 1 (Washington, DC: Woodrow Wilson International Center for Scholars, February 10, 2009), https://www.wilsoncenter.org/publication/new-evidence-north-koreas-chollima-movement-and-first-five-year-plan-1957-1961

11. Peter Moody, "Chollima, the Thousand Li Flying Horse: Neo-traditionalism at Work in North Korea," *Sungkyun Journal of East Asian Studies* 13, no. 2 (October, 2013): 211–33.

12. Clark W. Sorensen, "Success and Education in South Korea," *Comparative Education Review* 38, no. 1 (1994): 16.

13. Tim Kane, "Global U.S. Troop Deployment, 1950–2005" (Washington, DC: Heritage Foundation, May 24, 2006), 7, https://www.heritage.org/defense/report/global-us-troop-deployment-1950-2005

14. "ForeignAssistance.Gov—Country Summary," USAID Development Data Library, June 21, 2022, https://data.usaid.gov/Administration-and-Oversight/ForeignAssistance-gov-Country-Summary/k87i-9i5x

15. Alex Van Trotsenburg, "Korea and the World Bank Group: Life Starts at 60," World Bank Blogs, June 8, 2015, https://blogs.worldbank.org/eastasiapacific/korea-and-world-bank-group-life-starts-60

16. Katharine H. S. Moon, *Sex Among Allies: Military Prostitution in U.S.–Korea Relations* (New York: Columbia University Press, 1997).

17. Cha, *The Impossible State*, updated edn, 112.

18. Hans M. Kristensen and Robert S. Norris, "A History of US Nuclear Weapons in South Korea," *Bulletin of the Atomic Scientists* 73, no. 6 (November, 2017): 350.

19. Han Yong-Sup, "The May Sixteenth Military Coup," in Byung-Kook Kim and Ezra Vogel, eds., *The Park Chung Hee Era: The Transformation of South Korea* (Cambridge, MA: Harvard University Press, 2011), 50.

20. "Coup in South Korea," *New York Times*, May 17, 1961, sec. Archives, https://www.nytimes.com/1961/05/17/archives/coup-in-south-korea.html

21. Kim Hyung-A, "State Building: The Military Junta's Path to Modernity through Administrative Reforms," in Kim and Vogel, eds., *The Park Chung Hee Era*, 91–3.

22. "제1차 경제개발 5개년 계획 (1962–1966)" (First Five-year Economic Development Plan [1962–1966]), National Archives of Korea, n.d., https://theme.archives.go.kr/next/economicDevelopment/primary.do

23. The *chaebol* are family-owned industrial conglomerates spanning different economic activities and sectors, which have been dominant features of the South Korean economy since the 1960s.

24. *The Saemaul Undong Movement in the Republic of Korea: Sharing Knowledge on Community-Driven Development* (Mandaluyong City: Asian Development Bank, 2012), https://www.adb.org/sites/default/files/publication/29881/saemaul-undong-movement-korea.pdf

25. "Inter-Korean Dialogue, 1971–1972," Wilson Center Digital Archive, 2022, https://digitalarchive.wilsoncenter.org/collection/124/inter-korean-dialogue-1971-1972

26. Constitution of the Republic of Korea, December 27, 1972, https://en.wikisource.org/wiki/Constitution_of_the_Republic_of_Korea_(1972)

27. Kim Dae-jung, *Conscience in Action: The Autobiography of Kim Dae-Jung*, trans. Jeon Seung-hee (London: Palgrave Macmillan, 2019), 187–91.

28. Kane, "Global U.S. Troop Deployment, 1950–2005," 7.

29. Kim Seung-Young, "Security, Nationalism, and the Pursuit of Nuclear Weapons and Missiles: The South Korean Case, 1970–82," *Diplomacy & Statecraft* 12, no. 4 (December, 2001): 53–80.

30. Park Chung-hee, quoted in Don Oberdorfer, *The Two Koreas: A Contemporary History* (New York: Basic Books, 2001), 56.

31. Andrew H. Malcolm, "South Korea Is a Test of the Human Rights Issue," *New York Times*, May 1, 1977, sec. Archives, https://www.nytimes.com/1977/05/01/archives/south-korea-is-a-test-of-the-human-rights-issue.html

32. Henry Scott Stokes, "Foe of Seoul Regime Asks Decisions by U.S.," *New York Times*, September 16, 1979, sec. Archives, https://www.nytimes.com/1979/09/16/archives/foe-of-seoul-regime-asks-decision-by-us-opposition-chief-facing.html

33. Chun Young-gi and Kang Jin-kyu, "The Inside Story of the Park Chung Hee Killing," *Korea JoongAng Daily*, November 2, 2015, https://koreajoongangdaily.joins.com/2015/11/02/politics/The-inside-story-of-the-Park-Chung-Hee-killing/3011054.html

34. Kim Il-sung, "On Socialist Construction in the Democratic People's Republic of Korea and the South Korean Revolution," in *Kim Il Sung: Works*, vol. 19 (Pyongyang: Foreign Languages Publishing House, 1984), 236–84.

35. James F. Person, "The 1967 Purge of the Gapsan Faction and Establishment of the Monolithic Ideological System," North Korea International Documentation Project (Washington, DC: Wilson Center, 2014), https://www.wilsoncenter.org/publication/the-1967-purge-the-gapsan-faction-and-establishment-the-monolithic-ideological-system

36. Kim Il-sung, "Ten Principles for the Establishment of a Monolithic Ideological System" (Pyongyang: Foreign Languages Publishing House, 1974).

37. "Report on Work of Central Committee to the 5th Congress of Workers' Party of Korea," *Rodong Sinmun*, November 3, 1970.

38. *Rodong Sinmun*, April 11, 1963.

39. Cha, *The Impossible State*, updated edn, 190–2.

40. Ibid., 117.

41. Kim Il-sung and Lee Hu-rak, "Conversation Between Lee Hu-Rak and Kim Il Sung" (Pyongyang Government Building, November 3, 1972), South Korean Foreign Ministry Archive, History and Public Policy Program Digital Archive, https://digitalarchive.wilsoncenter.org/document/113235

42. *The Socialist Constitution of the People's Republic of Korea*, December 27, 1972, rev. 2016, https://www.constituteproject.org/constitution/Peoples_Republic_of_Korea_2016?lang=en

43. The Supreme People's Assembly of the Democratic People's Republic of Korea, "The Letter to the Congress of the United States of America," March 25, 1974, https://digitalarchive.wilsoncenter.org/document/letter-government-north-korea

44. Zhihua Shen and Yafeng Xia, *A Misunderstood Friendship: Mao Zedong, Kim Il-Sung, Sino-North Korean Relations, 1949–1976* (New York: Columbia University Press, 2018).
45. Kim Il-sung, "Ten Principles for the Establishment of a Monolithic Ideological System."

4: Change vs Continuity

1. Henry Scott Stokes, "South Korea Calls Presidential Vote," *New York Times*, November 10, 1979, sec. Archives, https://www.nytimes.com/1979/11/10/archives/south-korea-calls-presidential-vote-acting-chief-urges-constitution.html
2. Henry Scott Stokes, "7 Top Generals Are Held in Seoul: Military Power Struggle Is Seen," *New York Times*, December 14, 1979, sec. Archives, https://www.nytimes.com/1979/12/14/archives/7-top-generals-are-held-in-seoul-military-power-struggle-is-seen.html
3. "History," National Human Rights Commission of Korea, accessed August 11, 2022, https://www.humanrights.go.kr/site/homepage/menu/viewMenu?menuid=002001001002
4. Ibid.
5. Don Oberdorfer and *Washington Post* Staff Writer, "Blast Kills Top Aides to South Korean President," *Washington Post*, October 10, 1983.
6. "N. Korea's Flood Relief Aid for S. Korea in 1984," *KBS World*, March 22, 2018, http://world.kbs.co.kr/service/contents_view.htm?lang=e&menu_cate=history&id=&board_seq=275253
7. C.I. Eugene Kim, "South Korea in 1985: An Eventful Year Amidst Uncertainty," *Asian Survey* 26, no. 1 (1986): 72.
8. Special Reporting Team, "30 Years on, Son's Murder Still Haunts Family," *Korea JoongAng Daily*, January 12, 2017, https://koreajoongangdaily.joins.com/2017/01/12/socialAffairs/30-years-on-sons-murder-still-haunts-family/3028599.html
9. Fred Hiatt, "Death of Student Triggers Renewed Clashes in Seoul," *Washington Post*, July 6, 1987, https://www.washingtonpost.com/archive/politics/1987/07/06/death-of-student-triggers-renewed-clashes-in-seoul/511f991f-0eb7-491c-97c4-704563e3c73f/
10. Statistics Korea, "출생아수와 합계출산율" (Number of Births and Total Fertility Rate), 2022, https://kosis.kr/statHtml/statHtml.do?mode=tab&orgId=101&tblId=DT_POPULATION_06
11. "(6.29 선언) 직선제 개정관련 특별선언발표" ([June 29 Declaration] Announcement of a Special Declaration Related to the Amendment of the Direct Election), *MBC News*, June 29, 1987.
12. "The Apprenticeship," *KBS World Radio*, 2020, https://world.kbs.co.kr/special/northkorea/index.htm?lang=e.
13. Cha, *The Impossible State*, updated edn, 119.
14. *Rodong Sinmun*, November 25, 1981.
15. Kim Jong-il, *On the Juche Idea* (Pyongyang: Foreign Languages Publishing House, 1982).
16. William Chapman, "North Korean Leader's Son Blamed for Rangoon Bombing," *Washington Post*, December 3, 1983, https://www.washingtonpost.com/archive/politics/1983/12/03/north-korean-leaders-son-blamed-for-rangoon-bombing/ddec34cc-9c12-4fc6-bf75-36057091aa4e/
17. International Institute for Strategic Studies, *North Korea's Weapons Progammes: A Net Assessment* (London: Palgrave Macmillan, 2004).
18. Sergey Radchenko, "Sport and Politics on the Korean Peninsula—North Korea and the 1988 Seoul Olympics," North Korea International Documentation Project,

December 2011, https://www.wilsoncenter.org/sites/default/files/media/documents/publication/NKIDP_eDossier_3_North_Korea_and_the_1988_Seoul_Olympics.pdf

19. Kongdan Oh and Ralph Hassig, "North Korea Between Collapse and Reform," *Asian Survey* 39, no. 2 (1999): 287–309.

20. Clyde Haberman, "Koreans Install a New President," *New York Times*, February 25, 1988, sec. World, https://www.nytimes.com/1988/02/25/world/koreans-install-a-new-president.html

21. "2018_V_Industrial Relations," Korea Labor Institute, November 22, 2018, https://www.kli.re.kr/kli_eng/selectBbsNttView.do?key=381&bbsNo=35&nttNo=134320&searchY=&searchCtgry=&searchDplcCtgry=&searchCnd=all&searchKrwd=&pageIndex=1&integrDeptCode

22. Kim Hunjoon, "Seeking Truth After 50 Years: The National Committee for Investigation of the Truth About the Jeju 4.3 Events," *International Journal of Transitional Justice* 3, no. 3 (2009): 414.

23. "2018_V_Industrial Relations."

24. "2 Parties in Seoul Agree to a Merger with Ruling Group," *New York Times*, January 23, 1990, sec. World, https://www.nytimes.com/1990/01/23/world/2-parties-in-seoul-agree-to-a-merger-with-ruling-group.html

25. Victor Cha, *Beyond the Final Score: The Politics of Sport in Asia* (New York: Columbia University Press, 2009).

26. Roh Tae-woo, "화해와 협역의 새 시대 리관유 싱가폴 수상내외를 위한 만찬 만찬사" (A New Era of Reconciliation and Cooperation: Dinner for Prime Minister Lee Kuan Yew of Singapore), July 6, 1988.

27. Cha, *The Impossible State*, updated edn, 122.

28. Jacopo Prisco, "Ryugyong Hotel: The Story of North Korea's 'Hotel of Doom'," *CNN*, August 9, 2019, https://www.cnn.com/style/article/ryugyong-hotel-architecture-origins/index.html

29. Nicholas D. Kristof and Special Correspondent to the *New York Times*, "North Korea Bids Hello to the World," *New York Times*, July 1, 1989, sec. World, https://www.nytimes.com/1989/07/01/world/north-korea-bids-hello-to-the-world.html

30. David Holley, "Student Flies to N. Korea to Attend Event: S. Korea Dissident Defies Festival Ban," *Los Angeles Times*, July 1, 1989, https://www.latimes.com/archives/la-xpm-1989-07-01-mn-2269-story.html

31. Cha, *The Impossible State*, updated edn, 120.

32. Nicholas D. Kristof, "Crackdown in Beijing; Troops Attack and Crush Beijing Protest; Thousands Fight Back, Scores Are Killed," *New York Times*, June 4, 1989, sec. World, https://www.nytimes.com/1989/06/04/world/crackdown-beijing-troops-attack-crush-beijing-protest-thousands-fight-back.html

33. "Nicolae Ceaușescu," 2022, https://www.britannica.com/biography/Nicolae-Ceausescu

5: Diverging Paths

1. Conversation with regular visitor to North Korea, July 24, 2022.

2. Marcus Noland, "Famine and Reform in North Korea," *Asian Economic Papers* 3, no. 2 (2004): 4–5.

3. Sam Jameson, "Yeltsin Ends S. Korea Visit with Treaties," *Los Angeles Times*, November 21, 1992, https://www.latimes.com/archives/la-xpm-1992-11-21-mn-752-story.html

4. "Agreement on Reconciliation, Non-aggression, and Exchanges and Cooperation Between South and North Korea," United Nations Peacemaker, December 13, 1991, https://peacemaker.un.org/korea-reconciliation-nonaggression91

5. Yoon Dae-Jyu, "The Constitution of North Korea: Its Changes and Implications," *Fordham International Law Journal* 27, no. 4 (2003): 1289–305.
6. Kristensen and Norris, "A History of US Nuclear Weapons in South Korea," 350.
7. Kang Yoon-seung, "Samsung Chief Lee, Staunch Force Behind S. Korea's Rise to Tech Powerhouse, Dies," *Yonhap News Agency*, October 25, 2020, https://en.yna.co.kr/view/AEN20201025001354320
8. Kim Suk-Young, *K-Pop Live: Fans, Idols, and Multimedia Performance* (Stanford, CA: Stanford University Press, 2018).
9. Josette Shiner, "Kim Il-Sung Asks for Thaw in Ties with the U.S.," *Washington Times*, April 15, 1992.
10. "Fact Sheet on DPRK Nuclear Safeguards," International Atomic Energy Agency, July 25, 2014, https://www.iaea.org/newscenter/focus/dprk/fact-sheet-on-dprk-nuclear-safeguards
11. "IAEA and DPRK: Chronology of Key Events," International Atomic Energy Agency, July 25, 2014, https://www.iaea.org/newscenter/focus/dprk/chronology-of-key-events
12. Interview with Ministry of Foreign Affairs of the Republic of Korea official, Seoul, September 18, 2008.
13. Barbara Demick, "Some Grief over Death of North Korea Leader False, Defectors Say," *Los Angeles Times*, December 21, 2011, sec. World & Nation, https://www.latimes.com/world/la-xpm-2011-dec-21-la-fg-korea-fake-mourning-20111222-story.html; Chico Harlan, "North Korea Invokes Great Leader, Kim Il Sung, in Power Transfer to Grandson," *Washington Post*, December 24, 2011, https://www.washingtonpost.com/world/asia_pacific/north-korea-invokes-great-leader-kim-il-sung-in-power-transfer-to-grandson/2011/12/23/gIQAUVDDFP_story.html; Kim In-hua, "Ask a North Korean: Were North Koreans Genuinely Grieving When Kim Il Sung Died?," *NK News*, January 30, 2020, https://www.nknews.org/2020/01/ask-a-north-korean-were-north-koreans-genuinely-grieving-when-kim-il-sung-died/; Thae Yong-ho, *Passcode to the Third Floor: An Insider's Account of Life Among North Korea's Political Elite*, trans. Robert Lauler (New York, NY: Columbia University Press, 2024). The book will be published this April: https://cup.columbia.edu/book/passcode-to-the-third-floor/9780231198868.
14. Joel S. Wit, Daniel B. Poneman, and Robert L. Gallucci, *Going Critical: The First North Korean Nuclear Crisis* (Washington, DC: Brookings Institution Press, 2004), 257, 281, 314.
15. Andrew Pollack, "New Korean Leader Agrees to Pardon of 2 Ex-dictators," *New York Times*, December 21, 1997, sec. Archive World, https://www.nytimes.com/1997/12/21/world/new-korean-leader-agrees-to-pardon-of-2-ex-dictators.html
16. The Washington Consensus was a series of market-friendly policies promoted by the IMF, the World Bank, and the US Department of the Treasury—three institutions located in Washington, DC, within walking distance of each other. The policies included liberalization, deregulation, and privatization of the economy, considered to be necessary for the economy to function properly and for developing countries to become developed.
17. "공식활동 개시" (Start of Official Activities), *KBS News*, December 12, 1996.
18. Kongdan Oh and Ralph C. Hassig, *North Korea through the Looking Glass* (Washington, DC: Brookings Institution Press, 2000), 52.
19. Ibid., 97–9.
20. Lee Shin-Wha, "Responses to North Korea's 'Food Refugees,'" *Security Dialogue* 30, no. 1 (1999): 122–4.
21. Cha, *The Impossible State*, updated edn, 193.
22. Ibid., 197.
23. See annual *Food Aid Flows* reports from the World Food Programme, at https://www.wfp.org/fais

24. Mary Jordan, "President's Son Jailed in S. Korea," *Washington Post*, May 18, 1997, https://www.washingtonpost.com/archive/politics/1997/05/18/presidents-son-jailed-in-s-korea/f1357937-41a9-43eb-9b30-5516f1afc76d/

25. "Letter of Intent of the Government of Korea," International Monetary Fund, December 3, 1997, https://www.imf.org/external/np/loi/120397.htm

26. *The Jangmadang Generation*, documentary film, 51 mins, January 2017, https://www.nkmillennials.com/

27. Barbara Demick, *Nothing to Envy: Ordinary Lives in North Korea* (New York: Spiegel & Grau, 2009).

28. Lee Kyu-Sung, *The Korean Financial Crisis of 1997: Onset, Turnaround, and Thereafter* (Washington, DC: World Bank Publications and the Korea Development Institute, 2011), 114.

29. Soohyun Christine Lee, "Democratization, Political Parties and Korean Welfare Politics: Korean Family Policy Reforms in Comparative Perspective," *Government and Opposition* 53, no. 3 (2018): 518–41.

30. Robyn Klingler-Vidra and Ramon Pacheco Pardo, "Legitimate Social Purpose and South Korea's Support for Entrepreneurial Finance Since the Asian Financial Crisis," *New Political Economy* 25, no. 3 (2020): 337–53.

31. *The Socialist Constitution of the People's Republic of Korea.*

32. Bill Clinton, *My Life* (London: Hutchinson, 2004), 938.

33. Kim, *Conscience in Action*, 508–10.

34. "Perry Testimony on North Korea," U.S. Department of State Archive, October 12, 1999, https://1997-2001.state.gov/policy_remarks/1999/991012_perry_nkorea.html

35. Calvin Sims, "North and South Koreans Meet on a Mountain Path," *New York Times*, February 15, 2000, https://archive.nytimes.com/www.nytimes.com/library/world/asia/021500nkorea-skorea.html

36. Koreanet, *The Reunion Awaited for Half a Century (2000)*, film, 47 mins, 2018, https://www.youtube.com/watch?v=TFaeLdD2fd4

37. See data from the Ministry of Unification of the Republic of Korea, https://www.unikorea.go.kr/eng_unikorea/

38. Kim Suk Hi and Im Eul-Chul, "The Kaesong Inter-Korean Industrial Complex: Perspectives and Prospects," *North Korean Review* 5, no. 2 (2009): 83.

39. "Japan-DPRK Pyongyang Declaration," Ministry of Foreign Affairs of Japan, September 17, 2002, https://www.mofa.go.jp/region/asia-paci/n_korea/pmv0209/pyongyang.html

40. Lee Jong-Heon, "Analysis: Hyundai Facing Payments Scandal," *UPI*, February 27, 2003, https://www.upi.com/Business_News/2003/02/27/Analysis-Hyundai-facing-payments-scandal/72521046368610/

41. Kim and Im, "The Kaesong Inter-Korean Industrial Complex: Perspectives and Prospects," 82–3.

42. Kim, *Conscience in Action*, 733–7.

43. George W. Bush, "President Delivers State of the Union Address," White House President George W. Bush Archives, January 29, 2002, https://georgewbush-whitehouse.archives.gov/news/releases/2002/01/20020129-11.html

44. Don Oberdorfer, "My Private Seat at Pyongyang's Table," *Washington Post*, November 10, 2002, https://www.washingtonpost.com/archive/opinions/2002/11/10/my-private-seat-at-pyongyangs-table/824c6e6f-4971-4784-b14c-d771b1cf49ac/

45. "About Us: Our History," KEDO (Korea Peninsula Energy Development Organization), 2022, http://www.kedo.org/au_history.asp

46. Youngshik D. Bong, "The Gay Rights Movement in Democratizing Korea," *Korean Studies* 32 (2008): 86–103.

47. "History," KEDO.
48. Don Kirk, "Road Accident Galvanizes the Country: Deaths in Korea Ignite Anti-American Passion," *New York Times*, July 31, 2002, sec. World, https://www.nytimes.com/2002/07/31/news/road-accident-galvanizes-the-country-deaths-in-korea-ignite.html
49. "Growing Anger of Koreans over Acquittal of US Solders [*sic*] who Killed School Girls," *Dong-A Ilbo*, December 2, 2002, https://www.donga.com/en/article/all/20021202/226116/1
50. "Korean Students Attack US Troops," *BBC News*, July 30, 2002, sec. Asia-Pacific http://news.bbc.co.uk/1/hi/world/asia-pacific/2161150.stm
51. Stephan Haggard and Marcus Noland, "Repression and Punishment in North Korea: Survey Evidence of Prison Camp Experiences," East-West Center Working Papers—Politics, Governance and Security Series 20 (October 2009), https://www.eastwestcenter.org/publications/repression-and-punishment-north-korea-survey-evidence-prison-camp-experiences
52. Park Yoon-bae, "Kim Jong-Un's Fears about Hallyu," *Korea Times*, August 4, 2021, https://www.koreatimes.co.kr/www/opinion/2022/07/164_313356.html
53. Statistics Korea, "출생아수와 합계출산율" (Number of Births and Total Fertility Rate).
54. Eleanor Jawon Choi and Hwang Jisoo, "Transition of Son Preference: Evidence from South Korea," *Demography* 57, no. 2 (2020): 627.
55. Cho Nam-Joo, *Kim Jiyoung, Born 1982*, trans. Jamie Chang (London: Liveright, 2020), 85.
56. Ibid., 85.
57. Cho Chi-hyoung, "[Law Talk] Abolishing the Hoju System," *Korea Herald*, April 6, 2010, https://m.koreaherald.com/view.php?ud=20050323000033
58. Oleg Dyachenko, "Hallyu, K-Pop! Inside the Weirdest, Most Lucrative Global Frenzy in Music," *Quartz*, July 30, 2016, https://qz.com/725161/kpop-feature/
59. See the yearbook of migration statistics issued by the Korea Immigration Service: "통계연보" (Statistics Annual Report), Ministry of Justice Korea Immigration Service, accessed August 12, 2022, https://www.immigration.go.kr/immigration/1570/subview.do?enc=Zm5jdDF8QEB8JTJGYmJzJTJGaW1taWdyYXRpb24l MkYyMjglMkZhcnRjbExpc3QuZG8lM0ZyZ3NCZ25kZVN 0ciUzRCUyNmJic0NsU2VxJTNEJTI2cmdzRW5kZGVTdHIlM0QlMjZpc-1ZpZXdNaW5lJTNEZmFsc2UlMjZwYWdlJTNEMSUyNmJic09wZW5Xcm RTZXElM0QlMjZzcmNNoQ29sdW1uJTNEJTI2c3JjaFdyZCUzRCUyNg%3 D%3D
60. OECD, *Recruiting Immigrant Workers: Korea 2019* (Paris: Organisation for Economic Co-operation and Development, 2019), 43–66, https://www.oecd-ilibrary.org/social-issues-migration-health/recruiting-immigrant-workers-korea-2019_9789264307872-en
61. See "통계연보" (Statistics Annual Report).
62. Seol Dong-Hoon and John D. Skrentny, "Ethnic Return Migration and Hierarchical Nationhood: Korean Chinese Foreign Workers in South Korea," *Ethnicities* 9, no. 2 (2009): 147–74.
63. Ha Shang E., Cho Soo Jin, and Kang Jeong-Han, "Group Cues and Public Opposition to Immigration: Evidence from a Survey Experiment in South Korea," *Journal of Ethnic and Migration Studies* 42, no. 1 (2016): 136–49.
64. "Policy on North Korean Defectors," Ministry of Unification of the Republic of Korea, accessed July 26, 2022, https://www.unikorea.go.kr/eng_unikorea/relations/statistics/defectors/

65. Timothy S. Rich et al., "South Korean Perceptions of North Korean Immigration: Evidence from an Experimental Survey," *Political Science* 72, no. 2 (2020): 77–92.
66. Anna Fifield, "Seoul Success," *Washington Post*, August 3, 2018, https://www.washingtonpost.com/graphics/2018/world/a-new-generation-of-north-korean-defectors-is-thriving-in-seoul/; *The Jangmadang Generation*, documentary film.
67. "DPRK Successfully Conducts Underground Nuclear Test," *KCNA*, October 9, 2006.
68. International Institute for Strategic Studies, *North Korea's Weapons Programmes*.
69. Gi-Wook Shin, *Ethnic Nationalism in Korea: Genealogy, Politics, and Legacy* (Stanford, CA: Stanford University Press, 2006), 91–2.
70. *The Socialist Constitution of the People's Republic of Korea.*
71. Suh Dae-Sook, "Military-first Politics of Kim Jong Il," *Asian Perspective* 26, no. 3 (2002): 145–67.
72. Interview with long-term resident in North Korea, July 9, 2021.
73. Demick, *Nothing to Envy.*
74. Prisco, "Ryugyong Hotel: The Story of North Korea's 'Hotel of Doom.'"
75. Kee B. Park and Edward I. Ham, "North Korea's Surprisingly Robust Healthcare System," *Global Asia* 16, no. 3 (2021): 66–72.
76. Alastair Gale, "Orascom Suffers Static in North Korean Venture," *Wall Street Journal*, January 1, 2016, http://www.wsj.com/articles/orascom-suffers-static-in-north-korean-venture-1451628004
77. "A Sick State," *Korea JoongAng Daily*, September 10, 2008.
78. "S. Side Urged to Receive NDC Inspection Group," *KCNA*, May 22, 2010.
79. The Joint Civilian–Military Investigation Group, *Investigation Result on the Sinking of ROKS* Cheonan (Seoul: Ministry of National Defense of the Republic of Korea, 2010).
80. "KPA Supreme Command Issues Communiqué," *KCNA*, November 23, 2010.
81. "North Korean Leader Kim Jong-Il Dies of 'Heart Attack,'" *BBC News*, December 19, 2011, sec. Asia, https://www.bbc.com/news/world-asia-16239693
82. Demick, "Some Grief over Death of North Korea Leader False, Defectors Say"; Harlan, "North Korea Invokes Great Leader, Kim Il Sung, in Power Transfer to Grandson"; Kim, "Ask a North Korean: Were North Koreans Genuinely Grieving When Kim Il Sung Died?"
83. "Kim Jong-Il State Funeral Held in North Korea," *BBC News*, December 28, 2011, sec. Asia, https://www.bbc.com/news/world-asia-16342315

6: An Open South, a Closed North

1. "Missiles of North Korea," *CSIS Missile Threat*, March 24, 2022, https://missilethreat.csis.org/country/dprk/
2. Taekbin Kim, "Who Is Purged? Determinants of Elite Purges in North Korea," *Communist and Post-Communist Studies* 54, no. 3 (September, 2021): 73–96.
3. "What is Known about North Korea's Brutal Purge?," *BBC News*, December 13, 2013, sec. Asia, https://www.bbc.com/news/world-asia-25362732
4. Jung Pak, *Becoming Kim Jong Un: Understanding North Korea's Young Dictator* (New York: Ballantine Books, 2020).
5. Choi Song Min, "Mandatory Military Service Extends to Women," *Daily NK*, January 28, 2015, https://www.dailynk.com/english/mandatory-military-service-extends/
6. "Report on Plenary of WPK Committee," *KCNA*, March 31, 2013.
7. Victor Cha and Lisa Collins, "The Markets: Private Economy and Capitalism in North Korea?," *Beyond Parallel*, August 26, 2018, https://beyondparallel.csis.org/markets-private-economy-capitalism-north-korea/

8. Ibid.; Jieun Baek, *North Korea's Hidden Revolution: How the Information Underground Is Transforming a Closed Society* (New Haven, CT: Yale University Press, 2016); *The Jangmadang Generation*, documentary film.

9. Interview with long-term resident in North Korea, July 6, 2021.

10. Choe Sang-Hun, "North Korea's Party Congress Explained: A Coronation for Kim Jong-Un," *New York Times*, May 5, 2016, sec. World, https://www.nytimes.com/2016/05/06/world/asia/north-korea-congress.html

11. Nathalie Alonso, "A Journalist's Unmatched Access," *Columbia College Today*, September 13, 2021, https://www.college.columbia.edu/cct/issue/fall-2021/article/journalists-unmatched-access

12. Interview with long-term resident in North Korea, June 28, 2021; interview with long-term resident in North Korea, July 6, 2021.

13. "Missiles of North Korea," *CSIS Missile Threat*.

14. "Kim Jong Un Makes New Year Address," *KCNA*, January 1, 2018.

15. Ramon Pacheco Pardo, *North Korea–US Relations: From Kim Jong Il to Kim Jong Un* (London: Routledge, 2019), 147–81.

16. Kim Gamel, "Trump Drafted Tweet on Pulling Military Dependents from S. Korea," *Stars and Stripes*, September 10, 2018, https://www.stripes.com/news/woodward-trump-drafted-tweet-on-pulling-military-dependents-from-s-korea-1.546846

17. Victor Cha, "Giving North Korea a Bloody Nose Carries a Huge Risk to Americans," *Washington Post*, January 30, 2018, https://www.washingtonpost.com/opinions/victor-cha-giving-north-korea-a-bloody-nose-carries-a-huge-risk-to-americans/2018/01/30/43981c94-05f7-11e8-8777-2a059f168dd2_story.html

18. Euan McKirdy, "North Korea's Ruling Family: Who Was Kim Jong Nam?," *CNN*, February 16, 2017, https://www.cnn.com/2017/02/16/asia/kim-jong-nam-profile/index.html

19. "Kim Jong-Nam: VX Dose Was 'High and Lethal,'" *BBC News*, February 26, 2017, sec. Asia, https://www.bbc.com/news/world-asia-39096172

20. "Remarks by President Obama and President Park of South Korea in a Joint Press Conference," Obama White House Archives, May 7, 2013, https://obamawhitehouse.archives.gov/the-press-office/2013/05/07/remarks-president-obama-and-president-park-south-korea-joint-press-confe

21. Park Geun-hye, "Opening a New Era of Hope," *Korea Herald*, February 25, 2013, https://www.koreaherald.com/view.php?ud=20130225000590

22. Madison Park, "What Went Wrong on Sewol?," *CNN*, May 15, 2014, https://www.cnn.com/2014/05/15/world/asia/sewol-problems

23. Ser Myo-ja, "Seven-hour Mystery About Park, Sewol Solved," *Korea JoongAng Daily*, March 28, 2018, https://koreajoongangdaily.joins.com/2018/03/28/politics/Sevenhour-mystery-about-Park-Sewol-solved/3046205.html

24. "2015 MERS Outbreak in Republic of Korea," World Health Organization, 2022, https://www.who.int/westernpacific/emergencies/2015-mers-outbreak

25. "South Korea's Presidential Scandal," *BBC News*, April 6, 2018, sec. Asia, https://www.bbc.com/news/world-asia-37971085.

26. Ock Hyun-ju, "More than 2 Million Take to Streets Calling for Park's Resignation," *Korea Herald*, December 3, 2016, sec. Social affairs, https://www.koreaherald.com/view.php?ud=20161203000136

27. Jacob Poushter and Nicholas Kent, "The Global Divide on Homosexuality Persists," Pew Research Center's Global Attitudes Project (blog), June 25, 2020, https://www.pewresearch.org/global/2020/06/25/global-divide-on-homosexuality-persists/

28. The World Values Survey has been tracing attitudes toward migration across multiple countries for decades. South Koreans' attitudes toward migration were

most positive in the last wave of the survey conducted in the country at the time of writing, dating back to 2018. More information on the World Values Survey and the data is available at https://www.worldvaluessurvey.org/wvs.jsp

29. The Games organizers added a capital C to the name of the county to avoid any confusion with the similar-sounding Pyongyang, the capital of North Korea.

30. Panmunjom Declaration for Peace, Prosperity and Unification of the Korean Peninsula, Panmunjom, April 27, 2018.

31. "Gender Wage Gap," OECD Data, 2021, https://data.oecd.org/earnwage/gender-wage-gap.htm

32. *Global Gender Gap Report 2022* (Geneva: World Economic Forum, July 2022), https://www.weforum.org/reports/global-gender-gap-report-2022/

33. "Workplace Anti-Bullying Law Takes Effect," *Yonhap News Agency*, July 16, 2019, https://en.yna.co.kr/view/AEN20190716001551315.

34. "Joint Statement of President Donald J. Trump of the United States of America and Chairman Kim Jong Un of the Democratic People's Republic of Korea at the Singapore Summit," Trump White House Archives, June 12, 2018, https://trump-whitehouse.archives.gov/briefings-statements/joint-statement-president-donald-j-trump-united-states-america-chairman-kim-jong-un-democratic-peoples-republic-korea-singapore-summit/

35. Donald Trump, "Remarks by President Trump in Press Conference | Hanoi, Vietnam," Hanoi, February 28, 2019, U.S. Embassy & Consulate in Vietnam, https://vn.usembassy.gov/20190228-remarks-president-trump-press-conference/

36. Interview with long-term resident in North Korea, July 6, 2021.

37. "S. Korea Remains No. 2 Most Popular Content Provider on Netflix in Q4 2021," *Yonhap News Agency*, accessed August 15, 2022, https://en.yna.co.kr/view/AEN20220120003800315

38. Julia Hollingsworth, "K-Pop Fans Are Being Credited with Helping Disrupt Trump's Rally. Here's Why That Shouldn't Be a Surprise," *CNN*, June 22, 2020, https://www.cnn.com/2020/06/22/asia/k-pop-fandom-activism-intl-hnk/index.html

39. Ramon Pacheco Pardo and Jeong-Ho Lee, "South Korea's COVID-19 Success: The Role of Advance Preparations," KF-VUB Korea Chair Policy Brief, May 2020, https://brussels-school.be/publications/other-publications/south-korea%E2%80%99s-covid-19-success-role-advance-preparations

40. Martin Kaufman and Krishna Srinivasan, "Strong Policies Help Korea Navigate Uncertain Times," *IMF News*, May 12, 2022, https://www.imf.org/en/News/Articles/2022/05/12/CF-Korea-strong-policies

41. Christian Davies and Song Jung-a, "Ukraine War Offers South Korea's Hanwha Opportunity to Break into Nato Defence Market," *Financial Times*, July 11, 2022, https://www.ft.com/content/c2d11ae9-a385-418c-aa18-e517992743a7

7: Unification and the Changing Regional Context

1. Samuel S. Kim, "North Korea in 1999: Bringing the Grand Chollima March Back In," *Asian Survey* 40, no. 1 (2000): 151–63; Samuel S. Kim, "North Korean Informal Politics," in *Informal Politics in East Asia*, ed. Lowell Dittmer, Haruhiro Fukui, and Peter N.S. Lee (New York: Cambridge University Press, 2000), 237–68.

2. Koo Youngnok, "Future Perspectives on South Korea's Foreign Relations," *Asian Survey* 20, no. 11 (November 1980): 1152–63.

3. "Foreign Relations of the United States, 1950, Korea, Volume VII," Office of the Historian of the U.S. Department of State, June 9, 1950, https://history.state.gov/historicaldocuments/frus1950v07/d46.

4. Oberdorfer, *The Two Koreas: A Contemporary History*.

5. Kim Hak-soon and Song Choong-sik, "脫정치·脫 이념·脫 패권의 統一모델 만 들자" (Let's Make a Model for Unification That Is Not Politicized, Idealized, or Hegemonic), *Kyunghyang Shinmun*, August 1, 1990, https://newslibrary.naver.com/ viewer/index.naver?articleId=1990080100329226001&editNo=3&printCount=1& publishDate=1990-08; "내년 選擧日程 조정검토" (Review of Next Year's Election Schedule Adjustment), *Kyunghyang Shinmun*, October 11, 1991, https://newslibrary. naver.com/viewer/index.naver?articleId=1991101100329101001&editNo=15&pri ntCount=1&publishDate=1991-10-11&officeId=00032&pageNo=1&printNo=14 195&publishType=00010; "집권땐 北 흡수통일" (If I Become Leader of the Government, North Korea Will Be Unified by Absorption), *Chosun Ilbo*, July 5, 1992, https://newslibrary.naver.com/viewer/index.naver?articleId=1992070500239 104002&editNo=1&printCount=1&publishDate=1992-07; "北韓 흡수통일해야" (North Korea Should Be Unified by Absorption), *Maeil Business Newspaper*, July 17, 1992, https://newslibrary.naver.com/viewer/index.naver?articleId=19920717000992 02004&editNo=2&printCount=1&publishDate=1992-07-17&officeId=00009&p ageNo=2&printNo=8159&publishType=00020; "金鍾泌 (김종필) 자민련 총재 국회연설 (요지)" (Kim Jong-Pil, President of United Liberal Democrats, Speech to the National Assembly [Summary]), *Dong-A Ilbo*, October 25, 1996, https:// newslibrary.naver.com/viewer/index.naver?articleId=1996102500209104006&edit No=45&printCount=1&publishDate=1996-10-25&officeId=00020&pageNo=4& printNo=23348&publishType=00010

6. Charles Wolf and Kamiljon T. Akramov, *North Korean Paradoxes: Circumstances, Costs, and Consequences of Korean Unification* (Washington, DC: RAND Corporation, May 3, 2005), https://www.rand.org/pubs/monographs/MG333. html; David S. Maxwell, "Should the United States Support Korean Unification and If So, How?," *International Journal of Korean Studies* 18, no. 1 (2014): 139–56; Marcus Noland, "Why North Korea Will Muddle Through," *Foreign Affairs* (July/ August 1997), https://www.foreignaffairs.com/articles/asia/1997-07-01/why-north-korea-will-muddle-through

7. Ahn Byung-joon, "The Man Who Would Be Kim," *Foreign Affairs* 73, no. 6 (December 1994): 94–108; Nicholas Eberstadt, "Hastening Korean Reunification," *Foreign Affairs* 76, no. 2 (April 1997): 77–92; Michael Green, "North Korean Regime Crisis: US Perspectives and Responses," *Korean Journal of Defense Analysis* 9, no. 2 (December 1, 1997): 209–10, https://doi.org/10.1080/10163279709464377; Robert Collins, "Patterns of Collapse in North Korea," *Combined Forces Command C5 Civil Affairs Newsletter*, Seoul, Korea (January 1996).

8. Selig S. Harrison, "Promoting a Soft Landing in Korea," *Foreign Policy*, no. 106 (Spring 1997): 57–75; Michael Haas, ed., *Korean Reunification: Alternative Pathways* (New York: Praeger, 1989); Kwak Tae-Hwan and Joo Seung-Ho, "The Future of the Korean Peninsula: Unification and Security Options for the 21st Century," *Asian Perspective* 23, no. 2 (1999): 163–96; Robert A. Scalapino, *North Korea at a Crossroads*, Hoover Essays in Public Policy, no. 73 (Stanford, CA: 1997); Lee Keun, "The Road to the Market in North Korea: Projects, Problems and Prospects," WIDER Working Paper Series (Helsinki: United Nations University World Institute for Development Economics Research, August 1997).

9. Victor Cha, *The Impossible State: North Korea, Past and Future*, 1st edn (New York: HarpersCollins Publishers, 2012).

10. *Costs and Benefits of Korean Unification* (in Korean) (Seoul: Institute for Korean Integration of Society, 2011), 9–10 (containing estimates of unification cost based on published reports from 1991 to 2011); Chun Hong-Tack, "A Gradual Approach Toward North and South Korean Economic Integration," KDI Working Paper (Seoul: Korea Development Institute, November 1993), https://www.kdi.re.kr/ research/reportView?&pub_no=921&pg=7&tema=K01&pp=10; Kwon Goohoon,

"Experiences with Monetary Integration and Lessons for Korean Unification," IMF Working Papers (International Monetary Fund, May 1, 1997), https://www.imf.org/en/Publications/WP/Issues/2016/12/30/Experiences-with-Monetary-Integration-and-Lessons-for-Korean-Unification-2228

11. For a good account of this period, see Patrick McEachern, *Inside the Red Box: North Korea's Post-totalitarian Politics* (New York: Columbia University Press, 2010), 67–75.

12. Hong Soon-young, "Thawing Korea's Cold War: The Path to Peace on the Korean Peninsula," *Foreign Affairs* (June 1999) https://www.foreignaffairs.com/articles/asia/1999-05-01/thawing-koreas-cold-war-path-peace-korean-peninsula; Moon Chung-in and David I. Steinberg, eds., *Kim Dae-Jung Government and Sunshine Policy: Promises and Challenges* (Seoul: Yonsei University Press, 1999).

13. For more on *minjung* ideology, see Shin, *Ethnic Nationalism in Korea*; Shin Soon-ok, "Engagement? Containment? The Role of Identity in the Formation of South Korea's Policy Toward Pyongyang," *North Korean Review* 9, no. 1 (2013): 83–99.

14. "Full Text of Moon's Speech at the Korber Foundation," *Korea Herald*, July 7, 2017, sec. Politics, https://www.koreaherald.com/view.php?ud=20170707000032

15. Seo Ji-eun, "Unification May Be Jackpot: Park," *Korea JoongAng Daily*, January 6, 2014, https://koreajoongangdaily.joins.com/news/article/article.aspx?aid=2983129

16. Park Geun-hye, "Speech by President Park Geun-Hye, 'An Initiative for Peaceful Unification on the Korean Peninsula' at Dresden University of Technology" (transcript of speech, Dresden University of Technology, Germany, March 28, 2014), https://overseas.mofa.go.kr/dk-en/brd/m_7038/view.do?seq=716122&srchFr=&amp%3BsrchTo=&amp%3BsrchWord=&amp%3BsrchTp=&amp%3Bmulti_itm_seq=0&amp%3Bitm_seq_1=0&amp%3Bitm_seq_2=0&amp%3Bcompany_cd=&amp%3Bcompany_nm=

17. *Economic Effects of Korean Unification* (Seoul: National Assembly Budget Office, 2014), 3.

18. "100 Policy Tasks Five-Year Plan of the Moon Jae-in Administration," *Korea.net*, August 2017, https://www.korea.net/Resources/Publications/About-Korea/view?articleId=7959#

19. Moon Jae-in, "Full Text of Moon's Speech at the Korber Foundation" (Old City Hall, Berlin, Germany, July 6, 2017), https://www.koreaherald.com/view.php?ud=20170707000032

20. Moon Jae-in, "Address by President Moon Jae-in at May Day Stadium in Pyeongyang" (May Day Stadium, Pyeongyang, North Korea, September 20, 2018), https://overseas.mofa.go.kr/hk-en/brd/m_1494/view.do?seq=756615&srchFr=&amp%3BsrchTo=&amp%3BsrchWord=&amp%3BsrchTp=&amp%3Bmulti_itm_seq=0&amp%3Bitm_seq_1=0&amp%3Bitm_seq_2=0&amp%3Bcompany_cd=&amp%3Bcompany_nm=&page=11

21. Victor Cha and Marie DuMond, "On Unification: North Koreans' Hope for the (Near) Future," *Beyond Parallel*, February 8, 2018, https://beyondparallel.csis.org/unification-north-koreans-hope-near-future/

22. Lee Sang Sin et al., "KINU Unification Survey 2021" (Seoul: Korea Institute for National Unification, July 2021), https://www.kinu.or.kr/pyxis-api/1/digital-files/87cb5812-a81a-4fdc-824c-8d359544e8f7

23. Kim Hak-jae et al., "2019 Unification Awareness Survey (2019 통일의식조사)" (Seoul: Institute for Peace and Unification Studies, Seoul National University, February 28, 2020), https://ipus.snu.ac.kr/wp-content/uploads/2020/04/2019-%ED%86%B5%EC%9D%BC%EC%9D%98%EC%8B%9D%EC%A1%B0%EC%82%AC_%EC%B5%9C%EC%A2%85%EC%9B%B9%EC%9A%A9.pdf

24. Becky A. Gates, "The Economy," in *East Germany: A Country Study*, ed. Stephen R. Burant (Washington, DC: Federal Research Division, Library of Congress, 1987),

478, https://tile.loc.gov/storage-services/master/frd/frdcstdy/ea/eastgermanycount00bura_0/eastgermanycount00bura_0.pdf

25. Susan Larson, "Government and Politics," in *East Germany: A Country Study*, ed. Stephen R. Burant, 478.

26. Holger Wolf, "Korean Unification: Lessons from Germany," in *Economic Integration of the Korean Peninsula*, ed. Marcus Noland (Washington, DC: Institute for International Economics, 1998), 170.

27. "Korea, North," in *The CIA World Factbook* (Central Intelligence Agency, July 19, 2022), https://www.cia.gov/the-world-factbook/countries/korea-north/#economy; "Korea, South," in *The CIA World Factbook* (Central Intelligence Agency, July 20, 2022), https://www.cia.gov/the-world-factbook/countries/korea-south/; "North Korea Statistical Indicators (북한통계)," Korean Statistical Information Service, accessed July 19, 2022, https://kosis.kr/bukhan/nkStats/nkStatsIdctChart.do?num=14&listNm=%EA%B5%AD%EB%AF%BC%EA%B3%84%EC%A0%95&menuId=M_01_02

28. For comprehensive lists of a number of studies on the costs of unification, see Marcus Noland, Sherman Robinson, and Li-gang Liu, "The Costs and Benefits of Korean Unification: Alternate Scenarios," *Asian Survey* 38, no. 8 (August 1998): 801–14; Deok Ryong Yoon, "The Economic Impacts of a North Korean Collapse," ASI Working Paper Series (Seoul: Ilmin International Relations Institute, 2010); Dong Cheon Shin and Deok Ryong Yoon, "The Unification Cost and the Optimal Distribution of Investment on North Korea (통일비용과 적정투자배분)," *Korean Economic Review* 47, no. 3 (1999): 143–63.

29. Wolf and Akramov, "North Korean Paradoxes."

30. "Korean Reunification to Cost over $3 Trillion," *Korea Times*, September 14, 2010, sec. National, https://www.koreatimes.co.kr/www/nation/2022/07/113_73029.html

31. Jang In-sung et al., "Unification Costs Based on Different Inter-Korean Exchange Scenarios and Subsequent Implications (남북교류협력 수준에 따른 통일비용과 시사점)" (Seoul, Korea: National Assembly Budget Office, n.d.), http://www.nabo.go.kr/system/common/JSPservlet/download.jsp?fCode=13002&fSHC=&fName=%EB%82%A8%EB%B6%81%EA%B5%90%EB%A5%98%ED%98%91%EB%A0%A5+%EC%88%98%EC%A4%80%EC%97%90+%EB%94%B0%EB%A5%B8+%ED%86%B5%EC%9D%BC%EB%B9%84%EC%9A%A9%EA%B3%BC+%EC%8B%9C%EC%82%AC%EC%A0%90.pdf&fMime=application/pdf&fBid=19&flag=bluenet.pdf

32. Yoon, "The Economic Impacts of a North Korean Collapse."

33. "Korea, North," "Korea, South," in *The CIA World Factbook*.

34. Ibid.

35. IP2Location, "Korea (Republic of) IP Address Ranges," accessed July 22, 2022, https://lite.ip2location.com/korea-(republic-of)-ip-address-ranges?lang=en_US

36. IP2Location, "Korea (Democratic People's Republic of) IP Address Ranges," accessed July 22, 2022, https://lite.ip2location.com/korea-(democratic-peoples-republic-of)-ip-address-ranges?lang=en_US

37. "Korea, North," "Korea, South," in *The CIA World Factbook*.

38. In 2018, the length of South Korea's oil and gas pipeline was 2,365 miles. North Korea's was just 3.7 miles. "Korea, North," "Korea, South," in *The CIA World Factbook*.

39. Aidan Foster Carter, *Korea's Coming Reunification: Another East Asian Superpower?*, Economist Intelligence Unit Special Report M212 (London: Business International Ltd, 1992), 102.

40. Jong W. Lee and Warwick J. McKibbin, "Korean Unification: Economic Adjustments under German Assumptions," *Asian Economic Policy Review* 14 (2019): 1–20.

41. International Institute for Strategic Studies, *The Military Balance 2022* (Routledge, 2022).

42. Park Young O, "한반도 통일 시 한국군 주도 군사통합 방안 : 독일, 예멘, 베트남 사례를 중심으로" (South Korea Leading Military Integration on the Unified Korea), 미래군사학회, 한국군사학논총 4 (December 2013): 215–50.
43. Nicholas Eberstadt, *Korea Approaches Reunification* (Armonk, NY: M. E. Sharpe, 1995), 112, 122.
44. Rhee Kang Suk, "Korea's Unification: The Applicability of the German Experience," *Asian Survey* 33, no. 4 (1993): 371.
45. "Policy on North Korean Defectors," "Children out of School (% of Primary School Age)," World Bank Databank, accessed July 26, 2022, https://data.worldbank.org/indicator/SE.PRM.UNER.ZS
46. Kim Jeongmin, "North Korean Defectors Continue to Close the Wage Gap in South Korea," *NK News*, February 8, 2022, https://www.nknews.org/2022/02/north-korean-defectors-continue-to-close-the-wage-gap-in-south-korea/; "South Korea: Monthly Salary of Employees in Seoul 2021," Statista, accessed July 26, 2022, https://www.statista.com/statistics/1290413/south-korea-monthly-salary-of-employees-in-seoul/
47. Park Han-sol, "Suicide Prevention Programs for North Korean Defectors to Be Developed," *Korea Times*, October 29, 2020, sec. North Korea, https://www.koreatimes.co.kr/www/nation/2022/07/103_298408.html.

Epilogue

1. Victor Cha and Lisa Collins, "The Markets: Private Economy and Capitalism in North Korea?" *Beyond Parallel*, August 16, 2018, https://beyondparallel.csis.org/markets-private-economy-capitalism-north-korea/
2. Andrew Yeo, *State, Society and Markets in North Korea* (New York: Cambridge University Press, 2021).

Postscript

1. Lee Haye-ah, "Yoon Arrives in Japan for G-7 Summit, Meetings with Biden, Kishida," *Yonhap News Agency*, May 19, 2023, https://en.yna.co.kr/view/AEN20230519000952315
2. Andrew Yeo, "South Korea as a Global Pivotal State," *Brookings*, December 19, 2023, https://www.brookings.edu/articles/south-korea-as-a-global-pivotal-state/
3. Washington Post Staff, "Miscalculations, Divisions, Marked Offensive Planning by U.S., Ukraine," *Washington Post*, December 4, 2023, https://www.washingtonpost.com/world/2023/12/04/ukraine-counteroffensive-us-planning-russia-war/
4. Ramon Pacheco Pardo, "South Korea is Sidestepping the Hub," *Foreign Policy*, August 3, 2023, https://foreignpolicy.com/2023/08/03/south-korea-seoul-united-states-arms-weapons-sales-military-alliance-diplomacy/
5. Robert Williams, "Why K-pop Rules Fashion Week," *CNN*, January 23, 2023, https://edition.cnn.com/style/article/k-pop-fashion-week-bof/index.html
6. Samuel Hine, "How K-pop Conquered Fashion Week," *GQ*, March 8, 2023, https://www.gq.com/story/how-k-pop-conquered-fashion-week#:~:text=Now%2C%20we%27re%20squarely%20in,out%20stadiums%20around%20the%20world
7. Hyunsu Yim, "Netflix to Invest $2.5 Billion in South Korea to Make TV Shows, Movies," *Reuters*, April 25, 2023, https://www.reuters.com/technology/netflix-invest-25-bln-south-korea-make-tv-shows-movies-2023-04-25/
8. "What We Watched: A Netflix Engagement Report," *Netflix*, December 12, 2023, https://about.netflix.com/en/news/what-we-watched-a-netflix-engagement-report

9. Patrick Brzeski, "Disney's Top Asia Exec on Bob Iger's Streaming Pivot and the "Gold Rush" for Korean Content," *Hollywood Reporter*, February 20, 2024, https://www.hollywoodreporter.com/business/business-news/disney-president-in-asia-iger-streaming-pivot-korean-content-1235831271//

10. Kang Yoon-seung, "FDI Pledges to S. Korea Hit Record in 2023: Data," *Yonhap News Agency*, January 4, 2024, https://en.yna.co.kr/view/AEN20240104002900320

11. Amanda Chu and Myles McCormick, "The Impact of the Inflation Reduction Act, One Year On," *Financial Times*, August 17, 2023, https://www.ft.com/content/6f83ed81-28a5-46e9-98c4-a2bcf3d5b9fc

12. Mi-sun Kang, "Lotte Energy Ups Elecfoil Factory Capacity in Spain to 30,000 Tons," *The Korea Economic Daily*, August 7, 2023, https://www.kedglobal.com/batteries/newsView/ked202308070017

13. Jin Eun-soo, "Samsung to Build $280 Million Chip Research Center in Japan," *Korea JoongAng Daily*, December 21, 2023, https://koreajoongangdaily.joins.com/news/2023-12-21/business/industry/Samsung-to-build-280-million-research-center-in-japan/1941885

14. The White House, "Press Briefing by Press Secretary Karine Jean-Pierre and NSC Coordinator for Strategic Communications John Kirby," January 20, 2023, https://www.whitehouse.gov/briefing-room/press-briefings/2023/01/20/press-briefing-by-press-secretary-karine-jean-pierre-and-nsc-coordinator-for-strategic-communications-john-kirby-8/

15. U.S. Department of the Treasury, "Treasury Sanctions Entities Tied to Arms Deals Between North Korea and Russia," August 16, 2023, https://home.treasury.gov/news/press-releases/jy1697#:~:text=The%20entities%20are%20Limited%20Liability,Russia%27s%20brutal%20war%20against%20Ukraine

16. Joseph S. Bermudez Jr., Victor Cha and Jennifer Jun, "Ongoing Arms Transfers Activity at Najin Port," *Beyond Parallel*, October 17, 2023, https://beyondparallel.csis.org/ongoing-arms-transfer-activity-at-najin-port/

17. Reuters, "North Korea Recognises Breakaway of Russia's Proxies in East Ukraine," *Reuters*, July 13, 2022, https://www.reuters.com/world/north-korea-recognises-breakaway-russias-proxies-east-ukraine-2022-07-13/

18. Victor Cha and Ellen Kim, "A Renewed Axis: Growing Military Cooperation Between North Korea and Russia," *Beyond Parallel*, September 6, 2023, https://beyondparallel.csis.org/a-renewed-axis-growing-military-cooperation-between-north-korea-and-russia/

19. Ibid.

20. Joseph S. Bermudez, Jr., *A History of Ballistic Missile Development in the DPRK*, Center for Nonproliferation Studies Occasional Paper No. 2, 1999, https://www.nonproliferation.org/wp-content/uploads/2016/09/op2.pdf

21. Ibid.

22. Kim Soo-yeon, "S. Korea's Spy Agency Confirms Hamas Suspected Use of N. Korean Weapons," *Yonhap News Agency*, January 8, 2024, https://en.yna.co.kr/view/AEN20240108002351315

23. Michelle Nichols, "After Veto on North Korea, China Says 'Let's See' on U.N. Action over a Nuclear Test," *Reuters*, June 9, 2022, https://www.reuters.com/world/asia-pacific/after-veto-north-korea-china-says-lets-see-un-action-over-nuclear-test-2022-06-09/

24. National Intelligence Council, *North Korea: Scenarios for Leveraging Nuclear Weapons Through 2030*, National Intelligence Council National Intelligence Estimate, January 2023, https://www.dni.gov/files/ODNI/documents/assessments/NIC-Declassified-NIE-North-Korea-Scenarios-For-Leveraging-Nuclear-Weapons-June2023.pdf

25. Kim Soo-yeon, "N.K. Leader Calls for Defining S. Korea as 'Invariable Principal Enemy' in Constitution," *Yonhap News Agency*, January 16, 2024, https://en.yna.co.kr/view/AEN20240116000653315

SELECT BIBLIOGRAPHY

Amsden, Alice H., *Asia's Next Giant: South Korea and Late Industrialization* (New York: Oxford University Press, 1989).

Baek, Jieun, *North Korea's Hidden Revolution: How the Information Underground Is Transforming a Closed Society* (New Haven, CT: Yale University Press, 2016).

Brown, Arthur Judson, *The Mastery of the Far East* (London: G. Bell and Sons, 1919).

Caprio, Mark E., *Japanese Assimilation Policies in Colonial Korea, 1910–1945* (Seattle: University of Washington Press, 2009).

Cha, Victor, *Powerplay: The Origins of the American Alliance System in Asia* (Princeton, NJ: Princeton University Press, 2016).

———— *The Impossible State: North Korea, Past and Future* (New York: HarperCollins, 2012).

Cha, Victor D., and David C. Kang, *Nuclear North Korea: A Debate on Engagement Strategies*, revised and updated edition (New York: Columbia University Press, 2018).

Chang, Pil-wha, and Kim Eun-Shil, *Women's Experiences and Feminist Practices in South Korea* (Seoul: Ewha Woman's University Press, 2005).

Ch'oe, Yôngho, Peter H. Lee, and Wm Theodore de Bary, eds., *Sources of Korean Tradition*, vol. 2 (New York: Columbia University Press, 2000).

Chung, Young-Iob, *Korea Under Siege, 1876–1945: Capital Formation and Economic Transformation* (Oxford: Oxford University Press, 2006).

Clifford, Mark, *Troubled Tiger: Businessmen, Bureaucrats, and Generals in South Korea* (Armonk, NY: M. E. Sharpe, 1994).

Cumings, Bruce, *Origins of the Korean War*, vol. 1: *Liberation and the Emergence of Separate Regimes, 1945–1947* (Princeton, NJ: Princeton University Press, 1981).

Demick, Barbara, *Nothing to Envy: Ordinary Lives in North Korea* (New York: Spiegel & Grau, 2009).

Eckert, Carter J., Lee Ki-baik, Lew Young Ick, Michael Robinson, and Edward W. Wagner, *Korea, Old and New: A History* (Seoul: Ilchokak, 1990).

Fields, David P., *Foreign Friends: Syngman Rhee, American Exceptionalism, and the Division of Korea* (Lexington: University Press of Kentucky, 2019).

Griswold, Alfred Whitney, *The Far Eastern Policy of the United States* (New York: Harcourt Brace & Co., 1938).

Halle, Louis J., *The Cold War as History* (New York: Harper & Row, 1967).

Han, JeongHun, Ramon Pacheco Pardo, and Cho Youngho, eds., *The Oxford Handbook of South Korean Politics* (Oxford: Oxford University Press, 2023).

Han, Sungjoo, *The Failure of Democracy in South Korea*, 1st edn (Berkeley: University of California Press, 1974).

Henderson, Gregory, *Korea, the Politics of the Vortex* (Cambridge, MA: Harvard University Press, 1968).

Jessup, Philip Caryl, *The Birth of Nations* (New York: Columbia University Press, 1974).

Kim, Byung-Kook, and Ezra F. Vogel, eds., *The Park Chung Hee Era: The Transformation of South Korea* (Cambridge, MA: Harvard University Press, 2013).

Kim, Byung-Yeon, *Unveiling the North Korean Economy: Collapse and Transition* (Cambridge: Cambridge University Press, 2017).

Kim, Eun Mee, Yang Ok Kyung, Lee Haiyoung, and Cho Hae Lim, *South Korea Advances Toward a Multicultural Society* (Seoul: Nanam, 2012).

Kim, Jinwung, *A History of Korea: From "Land of the Morning Calm" to States in Conflict* (Bloomington: Indiana University Press, 2012).

Kim, Samuel S., "North Korean Informal Politics," in *Informal Politics in East Asia*, ed. Lowell Dittmer, Haruhiro Fukui, and Peter N. S. Lee (New York: Cambridge University Press, 2000), 237–68.

Kim, Suk-Young, *K-Pop Live: Fans, Idols, and Multimedia Performance* (Stanford, CA: Stanford University Press, 2018).

Kim, Suzy, *Everyday Life in the North Korean Revolution, 1945–1950* (Ithaca, NY: Cornell University Press, 2013).

Ku, Dae-yeol, *Korea under Colonialism: The March First Movement and Anglo-Japanese Relations* (Seoul: Royal Asiatic Society, 1985).

Lee, Chong-Sik, *The Politics of Korean Nationalism* (Berkeley: University of California Press, 1963).

Matray, James I., "Hodge Podge: American Occupation Policy in Korea, 1945–1948," *Korean Studies* 19 (1995): 17–38.

McEachern, Patrick, *Inside the Red Box: North Korea's Post-totalitarian Politics* (New York: Columbia University Press, 2010).

McWilliams, Wayne C., *Homeward Bound: Repatriation of Japanese from Korea after World War II* (Hong Kong: Asian Research Service, 1988).

Mercer, Jonathan, "Emotion and Strategy in the Korean War," *International Organization* 67, no. 2 (April, 2013): 221–52.

Merrill, John, "The Cheju-Do Rebellion," *Journal of Korean Studies* 2 (1980): 139–97.

Moon, Katharine H. S., *Sex Among Allies: Military Prostitution in U.S.–Korea Relations* (New York: Columbia University Press, 1997).

Oberdorfer, Don, *The Two Koreas: A Contemporary History* (New York: Basic Books, 2001).

Office of the Historian of the U.S. Department of State, "Foreign Relations of the United States, 1950, Korea, Volume VII," June 9, 1950. https://history.state.gov/historicaldocuments/frus1950v07/d46

Oh, Kongdan, and Ralph C. Hassig, *North Korea through the Looking Glass* (Washington, DC: Brookings Institution Press, 2000).

Pacheco Pardo, Ramon, *North Korea–US Relations: From Kim Jong Il to Kim Jong Un* (London: Routledge, 2019).

—— *Shrimp to Whale: South Korea from the Forgotten War to K-Pop* (London: Hurst, 2022).

Paine, S.C.M., *The Sino-Japanese War of 1894–1895: Perceptions, Power, and Primacy* (Cambridge: Cambridge University Press, 2002).

Pak, Jung H., *Becoming Kim Jong Un: A Former CIA Officer's Insights into North Korea's Enigmatic Young Dictator* (New York: Ballantine Books, 2020).

Rusk, Dean, *As I Saw It*, edited by Daniel S. Papp, 1st edn (New York: W. W. Norton & Co., 1990).

Shin, Bok-ryong, *The Politics of Separation of the Korean Peninsula, 1943–1953* (Seoul: Jimoondang, 2008).

Shin, Gi-Wook, *Ethnic Nationalism in Korea: Genealogy, Politics, and Legacy* (Stanford, CA: Stanford University Press, 2006).

Shin, Soon-ok, "Engagement? Containment? The Role of Identity in the Formation of South Korea's Policy Toward Pyongyang," *North Korean Review* 9, no. 1 (2013): 83–99.

Stueck, William, "The United States, the Soviet Union, and the Division of Korea: A Comparative Approach," *Journal of American–East Asian Relations* 4, no. 1 (1995): 1–27.

Szalontai, Balázs, *Kim Il Sung in the Khrushchev Era: Soviet–DPRK Relations and the Roots of North Korean Despotism, 1953–1964*, 1st edn (Stanford, CA: Stanford University Press, 2006).

Wit, Joel S., Daniel B. Poneman, and Robert L. Gallucci, *Going Critical: The First North Korean Nuclear Crisis* (Washington, DC: Brookings Institution Press, 2004).

Wolf, Charles, and Kamiljon T. Akramov, *North Korean Paradoxes: Circumstances, Costs, and Consequences of Korean Unification* (Washington DC: RAND Corporation, May 3, 2005).

INDEX

Also by the same authors

Victor D. Cha

Alignment Despite Antagonism: The US–Korea–Japan Security Triangle
Nuclear North Korea: A Debate on Engagement Strategies
Beyond the Final Score: The Politics of Sport in Asia
The Impossible State: North Korea, Past and Future
Powerplay: The Origins of the American Alliance System in Asia
The Black Box: Demystifying the Study of Korean Unification and North Korea (forthcoming)

Ramon Pacheco Pardo

North Korea–US Relations: From Kim Jong Il to Kim Jong Un
Shrimp to Whale: South Korea from the Forgotten War to K-Pop
South Korea's Grand Strategy: Making Its Own Destiny